FINANCING AMERICAN ENTERPRISE

FINANCING

AMERICAN ENTERPRISE

The Story of Commercial Banking

PAUL B. TRESCOTT

HARPER & ROW, PUBLISHERS

NEW YORK AND EVANSTON

CONTENTS

[v]

AN INTRODUCTORY NOTE

CHARLS E. WALKER

Executive Vice President
The American Bankers Association

The year 1963 marks the centennial anniversary of the signing of the National Currency Act by Abraham Lincoln, sixteenth President of the United States. Throughout the year and throughout the nation commercial banks, large and small, will be commemorating this milestone in our financial development.

It seemed entirely appropriate and highly useful, on this one-hundredth birthday of the dual banking system, to review the highlights of its existence, to record its accomplishments, its shortcomings and the measures taken to overcome them, and most important of all, to recall those experiences from the past which will be most useful to us in meeting the problems which the future inevitably holds.

Paul B. Trescott, professor of economics at Kenyon College, distinguished historian as well as economist, undertook this difficult task at the invitation of The American Bankers Association's Centennial Commission. The story that he unfolds in these pages will bring nostalgia to many readers. For all it will serve as a timely reminder that change and progress are inevitable characteristics of a free and dynamic society.

FOREWORD

LESTER V. CHANDLER

Gordon S. Rentschler Professor of Economics
Princeton University

This is the story of American banking as it must be told if it is to be meaningful—as a part of the story of the social, political, and economic development of American society. As such, it is inevitably a story of change and adaptation. No more than other institutions have banks been insulated from the great forces and events that have shaped and reshaped our society—forces and events which in the power and scope of their effects have been no less than revolutionary. Among these have been the great growth of population; settlement of the vast frontier areas; revolutions in technology; huge accumulations of capital; revolutions in agricultural methods and organization; transportation revolutions on waterway, railroad, highway, and airway; revolutions in communications, commerce, and industry; marked changes in the forms and sizes of business firms; and far-reaching changes in the levels and distribution of family incomes. These are only examples of the many changing forces that have impinged on banking and continue to do so.

In part, therefore, this is a story of the adaptation of banking structures and practices to a constantly, and sometimes rapidly, changing environment. But this is only a part of the story, for bankers have not been mere passive adapters to changes over which they had no influence. They have also played important, and in some cases vital, roles in these developments. Some of the most interesting sections of this book deal with the banker as innovator and as supporter of innovators, sometimes assuming large risks in the process.

Paul Trescott has told the story of American banking with skill and objectivity. These pages attest to his competence as economist and historian and to his proficiency as a writer. Admirable too is his objectivity in dealing with controversial issues and events. Mistakes and shortcomings as well as achievements are dealt with frankly, fairly, and with a sophisticated understanding of the issues involved. This is an important contribution to our knowledge of American banking.

PREFACE

This study is written to fill a large gap in the history of the American economy. Not that historians have ignored banks—far from it. But the existing treatments of banking history, both by general historians and by economists, suffer from a grave imbalance. With few exceptions, existing studies have concentrated on the relation of the banks to the monetary system and have slighted the role of bank credit in capital formation and economic development.

There can be no doubt that the monetary performance of the banking system has at times been deficient, although historical accounts have often exaggerated the extent and importance of the deficiencies. These deficiencies were, however, intimately related to the efforts of the banks to adapt to the credit needs of the economy—needs which were in the long run at least as important as the need for monetary stability. To ignore the historical role of bank credit is inevitably to accept a distorted view of the position of the banks in our economic development.

To remedy this distortion, a large part of this book is devoted to setting forth the relation between bank credit and the development of our economy. The analysis is founded upon statistical aggregations, but I have tried to minimize the amount of space devoted to these. They make for dull reading; more important, they fail to convey any sense of the colorful and exciting character of the nation's development. To capture something of this quality, I have dwelt at length on the role of banks in the development of important firms, industries, and sectors of the economy. In the process, the operations of the banks can be shown in a broad context, instead of being treated in isolation. The evolution of bank services can be evaluated in terms of their functional contributions to the good performance of the economy. And the development of the structure of the banking system—number, size, location of banks—is related to the broader social and economic factors which shaped it.

However, this study does not ignore the other aspects of banking history. It deals with the monetary functions of the banks, showing how they provided most of the expanding money supply needed for growth, but also analyzing the incidence of monetary instability, bank failures, and panics. It shows how the banks' responsibilities toward money and toward credit were often mutually incompatible.

This study also deals with the evolution of government regulation of banks, with emphasis on the efforts to reconcile these two areas of responsibility. Other significant phases of regulation have been, first, the recognition that the problem is essentially a national one, and second, the conclusion that effective banking policy could best be achieved through the instrumentality of a central bank.

This study has been prepared under the sponsorship of the Centennial Commission of the American Bankers Association. Its publication commemorates the passage in 1863 of the National Currency Act, which created national banking in its modern sense. The book has benefited greatly from the interest and counsel of Casimir A. Sienkiewicz, president of the Central-Penn National Bank of Philadelphia. Members of the staff of the American Bankers Association have provided much assistance in preparation of the manuscript—

particularly Mr. Harold Cheadle, Dr. Carter Golembe, and
Dr. H. Jerome Cranmer. The members of the Centennial
Commission are listed in the Appendix on page 281.

In gathering material for this book I have received indispensable aid from a large number of research assistants:
Stanley Huff, John MacInnis, Samuel Richmond, William
Kuehl, Donald Doerge, Charles Albers, Donald Gray, Rod-
ger Drabick, John Kierzkowski, Brian Pattison, and Thomas
Fleming. Dorothy Longaker did much of the work of copy-
reading, proofreading, and other editorial assistance. My wife
Ruth has provided valuable help on matters of style and organization.

I am grateful for materials supplied to me by a large
number of banks, and to bankers who have been willing to
spend time talking about their activities, problems, and
viewpoints. Valuable materials were also furnished by Miss
Cynthia Sorrick of Robert Morris Associates, and by Professor Lance Davis. My thanks are also extended to the numerous members of the staffs of the Board of Governors,
Federal Reserve System, the office of the Comptroller of the
Currency, and the Federal Deposit Insurance Corporation
for their kindness and help.

A work of this sort depends critically on the grassroots
scholarship of many students of financial history. My debt
to Stewart Holbrook and to Allan Nevins for details of information and for support in a particular point of view will
be apparent to readers familiar with their work. The
abundant statistical materials published by the National
Bureau of Economic Research have also been indispensable.

It remains to assure the reader that, after the contributions of all those aforementioned, whatever may remain of
errors, omissions, inconsistencies, interpretations, sophist-
ries, and other enormities are the full responsibility of the
author.

P. B. T.

FINANCING AMERICAN ENTERPRISE

CHAPTER

1

COMMERCIAL BANKING
IN THE AMERICAN ECONOMY

THE STORY OF AMERICAN BANKING starts in the turbulent
years which gave birth to the American republic. The men
who founded the new nation founded its first banks as well,
to help it survive, grow, and prosper.

It was Robert Morris, burdened with the thankless responsibility for managing the finances of the Confederation
government, who took the lead in founding the nation's first
bank in 1781. Morris hoped the bank would help to support
the badly shaken credit of the government. And famed pub-
licist Thomas Paine was one of the most outspoken defenders of the bank against critics who disliked this strange
innovation.

Alexander Hamilton, still an obscure but rising young
man, was one of the leaders in establishing the Bank of New
York in 1784. And a few years later, as Secretary of the
Treasury, he prevailed upon the newly formed federal government to create a far-flung national bank, whose branches

reached from Boston to New Orleans. George Washington, who backed Hamilton's plan, became a stockholder in the Bank of Alexandria when it opened near his home. Hamilton's two prominent successors in the Treasury, Oliver Wolcott and Albert Gallatin, became noted bankers after their services to government financing.

It was Hamilton who perceived brilliantly the ways in which the welfare of the nation would be served by the development of banking. By increasing the circulation of money, banks would help to establish an efficient market economy and would contribute to the "vivification of industry." Bank credit would also play a vital role. In sum, "by contributing to enlarge the mass of industrious and commercial enterprise, banks become nurseries of national wealth," concluded Hamilton.

Hamilton's dream of the United States as a great industrial nation has come true. And the role of the commercial banking system in the nation's growth has amply fulfilled the ambitious prospect which he envisioned for it. The banks did this by their unique ability to extend *credit* by creating *money* in the form of bank notes (until the 1930's) and bank deposits. Bank deposits have furnished the largest proportion of the money needed to sustain an industrial economy organized into an intricate pattern of specialization and exchange. Bank credit has financed capital outlays of business, government, and consumers, which have enabled our economy to accumulate a vast treasure of useful and productive wealth and to achieve rising levels of productivity and real income. And the gradual expansion of the money supply by bank lending has sustained the growth in total demand needed to provide a market for the growing productive capacity of the nation.

The banking system and the country grew up together. As the frontier moved westward, banks multiplied. Their characteristics tended to reflect their surroundings. In the cities of the east coast, long established as trading centers and well endowed with wealthy merchants, the banks themselves were distinguished for stability and conservatism. Many of them had long and successful careers, and quite a few, like the Bank of New York, are still in operation.

But in the areas of recent settlement—and that covered a lot of territory—banking was more exciting. It has been the fashion also to say that it was pretty bad. From one point of view, it was. Bank failures were numerous, and some of the failures stemmed from naïve exuberance, from incompetence, or from downright dishonesty. But if these banks lived dangerously, it was for a reason; for they were located on the road to Eldorado. The banks were part and parcel of the colorful and often wildly disorderly process which captured the imagination and energy of Americans in the years between Saratoga and Sarajevo—discovering and developing the fabulous resources of a virgin continent and matching them with the talents of a vigorous and enterprising people.

The driving power of American enterprise was plainly visible in the nineteenth century. It was visible in the decisions of millions of immigrants to risk the hardships of coming to a new country, and in the steady westward flow of population into areas of agricultural and commercial opportunity. It was spectacularly evident in the careers of inventors and industrial leaders such as Eli Whitney, Cyrus McCormick, John D. Rockefeller, and Andrew Carnegie. Its results were most apparent in the enormous growth of population, the corresponding increase in cultivated acreage, and the rise of industry. Less obvious, but vitally important was a steady improvement in the living conditions of the population.

In the twentieth century, the character of American enterprise has changed. The exciting frontiers are scientific and technological rather than geographic. Industrial leadership has relinquished some of its brass-knuckles quality (and, correspondingly, some of its color and drama). But the steady improvement in the economic status of the population has been more evident than ever. Since 1910, the nation's output per person has doubled, and the total is more equally distributed. During the same period, American workers also achieved a dramatic reduction in work burden, as average hours worked per week have fallen from sixty to less than forty.

These unprecedented improvements in economic welfare, resulting chiefly from massive capital formation and technological progress, are the fruits of enterprise. Many factors can be cited as reasons why Americans have displayed so much economic enterprise and initiative: the selective influence of immigration, a stimulating climate, religious and cultural backgrounds stressing prudence, thrift, and effort. But in order that economic enterprise might be beneficial to the society as a whole, it has always been essential that men of vigor and new ideas should have access to capital funds. American commercial banking has been admirably suited to meet this need.

Among all industrial nations, the United States has been unique in having a banking system composed of a large number of independent banks. Throughout most of American history, it has been relatively easy to start a new bank. Banking itself attracted men of the same enterprising spirit evident in industry. Competition was vigorous among the banks to extend credit for promising ventures. Because of their predominantly local character, individual banks had a high interest in the progress of their local communities. American banks have been borrower-oriented; their boards of directors have often consisted of the principal users of credit in the locality—so much that the bank has often been a sort of committee for the economic development of the community.

But the characteristics that put bank credit abundantly at the disposal of enterprise sometimes impaired the ability of the banks to fulfill their monetary responsibilities. Easy entry into banking could be abused by frauds or incompetents; eagerness to lend for new enterprises could involve a bank unduly with risky or illiquid loans; undue expansion of bank credit as a whole could aggravate business fluctuations and render the banks vulnerable to panics.

A better understanding of the functions and problems of the banking system can be obtained by looking at the operations of an individual bank.

In the era of agricultural and industrial expansion which followed the Civil War, the number of American banks increased rapidly, rising from about three thousand in 1870 to thirty thousand in 1920. Like much of the American experience, this development was unique. In the industrial countries of Europe, banking was conducted by a small number of large institutions. By contrast, the American banking system was more democratic, more decentralized, and on occasion, more disorderly.

The vast majority of these were small banks located in small towns throughout the nation's heartland—from Texas up through Iowa, Illinois, and Minnesota. They sprang up, like the towns themselves, in response to the flood of settlement that poured into the plains states after the Civil War. By sheer weight of numbers, these constitute the typical American banks of historical experience. Moreover, a large proportion of present-day banks trace their origins to this period.

The typical bank was located in a town of about one thousand people, serving as a trading center for surrounding farms. Small as it might be, the town probably had one or two other banks as well. The bank was small. It had deposits of less than $100,000, and numbered its depositors at most in the hundreds. Fewer still were the borrowers, while the staff of the bank itself probably comprised not more than four or five people, working in one or two rooms. Save for a typewriter, the industrial revolution was not conspicuously represented. Bookkeeping and calculating were done by hand and brain.

The typical bank's operations revolved around loans and around deposits. Interest received on loans brought in the income to pay salaries, interest, and dividends. And the banker was proud of the contribution his loans made to the development of the local economy. Quite a few loans, though usually small ones, were made to farmers. Credit from the bank had helped bring the surrounding countryside into cultivation in the first place and was now being used to experiment with complicated forms of equipment—threshing machines, reapers, and for the adventurous, monstrous steam-driven tractors. Other loans covered seasonal expenses for feed, seed, or labor.

The bank's loan customers also included some of the town's merchants. Some borrowed to help meet expenses for their stock of goods on hand, or to finance credit which they extended to farmers and other customers. And the local produce dealers needed loans at harvest time to pay the farmers for crops to be marketed. Finally, a few of the bank's loans were made on local real estate, to finance purchases of lots and construction of houses or business buildings.

Like many of the townspeople, the banker had probably come from somewhere back East. He came West looking for opportunity, looking for a community which showed promise of growth and prosperity. Very likely he had a direct stake in such growth through ownership of real estate in the town or nearby. In any case, his bank would stand to benefit from community development, which would bring growth in deposits.

Under the circumstances, it would be hard for the banker to look only at the narrow aspects of a particular loan. To reject an application might mean to lose a depositor, or to handicap a promising farm or commercial enterprise. But often there were more applications than the bank's limited funds could accommodate. Ultimately, the bank's ability to make loans depended on the willingness of people to keep deposits in it. Most of the bank's deposits represented business funds. The number of personal accounts was growing, but the majority of the people in and around the town had precious little cash to begin with and preferred to keep what they had in tangible form.

Most of the bank's borrowers were also depositors. Indeed, the banker usually let it be known that this was a condition of obtaining credit. This arrangement greatly simplified the operation of lending. When granting a loan, the bank could simply credit the proceeds to the depositor's account. By writing figures in the books, the bank could increase the amount of spendable funds at the disposal of the depositor without taking them from anyone else. Thus, at any given time, a certain proportion of the bank's deposits represented funds "created" in lending, rather than cash paid in over the counter. But most of the funds created would soon be withdrawn to buy things from out of town.

Depositors imposed a fair amount of trouble upon the bank. Most of the time and effort of the teller and bookkeeper were devoted to keeping deposits and cash straight. And there was the problem of settling accounts with other banks when funds were transferred by check. However, the bank was able to cover some of its deposit expenses by charging "exchange" when depositors wanted to make payments to other communities.

If the bank was going to keep its depositors, it had to keep their confidence. They had to be certain that they could get cash when they wanted it. One way of assuring this would have been for the bank to keep enough cash in the safe to pay them off in full. This would, however, have pretty well put it out of business, for it would have cut its lending power drastically. However, the banker could usually expect that demands for withdrawals would not run more than a certain proportion of the deposits, and would ordinarily be offset by funds flowing in.

To prepare for withdrawals, the banker kept on hand enough cash to cover perhaps 10 per cent of deposits. In addition, he maintained a deposit account with a "correspondent" bank in a larger city about fifty miles away. This account earned interest and could also be drawn on for the sale of drafts to customers wishing to make payments in the city.

The bank's deposit position was a sensitive index of the state of the local economy. When the crops were good and sold for a high price, money would come pouring in. The farmers would pay up their debts to the town merchants and do a lot of buying for cash. Much of the cash would pass into the local banks, which could then enlarge their loans.

When the farmers had a bad year, everything was bad. Debts would drag on, unpaid. Both the banks and the local merchants would allow people an extension—if they could. Sometimes they could not. The merchants had bills to pay and debts of their own to meet.

Worse, the bank was likely to find itself short of cash. A poor farm year would mean a less-than-normal flow of cash into the area. Day after day, the banker would have to pay off on checks which went to other communities to buy dry goods and lumber, sugar, coffee, and canned fruits. Instead of cash, he had a safe full of slow loans. Should he try to sell some of the notes to the other local banks? They were in the same pinch, and would take notes only at a heavy discount if at all.

Should he hale the unhappy borrowers into court? That was a hateful resource, usually reserved for the careless or dishonest borrower. What good would it do the bank to take over a farm that could not be sold for anything like its fair value? Why dispossess a hard working and honest family which was doing as good a job with the property as anyone could?

Often the banks survived crises like this. They survived when they could themselves borrow elsewhere, perhaps from their city correspondents. They survived when their depositors did not lose confidence. They survived when the farm troubles were limited to one locality, and when they proved to be of short duration. One bad year the bank and the community could take in stride—and perhaps two.

Other times they were not so lucky. A few hints of trouble, rumors spreading among depositors, and the banker's worst nightmare might come true—a long line of glum and sullen depositors waiting for the bank to open.

Whether or not the bank was in trouble before, a sustained run would ruin it. The cash in the vault was soon exhausted. When it was gone, there was little chance to get more. If the trouble was localized, other banks would sometimes lend cash; if the troubles were widespread, and an atmosphere of panic prevailed, every bank knew that it might be next. Each one hoarded its own cash. And in the years before the coming of the Federal Reserve System in 1914, there was no source from which the banking system as a whole could get more cash when panic struck.

If the cash ran out, the banker was forced to close his doors. Sometimes they opened again; sometimes they did not. If the bank was forced into liquidation, the slow loans had to be foreclosed, probably yielding little enough compared with the misery they inflicted on distressed borrowers. Everyone suffered when the bank failed.

The fortunes of many of the nation's small-town banks waxed and waned with the state of the farm economy. During flush years like 1885-1887, their numbers soared and their credit flowed abundantly. When trouble came—grasshoppers, drought, or perhaps a serious depression in the economy, like that of the mid-1890's—the banks were hard hit.

Most of the twenty-five years which followed 1896 were good years for the farmers. Prices trended strongly upward. This was the golden age for the "main-street" banks. When the farm economy hit rough going after 1921, the tide began to turn against them. Then came the devastating economic collapse of 1929-1933. Thousands of banks, large and small, were swept away in an unprecedented financial disaster.

The foregoing description of a typical bank highlights the chronic problem which afflicted all banks to some extent during the years preceding the 1930's—how to reconcile their responsibilities toward credit with their responsibilities toward money. The former dictated liberality; the latter, conservatism. The clash between the two made itself felt most painfully with respect to the *liquidity* of the individual bank—its ability to pay depositors (and in times past, banknote holders) in cash on demand.

For more than a century, it appeared that the American public could not enjoy the benefits of banking without paying a high cost in panics and instability. There were and are a few critics who felt that the benefits of the system were not worth the cost and wanted it abolished, but most people were well aware of the potential benefits to the nation from bank money and bank credit services. They recognized that laissez faire in banking would be disastrous, but had little enthusiasm for the prospect of a government-owned and operated banking monopoly. Instead, from the earliest times, Americans experimented with a great variety of patterns of banking control, hoping to find one that would secure the vigor and enterprise possible under competitive private management, while at the same time protecting honesty, competence, and stability through government action.

These regulatory experiments differed greatly in the relative stress placed on the banks' responsibilities toward money and credit. Throughout American banking history, emphasis has shifted from one to the other and back again. Efforts to improve the monetary functions of the banks stressed the need to keep bank money convertible into cash and to adapt the quantity of bank money to the state of the economic system as a whole. These efforts frequently involved restrictions on bank credit, either in amount or in kind. This restrictive process was likely, in turn, to cause a steady increase in unsatisfied credit needs, which might produce a new banking policy oriented more toward credit expansion—but with greater risk of monetary disturbance. Implicitly, this oscillation reflected the fact that each responsibility was too important to be subordinated to the other.

By a process of trial and error, the banking system and bank regulation evolved. Among the notable steps along the way were the establishment of the national banking system in 1863 and the creation of the Federal Reserve System in 1913. State governments also instituted many measures of supervision and control. But none of these solved the problem of banking instability, and the nation's worst financial crisis occurred from 1929 to 1933.

Out of the searing crucible of the depression have come extensive changes in banking structure and policies, public and private, which appear to have solved the traditional banking problem. The crash greatly reduced the number of banks, and that number remains far below its peak of the 1920's. The survivors were a hardy lot, however, and they still constitute the majority of today's banks. The crisis of the 1930's brought the establishment of the federal program for insuring bank deposits. And it set the stage for the emergence of the present Federal Reserve System as a smoothly functioning central bank, exercising restraint against undue fluctuations in the volume of bank money and providing a source from which banks can obtain needed cash if hard-pressed by depositors. Bank failures have been few and far between since 1933, and the economy has experienced nothing remotely resembling a banking panic.

Today's commercial banking system consists of about 13,000 banks, located in approximately the same number of communities. While the number of banks has shown a slight downward trend in recent years, the number of bank offices has risen through the increase in branch operations.

Modern commercial banks have roots which go more deeply into the nation's past than most sectors of business. More than 3,000 of our banks trace their origins back beyond 1900. Among these are nearly four hundred which date from before 1860. More than half of New England's banks have been in operation for a century or more. The First Pennsylvania Banking and Trust Company traces its ancestry to the country's first bank, the Bank of North America, which opened in 1782. Chase Manhattan is the successor to the Manhattan Company, the charter for which was obtained in 1799 by Aaron Burr on promise of providing water supply to New York City.

The prevalence of "seasoned" banks contrasts with the age distribution of business in general, which is much "younger." The age pattern of banks demonstrates that many of the early American banks were well managed and able to survive the panics and crises of intervening years.

Modern commercial banks carry on a wide variety of functions. They manage savings accounts, maintain safe-deposit facilities, and offer a wide variety of trust services. But their basic functions remain essentially what they were when the first American bank opened in 1782. They provide the public with money (now in the form of checking deposits) and extend credit by making interest-bearing loans. Because banks need not keep 100 per cent cash reserves behind their deposit liabilities, they can actually create additional deposit money when they make loans. In times past, each bank printed up its own bank notes, which it handed over to the borrowers. Today, banks often make loans by adding the amount of the loan to the deposit account of the borrower. This is physically an easy matter for the bank—it involves only a bookkeeping operation—and the added deposit funds are just that much more spending money for the borrower. They are, as one bank felicitously advertises, "instant money," created by the act of lending.

The banks' power to create money is fraught with significance for the welfare of the economy. If too much money is created, the demand for the nation's output may rise to excess. Prices may increase, distorting the distribution of real income and real wealth and rubbing raw spots of social tension among economic groups. If the money supply is drastically reduced, falling expenditures can create depression and unemployment. Businesses fail; homes and farms may be foreclosed for debt. Depression brings poverty to people who would welcome a chance to help produce the goods they need.

American experience of the 1930's and 1940's displays the contrasting sides of monetary disturbance. The first decade was one of insufficient expenditure, part of a worldwide depression which created tensions contributing to World War II. Then the war and its aftermath produced excessive increases in money and expenditures, bringing sustained inflation of the price level.

Creation of money by each individual bank has traditionally been restrained by the probability that newly created deposits would be withdrawn to make payments elsewhere, thus draining the bank of cash. In the modern economy, however, the banks operate within limits imposed by government regulation. Banks must hold reserves in proportion to their liabilities, and no bank can expand its deposit liabilities unless it has sufficient reserves on hand to do so. The most important reserve requirements are those imposed by the Federal Reserve System. By reducing the required proportion of cash reserves the banks must hold, the Federal Reserve can increase their lending power, while raising reserve requirements would reduce lending power.

The Federal Reserve banks can also influence the amount of commercial-bank reserves by buying or selling United States government securities in so-called "open-market operations." And they may lend reserve funds directly to member banks. By these means, the Federal Reserve System attempts to control the total volume of bank money and credit in the interests of a stable and prosperous national economy. This is not an easy job, and we will see later on how well they have done it.

Commercial banks make a wide variety of loans. Loans to business and farming cover all the major areas of production, distribution, and services in the economy. Banks extend home-mortgage loans and consumer credit. Banks buy state and local government securities, helping to finance roads, schools, and other important projects. Finally, the banks hold large amounts of United States government securities, particularly short-term issues, which can be turned into cash in a hurry without much risk of capital loss.

Banks furnish many other services. They rent safe-deposit boxes for storage of valuables. They sell foreign exchange, making it possible for business firms or tourists to acquire foreign money for import purchases or travel. They also participate in marketing issues of state and local government securities.

Many banks provide trust services to individuals and business firms. They function as executors under wills, or administer property for the benefit of survivors (or for the creator of the trust, if he wishes). Trust services to corporations arise under terms of mortgage bonds and other types of securities, under which title to certain property is vested in the trustee to be held for the benefit of the security holders. In recent years, commercial banks have taken on management of large amounts of corporate pension funds set up to provide retirement benefits for employees.

This great variety of banking services has evolved over

time. The most important functions of the banks, however, are still those involving money and credit. Their importance in assuring good performance by the economic system is as vital as ever. Despite our impressive achievements, we need further growth in our economy to meet urgent needs for health and education facilities, housing, and recreational opportunities. More jobs must be created to reduce existing unemployment and employ a growing labor force. Despite our high current average incomes, one-eighth of families still have incomes below $2,000. And overriding all consideration of domestic economic welfare lie the urgencies of the Cold War and the economic revolution of the world's underdeveloped areas. The job of the banks in financing the capital needed for growth is far from over.

Our defenses against economic instability are far better than in the past, partly as a result of the unpleasant experiences of the 1930's and 1940's, but many problems remain to be solved there as well. Both price increases and unemployment have continued to be disquieting, if not calamitous. There has been great disagreement about the merits of using Federal Reserve control over bank credit and money as a major lever to keep the economy on an even keel.

Thus, our story of American banking looks forward as well as backward. It carries our attention to the major economic problems of today and tomorrow. And it is dedicated to the principle that an understanding of the past will improve our ability to cope with the problems of the future.

CHAPTER

2

AMERICAN BANKING BEFORE 1863

AMERICAN BANKING began with the achievement of independence—the British had prohibited chartered banking in colonial America—and the first bank was chartered in 1781 in hopes that it would furnish financial support for the Revolutionary effort. Additional banks were started in major port towns by merchants, and the system grew in a conservative fashion for thirty years. But during the financial disorder and inflation attending the War of 1812, the number of banks mushroomed, and this tendency continued under the stimulus of the great flood of population into the West after the war ended. By 1820, there were 300 banks; by 1840, 1,000; and by 1860, nearly 2,000.

The rapid growth of banks reflected more than anything else the great scarcity of capital in the underdeveloped United States—a scarcity particularly galling to imaginative and enterprising men well aware of the tremendous economic potentialities of the nation's resources. The establishment of banks became a device for enabling investment to transcend the limits of domestic saving and inflow of foreign capital. "It has come to be a proverb," wrote a shrewd observer in 1857, "that banks never originate with those who have money to lend, but with those who wish to borrow." [1]

By 1860, the amount of bank credit in existence (as measured by loans and securities) was about $800 million, equal to roughly 10 per cent of the nation's stock of productive capital assets. Bank credit flowed abundantly into the formation of merchant inventories, which were vital to the development of an economy based on specialization and exchange. Much credit also went into agriculture, which still furnished 60 per cent of national output and employment in 1860. Vital developments in transport facilities, particularly railroads, drew partly on bank finance. And bank credit contributed to key industrial enterprises, ranging from Eli Whitney's pioneering developments in mass production of firearms at the beginning of the century to the great iron works of Peter Cooper and Abram Hewitt at Trenton. [2]

The banks served as a means for channeling saving and foreign capital into domestic investment. Much saving was channeled through bank stock, which was a highly profitable asset for domestic and, at times, for foreign investors. But the larger proportion of bank funds came through the creation of money. Most banks created money in the form of bank notes, and these formed the principal circulating currency of the period. By 1860, however, bank deposits had achieved considerable importance and loans were made by crediting the deposit accounts of borrowers just as at present.

The capacity of the country to absorb bank credit without inflation arose from the great need for an increased supply of currency and deposits. At the end of the Revolutionary War, the country's economy consisted mainly of farms which were largely self-sufficient or which relied on exchanges not involving money. By 1860, the "transportation revolution" and the extension of commercial enterprise had created a national market economy giving full scope to specialization and exchange. Further, the size of the economy increased greatly—territorially more than three fold; in population, nearly eight fold, and in total output, eighteen fold, comparing 1790 with 1860.

Over the same period, the supply of money increased from perhaps $15 million to about $600 million. Of the latter, gold and silver constituted about one-fourth and bank notes and deposits three-fourths. Bank deposits, which had begun mainly as "deposits for safekeeping" (what we would call savings deposits), had become increasingly popular as a medium of active payment through the use of checks. "To keep a bank account was once the badge of a large mercantile business; it is now the habit of most shopkeepers, mechanics, doing a considerable business, and professional men," according to the 1860 report of the Massachusetts bank commissioners. Check clearings in New York City totaled $7 billion in 1860, a sum well in excess of the value of the nation's output. At that, deposits and checks were an instrument of business, rather than personal transactions. Coin and bank notes provided the hand-to-hand circulating medium for wages and consumer payments.

A forty-fold increase in the quantity of money between 1790 and 1860 seems impressive, but such an expansion was clearly needed for an economy that was growing rapidly and relying increasingly on specialization and exchange. That the added money was needed is best demonstrated by the fact that commodity prices in 1860 were roughly equal to those of 1790.

Despite the substantial contribution of the banks to meeting the nation's needs for money and credit, banking was associated from the start with the most violent controversy. Public attitudes ranged from the most naïve faith in the inevitable benefits of all banking operations to equally exaggerated denunciations which labeled banking "a mad, untamable beast," or "a withering, blighting, curse." Such polarity of viewpoint is well illustrated by the state of Wisconsin, which prohibited chartered banking entirely from 1841 to 1853, then adopted legislation permitting virtually unlimited proliferation of banks. The American public could not get along with its banks, nor get along without them. The country tended to divide between those who felt that banks could make everyone rich and those who feared they would make everyone poor, and neither side lacked for evidence to support its case.

Much of the antagonism to banks arose from the instability of bank credit and money over the business cycle. During periods of economic upswing, bank credit tended to expand too much. A booming economy tended to stimulate a high demand for loans and to create optimistic expectations among bankers and borrowers alike. Thus, expanding bank credit might aggravate an expansionary movement, furnishing fuel for speculations in lands, commodities, or securities, and creating a large volume of debt, which could be easily repaid only if there were further speculative rises in prices.

Even more distressing was the tendency of bank credit to worsen periods of downswing and depression in the economy. Periods of boom often gave way to periods of crisis and contractions; banks were pressed for payment by their depositors or note holders, and in turn struggled to liquidate their loans to business borrowers. Credit would become stringent, the money supply would contract, and bankruptcies and property liquidations were likely. Inability of borrowers to repay often meant insolvency for banks as well, and the rate of bank failures was very high in depression periods. Nearly one-half of the banks formed between 1810 and 1820 failed before 1825, and a similar proportion of the banks formed between 1830 and 1840 closed by 1845. In all, the problem of economic instability was a serious one, even in a primarily agrarian economy.

Every depression spawned a host of incendiary pamphlets, such as "Banking Bubble Burst," by the Reverend Theophilus Fisk, in which he argued that "If our circulation was gold and silver, it would be impossible to create those ruinous fluctuations in prices that cover the land with misery and desolation, every once in five or ten years. The moment a spirit of speculation can be excited, the banks increase the flame by pouring oil upon it; the instant a reaction takes place, they add to the distress a thousand fold." [3]

The instability of bank credit was inherent in the structure of the banking system and involved factors beyond the control of individual banks. Each bank was expected to keep a reserve of gold and silver coin, into which notes and deposits could be converted on demand. During normal times, there was not much demand for coin, and banks could safely expand credit. Once a crisis arose, however, demands for coin would increase sharply. Individual banks seldom had more than 10 or 20 per cent reserves; more serious, there was usually no source from which they could obtain more. By 1860, a close link between banks and the stock market added to the problem. Many banks invested reserve funds in short-term loans to stockbrokers. When the banks were pressed for payment, they would call these loans, which could easily cause a selling wave on the stock market.

Still, the banks were not the only cause of instability. Foreign investment funds flowed into the country in a large but fluctuating volume, and American export sales abroad also showed large ups and downs. At home, construction expenditures, especially for transportation projects, were highly unstable because of their sensitivity to changes (or expected changes) in the rates of growth of particular communities and regions. Speculation in various types of property added to the problem. There can be no doubt that the banking system tended to aggravate economic fluctuations, but eliminating the banks would not have eliminated instability, if the experience in the pre-bank eighteenth century is any criterion.

The banks were also subject to criticism for the quality of the bank-note currency they created. Virtually every bank issued its own notes; there was no standardization of size or design. Amid the confusion of more than one thousand valid types of notes, counterfeiting and fraud also flourished. Notes of defunct banks were also frequently kept in circulation, and non-bank business firms sometimes issued due bills intended to circulate as currency. There was no national paper currency; the only money supplied by the government was coin, although United States Treasury notes sometimes circulated as currency. Bank notes often circulated at varying discounts in areas away from home, and business men struggled to keep abreast of which were good and which were not. Newspapers carried lists of good and bad notes, and periodicals devoted entirely to evaluating notes came into existence.

The worst abuses of note issue were associated with the "wildcat" banks. Every banker knew that if he could keep his notes in circulation without having to redeem them, his opportunities for credit expansion were virtually unlimited. Logically enough, the less scrupulous developed techniques for evading redemption demands. They tried to put bank notes in circulation far away from home, while perhaps at the same time locating a bank's headquarters in some location where it was not likely to be found—"out among the wildcats," in other words.

The true wildcat bank was a frontier creature only for evasion purposes; it sought a legal domicile to which access was difficult. Its lending operations were generally conducted in the major cities, where there was usually abundant demand for credit by business men who were willing to accept depreciated notes. The banking authorities of Florida, describing a Southern Life Insurance and Trust

Company, chartered with banking powers in 1835, reported no knowledge of its operation, but noted that "it is said [to be] chiefly operating in New York." Nebraska, which forbade note-issue banking within its own borders, obligingly chartered note-issue banks intended to operate in Iowa, which had a similar prohibition. Banks in widely separate areas sometimes concluded reciprocal-trade agreements whereby they would use each other's notes for loans; thus Illinois was flooded with Georgia notes.

Early in the 1860's, one observer paid tribute to the currency of the American West:

There the frequently worthless issues of the State of Maine and of other New England states, the shinplasters of Michigan, the wildcats of Georgia, of Canada, and Pennsylvania, the red dogs of Indiana and Nebraska, the miserably engraved notes of North Carolina, Kentucky, Missouri, and Virginia, and the not-to-be-forgotten stumptails of Illinois and Wisconsin are mixed indiscriminately with the par currency of New York and Boston, until no one can wonder that the West has become disgusted with all bank issues . . .[4]

The bank-note problem represented a sacrifice of the monetary responsibility of the banks to their credit function. And bank-note abuses were intimately bound up with broader problems of sustaining a sufficient inter-regional flow of credit and payments. The demand for loans in the West was high, and many of the banks of New England and the East poured funds into such loans—"for circulation"—a tendency which state banking officials tended to deplore. Yet in a crude way, this process linked the more abundant savings of the East with the needs and potential productivity of the West.

To contemporaries, there appeared one obvious solution to the bank-note problem—assure that every note was convertible into coin on demand. Numerous government actions were directed toward this goal. And among the banks themselves, the older and more conservative banks frequently exerted their influence to curb wildcat operations, by which they were often the losers. The First and Second Banks of the United States during most of the period prior to 1833 furnished a rough-and-ready system for returning bank notes for redemption, and banks that refused to redeem found their notes rejected in payments to the government.

In New England, Boston's Suffolk Bank began in 1818 to collect and return notes of out-of-town banks, many of which came to maintain deposits with it for redeeming notes in Boston. In 1840, New York State required all country banks in the state to keep funds with New York City banks for note redemption. Many banks provided facilities for inter-regional payment through the sale of domestic exchange. For example, a merchant in New Orleans wishing to purchase goods from Boston could purchase from a local bank a draft payable in Boston. To support exchange transactions and note redemption, there developed an extensive network of correspondent relations among the banks, centered around a large volume of interbank deposits and concentrated increasingly in New York.

In both lending and money creation, the banks maintained very uneven standards of performance. Like the proverbial little girl, the individual bank was likely to be either very good or very bad. Of the 2,500-odd banks formed down through 1860, about a thousand closed within ten years of opening—but virtually the same number continued in operation for forty years or more. More than one-third of the banks formed prior to the War of 1812 reached the century mark. New England banks had an enviable record—nearly two-thirds of them survived at least forty years. These banks were able to maintain such good performance because they were in the more developed regions where shortage of capital was not such a desperate plight and where banks could find plenty of low-risk short-term commercial loans. Environment as well as managerial prudence contributed to their longevity. A list of the oldest banks still surviving is on page 279 in the Appendix.

Unstable banking moved with the frontier. There the demand for credit was linked to investment in fixed capital, which often combined high potential productivity with high risk. The first great banking "bubble" developed mainly in the area consisting of Pennsylvania, Ohio, Virginia, and Kentucky, which produced nearly one hundred bank failures during the troubled years following the War of 1812. During the 1830's boom-and-bust banking was particularly prevalent in two regions, one bounded by upstate New York, Ohio, and Michigan; the other on the southern frontier, including Georgia, Florida, and Mississippi. The third notable experience with banking crisis, in the 1850's, was heavily concentrated in the northwest, ranging from Indiana west through Illinois and Wisconsin and into the new areas of Nebraska and Minnesota.

Although it is not hard to find cases of outright fraud and dishonesty, many of the shortcomings of the early banks reflected imprudence and inexperience. The directors and stockholders of a bank were often favored borrowers, a situation that might be unfair and unsafe, but also hard to avoid in a rapidly changing community. Entry into banking was easy, and performance was bound to be uneven. Officials of a Massachusetts bank defended themselves against charges of irregularity by pleading that they were "not themselves capitalists, nor men of previous experience in banking; and acquired their first knowledge of its rules and principles in this comparatively humble institution." [5] A lot of their colleagues could have said the same thing.

Experience with banking instability led a prominent journalist to remark in the 1830's that "banks were the *principal* source of social evil in the United States," and found expression in 1853 in the hope of James Guthrie, Secretary of the Treasury, that the outpouring of gold from California would enable the country to dispense with bank money entirely in the near future.[6] Such an outcome was hardly consistent with the American spirit of enterprise. The gold that poured out of California was ample to furnish all the nation's monetary needs, but it rapidly left the country, sent on its way to buy the imports of capital goods needed for the nation's growth—including the iron to build the Louisville and Nashville Railroad, of which Mr. Guthrie was to serve for many years as president. Thus, it was literally the scarcity of real capital that kept bank money in circulation.

The link between money and credit was an uneasy alliance. Once people accepted the principle that bank credit could provide capital, they were not likely to limit their use of it to an amount determined by the community's need for circulating money. The urgent demand for capital encouraged banks to expand credit too much and to evade their responsibilities for keeping their notes and deposits convertible into coin. The public demanded stable money, convertible into coin; it also demanded abundant credit and condemned the banks if they could not provide both simultaneously. Georgia legislators carefully provided that the Central Bank of Georgia must maintain coin reserves equal to its note liabilities; its credit creation therefore was so inadequate that they closed it up again. In 1819, according to Bray Hammond, "The Maryland legislature . . . enacted a law against banks that refused to redeem their notes. Two days later . . . it enacted another against persons who demanded that they redeem them." [7] The better (and luckier) banks met the problem by keeping their loans fairly liquid; they loaned only at short term and refused to renew notes. But this did not accord at all with the country's hunger for long-term credit for industry, agriculture, and transportation.

The number of problems that arose in early American banking was exceeded only by the number and variety of solutions advanced to meet them. In general spirit, the pe-

riod prior to 1860 divides into two phases. The years prior
to the early 1830's may be characterized as the era of "central banking"; the later years, as an age of "free banking."
In the first period, responsibility for banking control was
exercised by the federal government; in the second, it rested
exclusively with the states. Bank charters during the first
period were generally granted to individual banks by special state legislative enactments, an arrangement which
limited entry and protected quality somewhat, especially
before 1811.

More important restraints were exercised, however, by
the First and Second Banks of the United States, chartered
by the national Congress. The First Bank of the United
States was established in 1791 at the urging of Alexander
Hamilton. Its purposes were a blend of public and private;
it was to serve the government as a source of credit and
manager of government funds and transactions, but was
also promoted frankly to increase banking facilities in the
country. It established branches in major port cities and
operated on a nationwide basis. It functioned to some extent as a national clearing house for the notes and checks of
other banks, insofar as these were received in payments to
the government. The state-chartered banks found it necessary to keep sufficient cash on hand to meet the continued
demands for cash arising when the First Bank presented
their notes and checks for payment.

Unfortunately, the First Bank's charter expired in 1811,
and by a narrow margin, Congress failed to renew it. Much
of the opposition arose from traditional Jeffersonian states'-
rights sentiment. Shortly after, the country plunged into the
War of 1812, which set off a rapid inflationary spiral. The
government borrowed heavily from the state-chartered
banks, and their notes and deposit liabilities were so expanded that, in 1814, many of them ceased to redeem in
coin. Suspension of specie payments, as it was called, removed any limit on credit expansion. When the war ended,

a boom in farm lands in the Ohio and Mississippi valleys spurred rapid creation of new banks. The country experienced its first flood of depreciated notes, and demands for reform were heard everywhere.

Consequently, in 1816 Congress chartered a Second Bank of the United States, similar to the First but much larger. This also established a nationwide branch system with the head office in Philadelphia. But it got off to a miserable start, expanding its own loans rapidly during the postwar boom, partly because some of the branches were under the influence of corrupt speculators. When a turn in the international financial situation drained off gold and silver in 1819, the country experienced its first monetary panic. The new bank undertook a vigorous contraction of credit, and became violently hated for its role.

In later years, however, the bank developed into a sophisticated instrument of banking control. Although most of its stock was privately owned, and its responsibility to the public interest was not clearly set forth, it became a "public bank" in the 1820's under the leadership of Nicholas Biddle. Biddle was able to vary the volume of the bank's lending to offset undue economic fluctuations. He improved the country's system of domestic remittances by hounding the state-chartered banks to keep their notes at par and by carrying on extensive transactions in domestic and foreign exchange. Gradually the abuses that had entered the system before 1820 were cleared away and an efficient credit and payments system developed.

This state of affairs was shattered by Andrew Jackson, who became President in 1829. Jackson shared the frontiersman's dislike for banks and for the arcane mysteries of credit creation; his antipathy had roots in some bad personal experiences during the era of suspended payments. Because he disliked all banks, he killed the one he could reach, by vetoing the bill to recharter Biddle's bank. Giving vent to the widely held fear of a "moneyed aristocracy,"

Jackson denounced the bank as an odious monopoly, operating "to make the rich richer and the potent more powerful." Such slogans helped Jackson to a triumphant re-election in 1832. But his veto removed the main force that had held money and credit relatively stable. New banks were rapidly formed, and the tempo of economic activity expanded at an unhealthy rate, only to culminate in a series of financial panics and a serious depression in the early 1840's. These events seemed to repudiate Jackson's policies; but as the bank, which had continued operations under a Pennsylvania charter, perished under rather unflattering circumstances, its enemies could find some vindication for Jackson's actions.

Jackson's dislike for "moneyed corporations" reflected an agrarian distrust for the swirling world of credit, finance, innovation, and trade. However, the "moneyed corporations" were also under assault from an opposite point of view, from ambitious newcomers who resented the entrenched position of the "establishment." For them the "monopoly" of existing chartered institutions was objectionable because it excluded them from easy access to opportunities. Existing state banks wanted to be free of the "monster" of Chestnut Street which was always subjecting them to inconvenient restraints, and the business community was eager for more banks and more credit. The latter sentiment became the dominant force in the movement for "free banking."

Efforts to establish another central bank in 1841 were blocked by John Tyler and presidential vetoes. Instead, the federal government withdrew entirely from any direct dealings with banks. The Independent Treasury System, established in 1846, provided that the government would not accept or use bank notes in its transactions, and that government funds would be kept in the custody of public officials, not deposited in banks. Thus the Jacksonian forces succeeded in discrediting the concept of a central bank, which did not make its way back into American monetary policy until the adoption of the Federal Reserve Act in 1913.

Withdrawal of the federal government left the responsibility for banking control to the states. Several of these retained the principle of central banking at the state level. The Bank of the State of South Carolina, established as early as 1812, was owned and controlled by the state government. It operated successfully until after the Civil War and contributed to a banking climate that kept the state relatively free from banking troubles. The respected State Bank of Indiana, established in 1834, was really a supervisory system over a large number of "branches" which were actually separate banks. Other successful state ventures in central banking occurred in Missouri, Iowa, and Ohio. By contrast, the first such state enterprise, in Vermont, failed within five years. During the depression years following 1819, Tennessee, Alabama, and Kentucky set up state-dominated banks to lend to hard-pressed debtors—precursors of the Reconstruction Finance Corporation—and these institutions became insolvent. Illinois sustained a series of bad experiences with state-dominated banks.

State governments tried in many ways to keep bank notes and deposits convertible into coin. Many required that a large portion of bank funds be derived from stockholder capital rather than note issues and deposits. However, banks could easily make this ineffective by permitting stockholders to pay for their stock with IOU's—"stock notes." In the 1830's, states began to require banks to hold cash reserves related to the quantity of liabilities. Louisiana's system, adopted in 1842, proved effective in safeguarding bank liquidity. It required a high proportion of cash and short-term loans behind both notes and deposits. Other states were less successful.

Many states attempted to enforce compliance with law and sound practice by sending public officials to make on-the-spot examinations of condition. Some tried to protect the quality of bank assets by imposing limitations on loans to stockholders and directors or to any individual borrower. But the Maine bank commissioners conceded in 1861 that "it is not expected that any board of bank commissioners should be competent to pronounce as to the goodness of a loan in any one bank."

Among all the state experiments, however, the one that most notably swept the country after Jackson's "Bank War" was free banking. Originated in New York, the policy had spread by 1862 to fifteen states. No longer was it necessary for each bank to obtain a special charter through legislation; the "free banking" legislation authorized administrative officers to grant charters automatically to projected banks, if they met certain minimum requirements, such as capitalization. The free banks were permitted to issue bank notes, but only if these were backed up 100 per cent (or more) by government securities or other approved earning assets deposited with state banking authorities. Where properly interpreted, this section was intended to protect note-holders against bank failures; if the bank proved unable to redeem its notes, the pledged assets could be sold. This provision had a second potential not lost on state treasurers—it opened up a large prospective market for state bonds.

Ideally, free banking represented an effort to allow banking resources to expand rapidly to meet the country's needs for capital, while at the same time safeguarding the money thereby created. In most cases, it added to the disorder and instability of banking. In areas such as Michigan and Illinois, where banking supervision in this early period was lax and the assets accepted for note security were not well defined, free banking spawned a host of "small, swindling concerns" guilty of the worst abuses of wildcatting.

Free banking stimulated rapid growth in the number of commercial banks. On the eve of the Civil War, there were nearly two thousand banks, about three-fourths of them chartered, and one-fourth "private" banks functioning without charters. Among the banks of 1860 were many distinguished veterans, including the country's three earliest banks—the Bank of North America (1782), the Bank of New York (1784), and the Massachusetts Bank (1784). But on the whole, the demography of the banking population before 1860 was characteristic of underdeveloped areas —high birth rates and high death rates. More than half of the banks operating in 1860 had been established within the previous decade.

By 1860, commercial bank deposits totaled about $300 million. Most of this sum represented the working cash of business men and business firms, and interest-bearing accounts were uncommon. However, in New England and New York, more than two hundred mutual savings banks were in operation, and held over $125 million in interest-bearing deposits. In other states, more than fifty stockholder-owned savings banks or deposit banks had arisen, catering both to personal savings and to business deposit requirements.

Bank notes in actual circulation totaled about $180 million, although the total would be higher if we included notes of failed banks, counterfeits, and other forms of waste paper in circulation. Even with such adjustment, it is clear that deposits had come to constitute a larger part of the money supply than bank notes. City banks stressed deposit business, while the bulk of note issue came from the smaller banks in smaller communities. In combination, bank notes and deposits composed about three-fourths of the nation's money by 1860.

By 1860, there had developed also a marked difference between the banking patterns of the North and South. In the northern states, widespread free banking or liberal issue of special charters produced a large number of banks, most of them small. Entry into banking was generally restricted in the southern states, and existing banks were permitted to develop into large branch systems. Whereas northern banks in 1860 reported a total of four branches, southern banks (including Missouri, Tennessee, and Kentucky) had 165—more branches than banks. (The state bank systems of Indiana, Ohio, and Iowa were not true branch systems.)

Free banking was consistent with the sentiment of freedom of trade and enterprise which prevailed in the northern states. It was a relatively democratic system that arose to extend to anyone access to bank credit or opportunity to enter the banking business itself. The proliferation of northern banks was thus a tribute to the driving force of business enterprise, and to its mass character. But the cost of this was that the northern banks did less well by their monetary responsibilities.

Under free banking statutes, it was frequently profitable to set up "banks of circulation" which functioned solely as paper-money factories. To form a bank, a group of individuals would pool their promissory notes to borrow funds for the initial capitalization. With those funds, they would purchase securities as required by law and print up an issue of notes, with which they would repay the initial capital loan. The result was a bank with one real asset—interest-bearing securities—and one very dubious asset, consisting of the stockholders' IOU's, likely to be defaulted at the first sign of trouble.

In 1860, Illinois boasted seventy-four chartered banks, of which sixty-three banks showed no loans and discounts whatever, and fifty-two had no deposit liabilities. As for specie reserves, thirteen banks reported none at all and twenty-eight more showed purely nominal amounts. Deposit liabilities of Illinois chartered banks were about $700,000, which was only about 8 per cent as large as note liabilities of $9 million. And these were honest-to-goodness banks by Illinois law—each one recognized by state authority, which certified the securities held by each one to back up its note issues. It must be admitted that their founders had a sense of humor, for their number included a Mississippi River Bank and an Ohio River Bank. Another of these institutions, the Bank of the City of Chicago, was established by Seth Paine, a fervent believer in spiritualism. He employed a medium to sit behind the counter and determine which loan applications should be granted.[8] After a spate of additional charters, no fewer than eighty-nine of the Illinois free banks failed in 1861-1862.

Some southern states also experimented with "free" or liberal banking policies, and these still prevailed in 1860 in Virginia and Georgia especially. But most rejected such policies after a bad experience, or never took the plunge in the first place. These states preferred to stick with a smaller number of large banks or to get along without chartered banking altogether. By 1860, Arkansas, Mississippi, and Florida were virtually devoid of chartered banks, and Texas had entered the Union in 1845 with a constitution which forbade their establishment. All these areas were served to some degree by private bankers. And they were invaded by armies of "carpetbaggers"—loan agents from banks in other states with their satchels full of bank notes, ready to make "loans for circulation."

The different trends in North and South reflected significant differences in the regional patterns of economic life. The South had passed through a period of vigorous, democratic enterprise when the Mississippi valley lands were opened up after the War of 1812. This was reflected in the banking boom and bust of the 1830's. But by 1860, southern enterprise had settled into a much more concentrated and aristocratic pattern. There were fewer and larger enterprises. The cotton trade, in particular, involved large loans to big plantations and cotton traders. Freedom of entry into banking and access to credit for small farmers and merchants were not matters of great concern in the South. Thus the sectional banking differences mirrored, in their small way, the great gulf of social systems and outlooks on life that divided North and South in 1860.

At its best, the southern pattern was more conducive to safe banking than that of the North. The Louisiana system of reserve requirements was more sophisticated than anything in the North, and the southern banking system as a whole managed to avoid the financial turbulence of the 1850's. Ultimately the Civil War destroyed the stable but concentrated banking pattern of the South. And the creation of the national banking system opened the way for the nationwide extension of a pattern similar to that of the North in 1860.

In addition to the chartered banks, private banks had assumed an important role by 1860. These were not corporations, and their proprietors were therefore subject to full personal liability for their debts. They were not (with a few exceptions) banks of note issue, but carried on deposit business. In the early 1860's, there were about five hundred private banks, accounting for about 20 per cent of all bank deposits.[9] Very few of these were in New England, where chartered banking facilities were ample. On the other hand, where chartered banks were insufficient in numbers or notoriously bad in quality, private banks flourished. There were about one hundred in Illinois, holding $7 million of deposits, which was ten times the deposits in chartered banks. It is safe to say that this was the real banking system of the state, by which local loan and deposit business was performed. Private banks were the only banks in Nebraska, Colorado, California, and Kansas, and far outnumbered chartered banks in Michigan and Minnesota. California, which entered the Union at the height of the gold-rush fever, expressed contempt for the paper-money banks of the East by outlawing banks of issue in the state constitution. There, banking was largely an adjunct to the express business, with Wells Fargo a leader. That firm (now one of the West Coast's major banks) added to its transport functions a business in accepting deposits of coin or bullion and making loans on cargoes of precious metals in shipment.

Many private bankers operated on a very small scale—some were merchant firms to whom banking was only a sideline. There were, however, some big firms as well—three held over $1 million of deposits each in 1863, including Jay Cooke's firm in Philadelphia. Among the larger firms, several still function as prominent banks. Riggs and Company in Washington is now the Riggs National Bank. S. A. Fletcher of Indianapolis has become the American Fletcher National, and Marshall and Ilsley of Milwaukee are represented by a bank of the same name a century later.

Many of the private banking houses were financial specialists. Jay Cooke, for instance, was noted chiefly for investment banking—marketing new issues of securities, a function he performed with notable success for the Treasury during the Civil War. Others were chiefly stockbrokers, or dealers in foreign exchange. One function common to many, both in city and small town, was dealing in bank notes—"note shaving," as contemptuous contemporaries called it. The chaotic quality of the circulation created opportunities for specialists who could keep abreast of which notes were good or bad and provide a market for them away from the place of redemption. Notebrokers were also commonly the publishers of the abundant "banknote reporters and counterfeit detectors" of the day. The most notable of such publishers was John Thompson of New York, whose private banking operations ran into difficulties during the panic of 1857, but who made an impressive comeback under the national banking system.

What about the earning assets of the banks? What kinds of industries and activities did they finance? In all areas, the preferred loans were commercial loans par excellence—that is, loans to merchants and dealers in commodities, mostly for short terms, possibly secured by the goods themselves. In the great commercial centers, such as New York and New Orleans, many banks could operate almost entirely on such safe and liquid credit. But there were many places where such loans were not in demand or did not yield much profit.

Many country banks made loans to farmers—on mortgage or personal security. The Farmers Bank of Maryland, which commenced in 1805 with headquarters in Annapolis, and the Farmers Bank of Delaware, opened in 1807 with headquarters in Dover, are both still in operation. They operated modest branch systems and prospered by loans to farmers and merchants. In the South, loans to plantation owners on real-estate mortgages were very common, and the state banks of Indiana, Iowa, and Ohio loaned extensively to farmers. Mortgage loans were not uncommon on urban real estate also, though the results for the banks were not always favorable.

In New England, bank credit was extended abundantly to manufacturing. By 1860, that region led the nation in industry, with textiles, boot and shoe production, and machinery manufacture as principal categories. All of these drew heavily on bank loans, particularly production loans of less than twelve months' duration. A recent study by Professor Lance Davis, covering eight cotton textile firms, reveals that commercial banks furnished about 55 per cent of the loan funds obtained by these firms from all sources in the years 1837-1860. They obtained an average of $1 million in bank loans annually during the years 1847-1860.[10]

These various categories of credit were abundantly represented in the names chosen by the banks—there were in 1860 more than sixty farmers' banks, fifty mechanics', forty-five merchants', thirty commercial (or commerce), twenty traders', fifteen manufacturers' (including overlaps involving practically every combination). There were banks for lumbermen, grocers, importers, miners, timber cutters, wheat growers, reapers, millers. New London boasted a Whaling Bank; and on Nantucket Island, the Pacific Bank

had been established to lend chiefly to whaling expeditions
to that faraway ocean—a bank which survives as the Pacific
National! Of the several Iron Banks of the era, two are still
in operation (in Falls Village, Connecticut, and Morristown,
New Jersey).

The railroad boom of the 1850's drew on a large amount
of bank credit. New England banks, for instance, found
western railroad construction a promising outlet for "loans
for circulation." And the Ohio Life Insurance and Trust
Company, the bank whose failure touched off the panic of
1857, was a heavy investor in railroad credits which turned
sour.

Besides direct loans to business firms, banks by 1860 were
also an important indirect source of equity capital. They
made loans to wealthy capitalists on stock collateral, and in
addition, particularly in New York, provided a large volume
of credit to stockbrokers in the form of "call loans." Such
loans, which were nominally payable at the demand of the
banks, were regarded as a safe and profitable form of "secondary reserve."

Finally, banks were important holders of government securities, which made up about 10 per cent of earning assets.
Such investments were the standard backing, of course, for
note issue under free banking. Most widely held were state
government securities, which were issued mainly to finance
public improvement projects. One factor in the financial
panic of 1860-1861 was that northern banks had heavy investments in southern state government securities and
feared (rightly) that these would be defaulted. The debt of
the federal government was relatively small prior to the
Civil War, and did not form a large element in bank portfolios. However, during business depressions (as in the late
1850's), federal deficits usually increased the supply of securities and banks commonly increased their holdings.

Thus, banks in 1860 were important lenders to business
firms, farmers, and government. They were the principal

source of the nation's money supply, and carried on some of the clearing and bookkeeping involved in the system of credit and payments. They were not involved to any great extent with *personal* loan or deposit business. Savings deposits were relatively small and provided by relatively few commercial banks. However, many New England savings banks were at this time virtually savings departments of the commercial banks, for they invested large sums in bank stocks, kept large deposits with commercial banks, and were often managed by the same people.

Commercial banks were not directly sources of consumer credit, but they contributed to it indirectly. Bank loans often enabled merchants to carry the sort of customers' accounts described in the following (Pennsylvania) illustration:

The importing merchant sold his merchandise largely to country storekeepers at the nominal credit of six months, but generally he could not obtain payment under twelve months or even longer. These accounts with country merchants were open-book accounts, very little being given in payment. The retail shopkeeper was in much the same situation as the wholesaler. He bought his stock of goods on a six months' note and sold the bulk of it on accounts current to people who did not expect to settle oftener than once a year.[11]

The commercial banks of 1860 were just beginning to develop trust business. In New York, the Farmers Loan and Trust Company was pioneering in the development of personal and corporate trust services, and the United States Trust Company had over $1 million of deposits.

On the whole, the banking system mirrored the society as a whole—diverse, disorderly, growing rapidly but at an uneven pace of fits, jerks, and starts—enterprising and progressive, but not always overly scrupulous. Bank credit had played a big role in financing the westward movement of population, cultivation, and transportation. It underwrote much of the high level of international commerce and shipping, and it contributed significantly to the capital needs of up-and-coming industrial development.

But there was widespread discontent with the monetary performance of the banks, particularly after the panic of 1857. The problem was deep-rooted; it stemmed in part from the insatiable credit needs of frontier enterprise and in part from the absence of a central bank to defend the liquidity of the banking system against panic. So long as public opinion opposed tight credit and central banking, it would be difficult to achieve the kind of monetary stability which was so widely demanded. No obvious remedy presented itself.

Nor was there any agreement as to who should be responsible. The Democrats, who dominated national politics for most of the thirty years prior to the Civil War, adhered to the faith that banking control was no responsibility of the federal government. The individual states had, of course, tackled the responsibility of banking reform, and had made some beneficial innovations. But individual states could not take actions to secure a monetary *system* for the nation as a whole—to create a uniform bank-note currency and an efficient nationwide flow of credit and payments. Individual state regulation could do nothing to curb the tendencies toward cyclical instability which were inherent in the structure of the banking system so long as it lacked an adequate central bank.

The problems that existed in 1860 were not new; they had been recognized in some areas for nearly half a century. Without some special stimulus, there would doubtless have been no drastic reforms. The shock of the Civil War provided the stimulus for change. It created a situation of acute financial disorder and inflation, in which the banks were widely criticized for their conduct. It created a fiscal crisis for the federal government, necessitating unprecedented expedients to cover its mushrooming expenditures. The war removed from power the die-hard defenders of laissez faire and states' rights, and enhanced in general the power and scope of federal responsibilities. One of the most important manifestations of the new era was the reassertion of federal authority over banking through the establishment of the national banking system.

3

ESTABLISHMENT OF THE
NATIONAL BANKING SYSTEM

O N FEBRUARY 25, 1863, President Abraham Lincoln signed into law "An Act to Provide a National Currency, Secured by a Pledge of United States Stocks, and to Provide for the Circulation and Redemption Thereof." It may be doubted whether the hand that had so recently signed the Emancipation Proclamation felt any particular sensation from its contact with this particular bill, as distinguished from accompanying enactments "authorizing the Secretary of the Treasury to pay Perry E. Brocchus his salary as judge of the supreme court of the United States for the Territory of New Mexico," or "authorizing the Navy Department to allow to Paymaster Gilbert E. Thornton $4,500, in settlement of his account for money stolen from him without fault or negligence on his part."

To be sure, Mr. Lincoln had urged the enactment of the national currency bill in his message to Congress a few weeks previous. And his secretary, John Hay, indicates that the President took a greater interest in the bank proposal than in most financial measures. But his mind was filled with the more direct problem of the war itself. After two years of incredible blood-letting, the contenders stood stalemated. A series of federal commanders had demonstrated their incapacity in the frustrating campaigns in Virginia, so close to the capital. Now the rebels were moving northward, threatening an invasion that might bring the federal government to accept an armistice and grant them their demands. The military crisis was so serious that the President had been obliged to demand a system of national military conscription—a degree of coercion without precedent in American history.

However, the adoption of the National Currency Act brought great elation to Lincoln's Secretary of the Treasury. Salmon P. Chase had come to the Cabinet without any particular financial training. He was a lawyer by training and a politician by trade, a big, sober, serious man whose character was notable for outspoken moral rectitude, vanity, and ambition. Chase had been elected governor of Ohio in 1856 as a Democrat, but his outspoken condemnation of slavery and his geographic origin earned him a Cabinet position in a Republican administration.

In financial matters, Chase displayed many of the hard-money emblems of Jacksonian democracy. He disliked and distrusted banks and was antagonistic toward the central-banking principle. In 1856, he had announced his belief that "The best practicable currency in my judgment would be a currency of coin, admitting the use of large notes only for the convenience of commerce. Such a currency, however, is only attainable through the legislation of Congress and the action of the General Government." In this vigorous endorsement of federal action, Chase went far beyond most of his Democratic contemporaries. Ultimately it was his leadership and influence that restored federal control to the banking system, and the resulting legislation became the most notable achievement of his uneven career.

The problems that Mr. Chase encountered upon taking office in 1861 would have staggered a financial genius. The government had levied no internal taxes of any sort for forty years; thus, there was no administrative system in existence to collect them and no existing tax legislation amenable to rapid rate increases. Tariff duties on imports, long the sole source of tax revenues, were drastically increased, but furnished only a minor fraction of the funds now needed. Under the Independent Treasury system, all federal transactions were required to be made in coin, or Treasury notes, if available. The system was designed to keep the government away from the "corrupting taint" of the banks, but it made for inefficiency in handling transactions and greatly complicated the operations involved in borrowing money.

All of these conditions would have been less disturbing had it not been for the astronomical growth of federal expenditures. In the 1850's, the government spent at most $70 million a year. In the single year 1862, expenditures rose to more than six times that level, and by the end of the war were running beyond $1 billion a year.

The traditional expedient for covering federal deficits was to borrow by issuing bonds. Immediately after taking office, Chase set to work trying to raise funds by this route. His insistence that bonds be paid for in coin soon led to a dispute with the banks, who wanted to pay for them with newly created deposits (as the loan legislation would probably have permitted). Nevertheless, many of them subscribed generously to the Treasury issues.

Though the banks paid for their bonds in coin, their deposits and note issues expanded. Funds lent to the government were rapidly spent, then to a large extent redeposited by private recipients; bank loans were extended to individuals buying securities; and as time passed, the stimulus of a war economy sent the volume of business loans upward.

Secretary Chase watched the banks with an unsympathetic eye. Although grateful for their support, he was alarmed at the increased quantity and decreased quality of the bank-note circulation that seemed to attend it. In his first annual report (December 1861), he advanced a novel proposal. Under existing free banking systems, banks were authorized to issue their own distinctive, unstandardized notes upon deposit of approved securities (including United States Treasury securities in most states). Why not create a uniform bank-note currency, issued under federal authority, which existing state-chartered banks would be permitted to put into circulation upon deposit of an appropriate sum in Treasury securities?

Before much attention could be given to this proposal, circumstances changed radically. A few days after Chase's report, the banks announced that they could no longer redeem their liabilities in coin. Such suspension of specie payments was bound to come. The banks were losing specie reserves, as financial disorder and the deterioration of the military situation led to hoarding of coin, and as exports of specie were spurred by the domestic inflation of prices. While their reserves declined, the banks were increasing their demand liabilities by public and private loans.

Nevertheless, the suspension was greatly annoying to Chase and to those in Congress who shared his preference for hard money and his distrust of the banks. Many congressmen felt that there was little point in selling bonds to the banks in exchange for inconvertible notes and deposits; let the government save itself the cost of interest payments and issue paper currency itself.

Let it be remembered that prior to the Civil War the federal government did not issue paper currency. To be sure, during the War of 1812 and during subsequent periods of depression deficits, the government issued short-term Treasury notes which sometimes circulated as currency (although they generally bore interest). But these were limited in amount, temporary in existence, and were not legal tender for private transactions. To advocate federal issues of legal-tender currency was to conjure up recollections, often romantically exaggerated, of the horrors of paper-money inflation in the Revolutionary era.

During 1861, the Treasury issued interest-bearing Treasury notes, as oft before. It experimented with a new type of "demand notes"—currency ostensibly convertible into coin on demand. These were not legal tender, however, and were not widely accepted—particularly after the Treasury proved unable to keep enough coin on hand to redeem the notes.

In early 1862, it was becoming painfully evident that the war would last much longer and cost vastly more than had previously been thought. Should the government attempt to cover its enormous requirements by further bond sales? The prospect did not appeal to most congressmen. They had visions of a repetition of the experiences of 1814-1815, when the government issued bond flotation after flotation at steadily increasing discounts and had been obliged to accept in payment bushels of bank notes of the most diverse quality—many of which were completely useless for making payments at the places where cash was needed.

Instead, a bill to finance government expenditures by the issue of legal-tender currency was introduced by Congressman E. G. Spaulding, president of the Farmers and Mechanics Bank of Buffalo, New York. He opposed further bond sales, arguing that under such an arrangement the government "must go into the streets shinning for the means, like an individual in failure of circumstances, and sure of being used up in the end by the avarice of those who may exact unreasonable terms." The proposed currency, he contended, would pay the troops and would also furnish a national currency with which people could pay their taxes, a currency suitable for use anywhere in the country at a time when bank notes, lacking convertibility, were not satisfactory for these purposes. Congress acquiesced, and on February 25, 1862, the President signed what was the first national currency act, authorizing the issue of $150 million of legal-tender notes—the renowned "greenbacks."

Although Secretary Chase disliked the legal-tender provision, he supported it as a necessary evil. Once empowered, he showed no reluctance to issue the new notes. Furthermore, he modestly decorated the $1 bill with his own portrait. Unsympathetic observers regarded this as an unfair method of campaigning for the presidential nomination, an accusation supported by the absence of contemporaries' pictures from the other notes. (Mr. Chase's portrait now graces the $10,000 bill, a denomination not issued in 1862.)

Ultimately a total issue of $450 million of the new currency was authorized, and the volume in circulation approached that level by 1863. These notes were not convertible into specie on demand; but they could be used to buy interest-bearing federal bonds payable in gold and redeemable after the war.

The new currency greatly eased the Treasury's burdens during the rest of 1862. Furthermore, a new system of internal taxes began to yield revenue in 1863. But expenditures were rising even faster; the pressure to raise funds was unremitting. At the same time, the economy was showing the unsettling effects of heavy federal deficits. Prices were rising at an increasing rate—wholesale prices increased 20 per cent in the last half of 1862.

The issue of government currency was directly inflationary; in addition, the greenbacks supported the expansion of bank credit. Since greenbacks were legal tender, the banks could use them in place of gold and silver to redeem their own liabilities or to hold as legal reserves, where these were required. Thus, the greenbacks became "high-powered money," in that each dollar of greenbacks deposited in banks could serve as the basis for several dollars of credit expansion. Congressman Hooper of Massachusetts warned that "just in proportion as the amount of United States notes [greenbacks] is increased, the bank circulation which is redeemable in those notes will be augmented, and both will depreciate together."

There was increasing discontent with the deteriorating quality of bank-note currency as well. "In 1862 there were fifteen hundred banks," noted Senator John Sherman of Ohio, "the notes of 253 of which had not been counterfeited. The variety of imitations was 1,861; of alterations, 3,039; of spurious notes, 1,685." [1]

In December 1862, Chase renewed his support for a national bank-note currency backed by United States securities. But now he urged that it be issued by "banking associations organized under national legislation"—with national rather than state charters. Existing state-chartered banks were to be encouraged to take national charters, and there was a vague suggestion that something more drastic would happen if they did not.

The immediate advantage of the proposal to the government, Chase noted, "will be found in the market created for bonds, and the support thereby given to the national credit." And once the war was over, a bank-note currency would be superior to the greenbacks, which were liable to excessive issue and which would, he felt, not respond properly to the needs of the economy. Thus the greatest benefits would come, he concluded, when the proposed bank notes "shall become the established and sole national circulation of the country."

The national-bank plan soon received the vigorous endorsement of President Lincoln. But in Congress, opposition arose from several quarters. Some legislators saw no reason to desist from the issue of greenbacks as a proper national currency. Others attacked the measure as unduly oppressive. What would happen, they asked, to all the state securities presently held to back note issues? Among the banking community, there was much opposition, particularly in New York. The city bankers feared the measure would encourage

the formation of small and unwholesome "banks of circulation," and possibly lower banking standards rather than
raise them.

As time passed, however, the proposed bill picked up
more and more safeguards. Mr. Chase insisted that the
measure was essential to promote bond sales. Outside the
government, he was vigorously supported by Jay Cooke,
the country's leading private banker, who was performing
yeoman service in selling bonds. Partly through the influence of Jay Cooke and his brother, Henry, the powerful support of Senator Sherman was brought behind the measure.
On February 25, 1863—precisely a year after creation of the
first national currency—the National Currency Act became
law.

The resulting law was long and complex, but far-reaching
in scope. It authorized the United States government to
charter banks ("associations" was the term used in the act),
provided they could muster $50,000 of capital, of which at
least $30,000 must be invested in Treasury securities. The
"national currency" created by the law was to take the form
of national bank notes, uniform in design and engraved under the direction of the government, but to be put into actual circulation by individual banks. Banks could obtain a
supply of notes from the government only by pledging
Treasury bonds as security, and note issues could not exceed 90 per cent of the face value of the bonds so pledged.
Each bank would then issue the notes, imprinted with its
own name, and was charged with the duty of redeeming
them on demand into "lawful money"—that is, greenbacks.
Should a bank be unable to redeem its notes, the bonds
pledged as security would be sold (or redeemed) by the
government and the proceeds used to pay the noteholders.

The government would accept national bank notes at par
for internal revenue taxes or loans; in addition, every national bank was required to accept at par the notes of all
the others. The notes would thus have uniform design and

wide geographic acceptability. Consequently, they would be preferred by the public, and the banks would naturally want to become eligible to issue them. This would provide an incentive for banks to join the system (for there was no compulsion for them to do so), and encourage them to buy Treasury bonds as a basis for note issues.

The bill followed the standard pattern of state free-banking policies. However, the national banking system was to be carefully safeguarded against abuse. First, national banks were required to maintain cash reserves as a proportion of notes and deposit liabilities. However, banks outside the major cities were allowed to count as part of their legal reserves funds held on deposit with city banks. Second, the banks were made subject to a number of carefully designed "quality controls" over their lending operations, and a special federal agency—the office of the Comptroller of the Currency—was created within the Treasury department to supervise and examine the banks in order to make sure the requirements were carried out. Third, rigid limits were imposed on the amount of notes issued by individual banks and by the entire system.

On June 20, the first charter was issued, for the newly created First National Bank of Philadelphia. The bank was largely the creation of Jay Cooke, assisted by his former employer, the private banking firm of E. W. Clark and Company of Philadelphia, but its corporate identity was, of course, separate from their private operations. Actually, the first application was from the First National Bank of New Haven, whose management graciously stepped aside to allow Mr. Cooke to receive Charter Number One. The Philadelphia First enjoyed a long and distinguished career, operating very near the country's first bank—The Bank of North America. The distinctive façades of the two now stand side by side on Chestnut Street—both now occupied by the First Pennsylvania Banking and Trust Company, into which they have been absorbed in the twentieth century. Charter Number Two has weathered a century and now operates as the First New Haven National Bank. Also chartered on June 20 were the First National banks of Youngstown, Ohio, and Stamford, Connecticut. The latter is still in operation as the State National Bank of Connecticut.

The public's attention was not greatly aroused by the commencement of the new banking system. Lee's army was moving north through the Cumberland and Shenandoah Valleys in its most audacious campaign, aiming to split the North and strike at Washington from the rear. A few miles southwest of Harrisburg, Meade was waiting for him. For four days the battle raged at Gettysburg; the northern lines held, and the southern tide was repulsed. A few days later came news of the fall of Vicksburg. From then on, the tremendous economic and logistic superiority of the northern forces asserted itself increasingly.

Nevertheless, much of the region west of Washington remained subject to Confederate control. In the summer of 1864, as the economic straits of the Confederacy became increasingly pressing, troops under command of Jubal Early seized a number of towns in Maryland and Pennsylvania and demanded ransom in cash or goods on threat of destruction. At Chambersburg, Pennsylvania, a demand for $500,-000 was refused, and the town was put to the torch. At Frederick, Maryland, however, the ransom of $200,000 was raised by loans from the town's five banks. This action probably saved a large quantity of federal supplies stored in the town and delayed a movement toward Washington sufficiently to allow necessary reinforcement of the capital's defenses. Memory of the incident has been kept alive by the repeated efforts of the town to obtain reimbursement from the federal government.[2]

Growth of the new national banking system was slow. Some existing chartered banks took national charters, including the Hartford, Youngstown, and Stamford "Firsts". But generally there was no rush by existing banks to join the system. Many were put off by the stuffy insistence of the Treasury that they give up their historic names in exchange for anonymous numerals. City banks generally were not large issuers of notes, and thus were indifferent to the note-issue privileges. Finally, bankers in New York had come to dislike Mr. Chase; and they were not pleased by the strain of anti-bank sentiment that they detected in the measures of 1862 and 1863.

Jay Cooke traveled widely and worked hard to promote national banking—an activity which served both his friendship with Chase and his interest in bond sales. He sponsored prominent national banks in Washington, D. C., and in New York City. In addition, Secretary Chase had the good fortune to secure the services of Hugh McCulloch as his first Comptroller of the Currency. McCulloch had been president of the Bank of the State of Indiana; he had come to Washington in 1862 to fight the national banking bill, but stayed on to direct its operations. He was a respected banker, but a public banker as well, experienced with regulatory as well as profit-seeking activities.

By November 1863, only 134 national banks had been formed, and five-sixths of these were new institutions, rather than conversions. A report of the New York Clearing House Association looked upon the newcomers with scorn: "Your committee knows of very few which are designed to do a legitimate banking business. There may be others, but from the small amount of capital of more than a hundred of them, and the localities of several, your committee strongly suspects them of being intended for banks of circulation only, not regular banks for deposits and discounts."

A number of the new banks were sponsored by private bankers like Jay Cooke. The First National of Davenport, Iowa, which was the first national bank actually to open for business, was largely sponsored by Corbin and Dow, private bankers, while the First National Bank of Cleveland was developed by S. W. Crittenden and Company. Such firms found the note-issue privilege attractive; shrewd men could foresee that the national bank notes would remain in circulation, since the public would have no incentive to convert them. The notes would enable the banks to hold government bonds and receive the interest on them, which was high and payable in gold, while incurring virtually no expense. For existing state banks, however, this advantage was offset by the necessity to withdraw their old notes from circulation.

The sizes and locations of the earliest national banks did give some cause for concern, and a few of them did turn out to be merely "banks of circulation." But the records show unmistakably that most of the first "Firsts" meant business. The accounts of the first fifty banks to receive national charters show in October 1865, $25 million of private deposits to $10 million of notes. Even excluding eight big banks which provided two-thirds of the totals, we find deposits running almost 50 per cent ahead of notes. The first fifty also have a good survival record—nearly half of them have reached the century mark. A list of the survivors is found on page 280 in the Appendix.

The slow growth of the system in 1863 led Chase, McCulloch, and their allies to work for revisions in the law, and it was thoroughly reconstructed in June 1864. The new law increased some of the safeguards against wildcatting—it prohibited real estate loans, raised the minimum capital for city banks, and increased the proportion of capital that had to be paid in before a bank could open for business. On the other hand, the legal cash reserve requirement was reduced. Banks were authorized to keep distinctive parts of their former names.

This legislation speeded up conversions, but the rate was still unimpressive. By late 1864, nearly six hundred national banks had been formed, but less than two hundred were conversions. Most of the national banks were small, while the major banks in leading cities remained aloof. In New

York City, for instance, the First National Bank was organized as a new bank under the leadership of John Thompson, former private banker and publisher of a leading bank-note reporter. For a time his bank was an outcast in the New York banking community; but ultimately it prospered, and Thompson went on to become one of the founders of the Chase National Bank.

With the end of the war in sight, Congress and the administration resolved to carry through reform of the monetary system to its logical conclusion. "The national banks were intended to supersede the State banks," thundered Senator Sherman. "Both cannot exist together." [3] In March 1865, the government employed for the first time Chief Justice Marshall's principle that "the power to tax is the power to destroy." By a narrow margin, Congress voted to impose a tax of 10 per cent on all further issues of bank notes, other than those authorized by the National Currency Acts.

As expected, applications for charter conversion accelerated. The big city banks were not much affected by the tax itself—the Bank of Commerce, the biggest bank in the country, issued no notes—but they had an inducement to follow country banks into the system. The latter would need city correspondents to hold their reserve deposits, and only national banks would be eligible. More than seven hundred banks shifted to national charters in 1865, and many of the remaining banks simply closed up shop.

By the end of the war, the inflationary process of federal finance had carried the money supply—government currency, bank notes, and bank deposits—to a level double that of 1860. With the great rise in money and total expenditures came a large increase in prices. By 1865, the cost of living was 75 per cent above 1860, and wholesale prices at their peak were more than twice the prewar levels. Even so, the price inflation in the North was mild compared to that in the South, where currency issues were the chief means of finance. In the Confederacy, prices in 1864 were forty times what they had been in 1861. With defeat came repudiation of the Confederate currency and bonds, ruining many financial institutions in the South.

The greenbacks and national bank notes soon took the appearance of competing forms of currency, each with its partisans. In the immediate postwar years, great controversy raged over their relative roles, and over the desirability and means of restoring them to full par value in terms of gold and silver. We will return to this subject in Chapter 7.

How much the creation of the national banking system added to the market for Treasury bonds during the war is hard to determine—perhaps $100 million. To the extent that bond purchases led to the expansion of bank notes and deposits, there must have been some addition to inflationary pressure, though perhaps not so much as through greenback issue. However, the northern banks did make numerous beneficial contributions to the assistance of war finance, for which they were praised by Comptroller Hulburd in 1866. "They now hold one-fourth of the entire indebtedness of the United States," he pointed out. "They have redeemed and returned to the Treasury . . . over fourteen millions of mutilated legal-tenders, and have redeemed twenty-five millions of seven-thirty [bond interest] coupons, to the very great convenience of both the public and the Treasury Department. They have been instrumental in placing in the hands of the people more than eleven hundred millions of United States securities. They have received and disbursed from the revenue seventeen hundred and seventy-four millions of public moneys free of expense to the government." [4] Furthermore, the banks were heavily taxed during the war.

By the end of 1866, more than sixteen hundred banks were functioning under national charters. Perhaps two hundred chartered banks remained outside the national system. The trust companies stayed out by necessity, for national banks were not authorized to perform trust functions. Also remaining outside were a number of stockholder-owned savings and other deposit banks such as the Boatmen's Bank of St. Louis. Equally important, there remained outside the national system a large number of private banks. Some of these served as sponsors and managers of national banks but kept their private operations going as well.

Thus, the national banking system was never universal. But in the late 1860's, it did cover about three-fourths of the country's banking resources. By 1870, the formative stage of the system was completed. National banks were operating in about a thousand communities, and their size distribution was similar to that of northern banks of 1860.

The National Banking Acts of 1863 and 1864 made no allowance for branch banking, and McCulloch and Chase took the position that it was to be discouraged. The bank-of-the-state system of Ohio, Indiana, and Iowa dissolved and most of their components took national charters as unit banks—giving rise to the odd name of the National Branch Bank of Madison, Indiana (now the Madison Bank and Trust Company). In West Virginia, the branches of the Northwest Bank of Virginia took unit charters, as did the components of the Merchants and Mechanics Bank of Wheeling.

Most of the southern branch banks had been ruined by the war, with the chief exception of those in Kentucky— and even there, state legislation soon barred further branch operations. In 1865, however, Congress authorized state banks to enter the national system with existing branches; and in 1866, a national charter was granted to the Bank of the State of Missouri, with eight branches. (The branch at St. Joseph split off and took a unit charter.) The Missouri bank, with head office in St. Louis, was the largest bank outside New York City, and the largest issuer of bank notes in the country. The circumstances leading to its failure in 1877 will be examined in the following chapter.

With this exception, the national banking program

worked against branch banking, which was, consequently, almost nonexistent in the United States during the latter part of the nineteenth century.

On the whole, the standards met by the early national banks compared favorably with those of the prewar period. By 1870, a total of fifteen national banks had failed, chiefly because of alliances with private banking operations. This was a big improvement over the failure record of the 1850's. The Comptroller's office boasted that it screened the banks before granting charter applications, and periodic, unannounced examinations were inflicted on the national banks. Gradually and without fanfare the Comptroller's office began to develop improved standards of asset quality to be applied in bank examination, a process which helped raise standards used by many state authorities as well. An impressive array of bright young bank examiners moved from federal service into positions with leading banks.

The banking legislation of the 1860's was first and foremost aimed at reforming the bank-note circulation, and in this respect it was outstandingly successful. The punitive tax ended once and for all the chaos and confusion that had plagued the currency for half a century before. The national bank notes were safe and uniform, and enjoyed the full confidence of their holders. Since the notes were in effect backed by the faith of the United States government, note holders never had any incentive to panic and to "run" on banks to convert these notes into other forms of cash. And, indeed, no holder of national bank notes suffered any loss from bank failure or suspension.

Furthermore, counterfeiting and fraud were greatly reduced. In place of the thousands of varieties of notes, there were now a very few with which everyone could be familiar, and their paper and engraving were much harder to duplicate. In addition, counterfeiting these notes became a federal crime. The Secret Service was created in 1865 to police violations, and under the direction of the swashbuckling William Wood, rounded up more than two hundred counterfeiters within a year.

Finally, the note-issue reform did much to raise the standards of banking generally. The wildcat banks of earlier times were invariably note-issue banks. Now note issue was completely hedged by safeguards. To be sure, non-national banks could and did continue to operate purely on the basis of deposits, but a bank had to display some solidity and integrity, or people would not keep deposits with it. One of the paradoxical tendencies of the national banking legislation was the great shift toward deposit banking which resulted from the limitations on note issue.

On the other hand, the national bank-note currency presented management problems of its own. Framers of the legislation were impressed by the need to avoid unlimited currency inflation, and wrote into the laws a maximum limit of $300 million. Treasury officials faced the task of parceling this out among the banks, and by 1866 had reached the upper limit. Most of the original circulation was allocated to banks in the northeast, where both conversions and new bank formations were most numerous. In the South, banking was slow in reviving after the war, and southern applications to establish national banks did not come in any volume until the currency quota had been used up. By then, many rapidly growing areas in the West desired national banks as well. Exhaustion of the note-issue quota caused a virtual halt to the granting of charters, until new legislation in 1870 enlarged the authorized note circulation and gave preference to the "under-banked" areas.

Other problems emerged before long. The mechanism of note issues provided no means of dealing with seasonal variations in demand for currency, nor of expanding the circulation to match the growth of the economy. Indeed, once the war was over and the government began to reduce the national debt, note issue tended to contract.

Notwithstanding these disadvantages, the currency reform of the 1860's worked a vast improvement. In so doing, it went to considerable lengths to subordinate the credit functions of the banks to their monetary function. The banks were effectively prohibited from extending private credit through note issue. National banks were prohibited from making mortgage loans, a measure prudent from the standpoint of liquidity and safety, but one which left a vast area of credit demand closed to national banks. They were prohibited from making loans on the security of their own stock. They were forbidden to lend to one borrower a sum in excess of 10 per cent of their capital accounts.

Still, subject to all these restraints, the national banking legislation effectively opened the entire country to free banking. No longer could state authorities limit or forbid chartered banking within a state. Indeed, their response after 1866 was frequently to ease the way for the formation of state banks.

During the latter 1860's, national banking was generally quite profitable, and few bankers felt the restrictions unduly onerous. With gold at a substantial premium, the banks found it remunerative to hold government bonds. National banks furnished ample credit facilities to the northeastern section of the country, where most production and trade occurred.

But the national banking system was very poorly designed to meet the credit needs of southern reconstruction. Local funds were inadequate to meet the minimum capital requirements—besides, southern banks had typically been note-issue banks, and the public was not prepared to hold deposits sufficiently to permit creation of much private credit. Top this with the exhaustion of national bank-note quotas in the late 1860's, and you have the explanation of the striking fact that in 1870, out of sixteen hundred national banks, fewer than one hundred were located in eleven Southern states. There were none at all in Mississippi and Florida, and only twenty-seven in Arkansas,

Texas, Louisiana, Alabama, Georgia, and the Carolinas combined.

Many observers have ranked the failure to provide for an adequate credit system in the South as one of the most serious deficiencies of the Reconstruction program. Such outside credit as entered the region was largely mercantile; northern firms extended commercial credit to southern merchants, who in turn sold goods to the impoverished farmers, white and colored, on credit. In return, the merchants marked up their prices enormously, insisted on crop liens or mortgages for security, and kept their debtors rigidly tied to the cash crops of cotton and tobacco, with the attendant curses of malnutrition, soil depletion, and market instability. Farmers by the thousands slipped into tenancy as their debt burdens and terms became too onerous to fulfill—a development accentuated by the downward trend in the prices they received.

In the West, the problem was not reconstruction out of dire poverty, but development of vast potential wealth. The wealth was mostly in the form of land, however, and national banks could not make loans on mortgage. The farmers of the middle border wanted money they could hold in their hands, but extension of credit through bank-note issues was now barred. The minimum capital requirements were hard to meet west of the Mississippi, as in the South.

From these regions there came, almost from the start, an unremitting antagonism toward the national banking system. Clearly the pendulum of public opinion was swinging. Public dissatisfaction with bank failures and monetary instability in the years prior to 1863 had been responsible for the imposition of banking safeguards which were particularly restrictive to the kinds of credit demanded on the agrarian frontier. Now these restrictions were in turn under fire.

However, the critics were also attacking, by implication, the failure of Congress to create a "national" banking system—that is, a system that would facilitate the movement of loanable funds over the country as a whole, so that the "underdeveloped" regions of South and West could draw on the abundant saving of the northeast. One possible solution might have been to permit branch banking across state lines. But there was no support for this idea, which smacked so much of the old Bank of the United States. Considering the experience with interstate loan companies in the 1880's, and with the Freedman's Savings and Trust Company (described on p. 61), it may be doubted whether such an arrangement would have worked. Such operations would certainly not have been popular in South and West, one may be sure.

Some capital did move when banks in less-developed areas sold their stock to investors in wealthy areas. But national bank stock was not ideal for this purpose. To safeguard creditors, Congress had provided that stockholders might be assessed, in event of bank failure, for an amount equal to the initial par value of their stock. Thus the stock might turn into a liability. To avoid this danger, stockholders had to keep well informed about the condition of a bank and the character of its management—something not easy to do at a distance. Consequently, bank stock tended to remain close to home. A report by the Comptroller in 1876 showed that only 10 per cent of national bank stock was owned by out-of-state investors, and the proportion was only slightly above the average in South and West.[5]

A number of expedients developed to meet the needs for mobility of credit. Eastern banks and financial institutions carried on lending operations outside their home areas. Borrowers issued readily negotiable commercial paper, which often gravitated from West to East. The major means for promoting mobility of funds, however, was through correspondent banking relations. These existed principally to provide country banks with reserve and note-redemption facilities. But the big banks, especially in New York and the northeast, often made loans to banks in other areas, frequently by purchasing interest-bearing "certificates of deposit" from them. However, critics noted that funds often flowed "uphill"—that is, country banks sent off funds to their city cousins to be used for stock-market lending.

That the mobility of funds into the West was not very satisfactory during the last third of the nineteenth century is evident from the high interest rates that prevailed. As late as 1908, Woodrow Wilson was critical of the relatively slight development of branch banking. "The local bank is built up by local resources," he pointed out. "Only the local resources for the most part can be called upon for local advantages. Every community is as poor as its own resources. You cannot get the riches of the country in order to make it rich until it gets rich enough to establish a bank. It cannot get credit in the money centers until there accumulates enough capital to make it practically independent of that credit." [6]

We do have one case of an interstate branch bank which was established under federal auspices—the Freedman's Savings and Trust Company. This institution received a special charter from Congress in March 1865, and was entirely separate from the national banking program. Its purpose was to provide savings-deposit facilities for ex-slaves and their descendents. Its structure was essentially that of a mutual savings bank, managed by trustees, with no stockholder capital. The institution was to invest in United States securities, but up to one-third of the deposits might be employed without restriction. No adequate provisions for reserves or supervision were imposed.

The Freedman's Savings and Trust opened its main office in New York City, but soon was operating thirty-three additional offices, chiefly in the South. It provided checking deposit facilities and made no effort to limit its operations to Negroes. The management succeeded in attracting a lot of deposits by stressing the supposed "official" character of the institution. In 1870, Congress amended the charter to permit mortgage loans and real estate operations—an interesting contrast to the national banking restrictions. By 1873, the organization held over $4 million in deposits.

During the panic of 1873, the institution was hit by heavy depositor withdrawals and by heavy losses on its real estate and other loans. Evidences of incompetent and dishonest management were beginning to come to light. It went into liquidation in 1874, owing $3 million to more than 60,000 depositors, many of whom had very small accounts. Ultimately they received about two-thirds of their money, though many failed to file claims properly and received nothing.[7]

This episode, revealing as it is of the frailties of public and private men in the days of Reconstruction, does not prove that honest and productive interstate banking could not have developed. But certainly the rule of thumb, "one bank-one office," vastly facilitated careful examination of banks by government officials, and made it easy for bank management to know what was going on. The subsequent abuses that arose under chain banking suggest problems which might well have afflicted a system providing for interstate branch banking at that time.

All in all, the creation of the national banking system and the suppression of state-bank note issues constituted a momentous change in the nation's monetary and banking system. Although much of the incentive for banking reform arose out of the instability of the 1850's, the decisive support for federal action came only because of the government's desperate need for funds—a need, paradoxically, which the national banking legislation did not really do much to meet. The National Banking Acts and the tax on state-bank notes reversed the irresponsible attitude toward banking fostered by Jackson and his followers. The legislation of the 1860's established once and for all the principle that control of the quantity and quality of the nation's money was a national responsibility.

The changes in policy were radical, and it is not surprising that they were not altogether successful. From a monetary standpoint, the national banking program created a paper currency that fluctuated too little and a deposit structure that fluctuated too much. Furthermore, emphasis on the monetary responsibility of the banks led to measures that restricted their ability to meet the needs for credit in the less developed sections of the country.

In the light of subsequent developments, one may argue that the national banking legislation actually over-regulated the banks. Its founders were imbued with the Jacksonian dislike of central banking—McCulloch boasted in 1864 that the new system "promises to give to the people that long-existing 'desideratum', a national currency without a national bank, a banknote circulation of uniform value without the creation of a moneyed power in a few hands over the politics and business of the country." [8] They sought instead to protect the liquidity and solvency of the banks by putting each one in a virtual strait jacket. Even so, the restrictions did not adequately provide a source from which the banking system as a whole could obtain cash in a crisis, nor did they eliminate the tendency for money and credit to fluctuate unduly.

Before many years had passed, the pressure of credit demands which the national banks could not satisfy provided the basis for the revival of state-chartered banks and trust companies, leading to a genuine "dual banking system." How the banking system evolved in relation to the economic changes that followed 1865, and how the banks participated in economic change and development, are the main themes of the chapters that follow.

CHAPTER

4

AMERICA'S AGE OF ENTERPRISE

Once the civil war was over, the nation embarked upon
a long period of remarkable economic growth. Despite interruptions caused by business depressions, particularly in
the 1870's and 1890's, the trend was maintained surprisingly
well down through the decade of the 1920's. In the process,
living standards were greatly increased and the character of
the economy altered almost beyond recognition.

The nation's total output of goods and services increased
rapidly. From an average volume of about $6 billion a year
in the late 1860's, it rose to $30 billion by the end of the
century, and by the late 1920's was averaging about $70
billion—after adjustments for price variations.

This rise in output reflected rapid increases in the productive capacity of the economy. The most important factor in this process was more people. In 1870, the nation's
population totaled about forty million; it had nearly doubled by 1900, and by 1928 stood around one hundred
twenty million. Natural increase contributed most of this
rise, particularly before 1900, when the family with eight

or ten children was not uncommon. But this was also the period of a vast tide of immigration. Between 1905 and 1914, immigrants poured in at the rate of one million a year —levels never matched before or since. By 1920, one-fifth of the people in the country over twenty-one years of age had been born abroad. Great numbers came from England, Germany and Scandinavia, from Italy, Poland, Russia, and central Europe. They came fleeing poverty and oppression in the old world, or seeking opportunity in the new. Most of them were in the prime of life, ready to work and to endure hardships, and they found plenty of both.

Although many people continued to suffer from low incomes, the nation's output was able to rise faster than the population, until production per capita in the late 1920's was nearly four times what it had been sixty years before.

The second factor on which the nation's phenomenal growth rested was land. Between 1860 and 1910, the vast resources of the continent were brought under cultivation, and the United States became the agricultural leader of the world. Area in farms increased from four hundred million acres in 1860 to nearly nine hundred million in 1910; and the number of farms rose from two million to six million. Total farm output more than tripled, with wheat, cotton, livestock, and dairy products contributing a major share of the expansion.

But most strikingly, the era that followed the Civil War was the period of America's industrial revolution. The number of manufacturing workers increased from two million in 1869 to ten million in 1929, and total manufacturing output rose nearly twenty fold. Industrialization was epitomized by the steel industry, just beginning its existence in the 1860's. Steel output reached 100,000 tons in 1872; by 1880, it had topped the million mark. It passed ten million tons in 1899, and in 1929 surpassed fifty million. Less dramatic but much closer to the average man's standard of living were the substantial increases and improvements in food processing and textile production.

Critically important to the whole process of economic growth and industrialization was the creation of a national transportation system. Railroad construction more than any other single factor furnished the driving force in the economy in the years between the Civil War and World War I. Railroad purchasing stimulated the construction, steel, and machinery industries. Western land-grant railroads took the initiative in encouraging rapid settlement. The short-run variations in railroad spending largely shaped the fluctuations in the economy in the post-Civil War years.

By 1920, the nation's railway network was essentially completed—a web of over 400,000 miles of steel, 90 per cent of which had come into existence since 1867. By 1920, the country had entered the automobile age. In the decade to follow, the tremendous growth of auto production and use set off repercussions through many other sectors of the economy—steel, petroleum, highway construction, rubber, glass—much as the railroads had done in earlier years. Similar as they were, however, the shift from the railway age to the automobile age was associated with far-reaching economic and financial changes. Railroad development spawned giant corporations, selling their services to the public under conditions often bordering on monopoly. With this came the rise of financial institutions oriented toward big business. The age of railroad development was marked by bitter social tensions and animosities, by a sense of class conflict between "the people" on one hand and "Wall Street and the trusts" on the other.

The coming of the automobile was associated with very different trends. Although the auto firms themselves achieved great size, the competitive tone of the industry, set by Henry Ford, worked spectacularly in the direction of lower price and improved quality. More subtly, the industry sold the buyer his own transport service, making him more independent, not less. It favored the rise of small businesses—

filling stations, auto dealerships—while the railroads had tended to favor the large. The spread of car ownership was broadly symptomatic of a new era of high-level mass consumption and of the emergence of a middle-class society. It brought with it a transformation in the outlook of banking and finance, with increasing emphasis on services to consumers—a transformation which was hastened by the events of the 1930's.

Whether the tone was being set by railroad or automobile, however, industrial growth created enormous energy requirements, met by greatly expanded output of coal and petroleum. Industrial production required raw materials, and men tore into the bowels of the earth with a vigor which was often alarming to send forth vast quantities of iron, copper, lead, zinc, and the precious metals.

America's industrial revolution was also critically dependent upon new ideas—the spectacular advances of technology, science, and engineering, which devised means of making better and cheaper steels; of refining petroleum and designing engines to burn it; of generating electricity, transmitting it, and putting it to work for energy and light.

And everywhere, the nation's economic growth required capital—in farming, in railroads, in industry. Capital appeared most dramatically in the huge steel mills of Pittsburgh, or the Ford plant near Detroit, or in the construction of the Pacific railways. But it was equally important in the forms of plows, reapers, and tractors, or the tools and inventories of millions of small business firms. Between 1880 and 1929, the amount of productive capital in use quadrupled; by 1929, the nation's economy was using $150 billion worth of capital goods. The added capital kept pace with the rising population and work force and, combined with technical improvement, supported impressive increases in output per man hour in industry and transportation.

To finance the capital growth essential to industrial progress also required a lot of money. As always, an impressive proportion of the total financing required came from the saving of the farmers and business men involved—plowing back personal effort and current income. But the period also saw an increase in the general importance of external sources of funds, as compared with the pre-1860 situation.

Vital to the management and financing of large capital growth was the growing use of incorporation. In the 1860's, railroads and other transport operations were the chief domain of large non-financial corporations. In the latter part of the century, however, the advantages of corporate status became increasingly compelling to many firms, especially as they grew in size. Then as now, corporate status possessed great advantages for acquiring external funds through security issues and for management of large-scale properties.

The rise of corporations meant the rise of stocks and bonds as instruments of capital financing. Many of these were sold abroad, as the period witnessed a large inflow of foreign capital. Large amounts were purchased by wealthy individuals, in an era when inequality in income and wealth was more extreme than in our own times. And a substantial amount of securities was sold to banks and other financial institutions. Railroads and industrial corporations also drew on shorter-term bank credit, sometimes to tide them over while new long-term securities were being issued. Still more bank credit flowed to them indirectly, through bank loans to individuals on collateral of stocks and bonds.

The banks were deeply involved in railroad and other corporate finance in other ways as well. New securities had to be marketed, and banking houses (particularly the important private bankers) did a large share of this business. Corporate finance also required elaborate trust services connected with stocks, bonds, and other financial instruments. Securities had to be registered, transfers of ownership effected, interest and dividend payments disbursed, and title to mortgaged property protected in the interests of bond-holders.

While the rise of big industrial firms was a dramatic aspect of the country's economic development, the important work of growing, processing, and distributing the nation's food and fiber remained principally the work of millions of small, local enterprises—farms, factories, and stores. Bank credit was an important financial resource to these firms, as it has continued to be ever since. And in the years down to 1900, such activities commanded the attention of most of the country's banks, and probably the bulk of bank credit.

The evolution of the American banking system was intimately bound up with the economic trends we have noted. The number of banks grew rapidly as the great vacant areas of the West were subdued by farmers and by the architects of a multitude of small towns. The number of national banks increased, but the expansion was much more spectacular among non-national banks, which were easier to start and less restricted in their operations. Equally impressive was the diversity in the types of banking and related institutions.

In the years prior to 1900, banking expansion was notable more in numbers than in size of institution. The number of banks grew from about two thousand in 1866, to over twelve thousand by 1900. However, the average size of commercial banks in 1896 was about half a million dollars of assets each—no larger than in 1870. The biggest New York bank boasted assets of $30 to $40 million, which was not much above the levels achieved in 1870. American banking almost everywhere was characteristically "main-street banking" in size and scope.

After 1900, the banking system seemed to split in half, following the divergent trends of small-town-farm growth on one hand and big-city-industrial growth on the other. The number of small-sized, small-town banks increased enor-

mously in the first twenty years of the century, so that by
1920 the country had 30,000 banks. At the same time, the
size of the largest institutions was increasing greatly, much
of the increase coming through mergers. In 1897, the National City Bank of New York merged with the Third National Bank and pushed its total assets over the $100-million
mark. Chicago's First National also expanded rapidly by
mergers. In the years following, additional consolidations
enlarged Guaranty Trust, Irving Trust, and (in the 1920's)
the Chase National. National City was the first to penetrate
the $1 billion-mark in the 1920's. Big banks sought to keep
pace with their giant industrial customers. And banking
growth was greatly facilitated by the development, about
the turn of the century, of machines to take over the enormous volume of calculations involved in handling checks
and deposit business. The first systematic programs of credit
analysis were instituted at about the same time.

The many and the huge! Main Street banks and Wall
Street banks—this dualism is greatly oversimplified, but it
does capture the essence of the major cross-currents affect-
ing banking. The pull of agricultural-commercial expansion
on the one hand and railroad-industrial growth on the
other had tremendous influence on the character and functions of banks—influence which tended to strain at the limitations imposed by the national banking system. In the
country, the pull was toward banks that could be formed
with small capital and could lend on mortgage. In the city,
the pull was toward investment banking and corporate trust
services. These opportunities created the vacuum into which
non-national banks expanded. In time the restraints on national banks were themselves relaxed, and the banks came
increasingly to take on the "department store" quality which
is now so apparent.

The details of the relation of banks to American economic
growth and change vary endlessly from case to case, but the
relation was usually close. New firms generally started up

on capital accumulated by the owner or by local capitalists willing to enter partnership. Once the firm was under way, bank credit was likely to play a major role in its growth, along with reinvested profits. On the other hand, newly created wealth, from whatever source, commonly spawned new banks. These relations are well exemplified by the petroleum industry, which became in several respects a prototype of the good and the bad elements in the age of enterprise.

The emergence of a petroleum industry coincided with the coming of the Civil War. "Colonel" Edwin Drake had come to western Pennsylvania to make the first experiments in drilling, partly at the instigation of James M. Townsend, president of the City Savings Bank of New Haven. When Drake's funds were exhausted, a last minute loan from a Meadville bank provided the margin needed to make a strike in 1859. Soon a mad rush of settlement, drilling, production, and speculation was on. New wells were brought in almost daily, with output increasing so rapidly as to outrun at times the facilities for storage and transportation. Boom towns sprang up out of nowhere. New banks were opened to provide deposit facilities for the new wealth, and to channel outside funds into profitable local opportunities. C. V. Culver, a Pennsylvania congressman, formed a banking syndicate in New York under the name of Culver, Penn and Co., which promoted a string of banks in the region. Culver funds were poured into town speculation and construction of a railroad.

Soon, major rail lines had extended into the region, but the oil was still being hauled from well to railroad in barrels loaded on wagons at fantastic expense. By 1864, transportation charges took 60 per cent of the New York delivered price of oil. Samuel Van Syckle, an oil buyer, borrowed $30,000 from the First National Bank of Titusville and set to work building a pipeline to reach the railroad. Despite sabotage by the local teamsters, the line was at once financially successful and economically beneficial. Soon pipelines became a significant medium for longer shipments as well.

In 1866, the bubble burst. Soaring production combined with the deflationary postwar trend of prices depressed the market, and much of the debt-founded speculation collapsed. The Culver bank chain failed, closing five banks in the area; its Venango National was only the second national bank to fail in the country. (In all fairness to Culver, we note he was also financially active in the First National Bank of Elkhart, Indiana, which originated in 1842 as the Bank of Elkhart, and which is still in successful operation.) The Titusville bank had to foreclose on the Van Syckle pipeline.

The oil boom also brought a tremendous growth in refining activity which soon witnessed the rise of petroleum's leading figure—John D. Rockefeller. Rockefeller had started in business as a youthful commission merchant in Cleveland. In 1860, he scouted the oil fields and came to the conclusion that the competitive chaos and instability made the production end a poor bet for outside investors. But refining was another story. Refinery facilities were sprouting in Cleveland, one of them operated by a friend, Samuel Andrews, who drew Rockefeller into the business to provide capital. The new firm was efficient and progressive technologically; under Rockefeller, expansion became a major objective. The profits were plowed back and bank loans utilized to the fullest degree. At first it was hard going—Rockefeller said later, "I had worn out the knees of my pants begging credit at the banks." Within a few years, it was a different story. As Allan Nevins put it:

since between three and four million dollars were now invested in the city's refining business, Cleveland bankers were willing to encourage so important a local industry—particularly when they could lend to a man as able and reliable as Rockefeller.

And Rockefeller was eager to borrow. He was determined to achieve leadership in [the industry]. In 1867 his and [his brother] William's names appeared together in the New York directory; thereafter his trips east were frequent, and his plans grew larger. Walking in Cleveland one day with H. S. Davis, president of the Y.M.C.A., he was talking of them when a leading banker drove down the street. Drawing up at the curb, the banker hailed the two young men and demanded: "Mr. Rockefeller, do you think you could use $50,000?"

This was a windfall indeed, but Rockefeller gazed dubiously at the financier, and seemed to be giving the question judicious consideration. Finally he replied: "We-l-l, Dan, can you give me twenty-four hours to think it over?" Inwardly he burned with anxiety for the money.

Next day he took the loan, which might have been lost by precipitate eagerness.[1]

In 1870, the organization became the Standard Oil Co. of Ohio, which had enlisted the considerable business talents of William Rockefeller and Henry Flagler. It formed the South Improvement Company, a holding company into which were merged most of the Cleveland refineries. Standard enjoyed the backing of three prominent Cleveland banks—the Merchants National, Commercial National, and Second National, and men prominent in these banks became substantial stockholders in the South Improvement venture. From then on bank credit played a dual role in the industry; it financed capital growth, but it also helped to underwrite the acquisition of competing facilities. In the process, Standard gained a dominant position in refining and acquired such valuable personnel as John D. Archbold and H. H. Rogers.

Bank loans helped Standard to buy out Tom Scott's Empire Transportation Company in 1878. Soon afterwards, independents built the Tidewater Pipeline across the Alleghenies, helped by large loans from the Second National Bank of Titusville. In 1882, Tidewater obtained $2 million from securities issued through a syndicate headed by the First National Bank of New York, but harassment by an inside minority which wanted to tie up with Standard hampered prospective bond sales to European investors. This in turn helped bring the pipeline into the Standard operation.

Although one of the Standard subsidiaries had a $500,000 loan outstanding from New York's First National Bank as late as 1885, Standard became increasingly independent of banks as it expanded and prospered. "I think a concern so large as we should have its own money and be independent of the 'Street'," said John D. Rockefeller in 1885.

The firm's profits were used to pay off its debts and to build up large holdings of cash and financial assets, a process which gave it increasing power as a supplier of funds to the financial markets. With these funds and their own ample resources, the "Standard Oil crowd" of William (but not John D.) Rockefeller, Rogers, Flagler, Archbold, and others soon became a major influence on Wall Street. In the 1890's, they formed a close alliance with James Stillman and the National City Bank and helped its meteoric rise to first place among American banks. Flagler poured millions into the development of Florida—railroads, hotels, and municipal improvements. In the early twentieth century the "crowd" shared hegemony on Wall Street with J. P. Morgan.

Standard Oil's dominant position in refining was widely denounced. The Sherman Antitrust Act of 1890 was aimed principally at Standard; and ultimately, in 1911, the Supreme Court handed down a momentous decree requiring geographical division of the firm into some thirty-eight companies. By then, however, new competition was arising, heralded by the gushers of 1901 at Spindletop, Texas, which soon shifted the center of gravity of the industry, and the coming of the automobile was to change the entire environment of the industry.

For all the criticism, the Standard Oil organization was a highly efficient firm which worked steady improvements in transporting and refining petroleum. The Rockefeller empire was founded on kerosene, and by improved refining and vigorous marketing it contributed to a lighting revolution which has all but been forgotten since the rise of electricity. Particularly after the introduction of the mantle around 1890, kerosene lamps provided good cheap household illumination in small towns and rural areas until the 1930's.

While Rockefeller was rising to fame as the master of the stream of oil rushing out of Pennsylvania hills, James Eads sought to master the waters of the Mississippi. If ever an illustration were designed to prove the principle that "bad banking made America great," it was the career of James B. Eads. Eads was one of the greatest engineering minds of American history, despite his lack of formal preparation. He started out before the Civil War in salvage, dredging, and snag removal on the Mississippi, and became prominent during the war as a producer of many of the ironclad gunboats which helped the Union forces to victory on the western waters.

The war over, Eads turned his imagination to an attempt to bridge the Mississippi at St. Louis. The city had long since become a booming river port and was now an important rail center for westward carriage. However, the railroads from the east stopped on the Illinois side of the river, and everything going across had to go by ferry. In 1865, Eads got a bridge company under way, and by 1866 had secured approval of Congress. But to protect river navigation, the law required the spans to be so high and wide that most engineers regarded the project as hopeless. Eads had to design much of his own equipment and hover over his suppliers to keep the steelwork up to specifications. But construction proceeded in 1867.

By then, Eads was also in the banking business. The state of Missouri had long owned the bulk of the stock of the Bank of the State of Missouri, one of the big branch banks of the country. In 1866, the state offered the stock at public sale, and a group headed by Eads successfully acquired ownership and control, with the help of a large loan from New York's National Bank of Commerce. The new owners promptly applied for a national charter, and their bank became the National Bank of the State of Missouri—and the largest issuer of bank notes in the country. As the bridge project ran into difficulties and delays, it drew increasingly on the bank for funds. By 1873, nearly $10 million had been spent on the bridge project, some of the funds coming all the way from Junius Morgan in London. At last the bridge was opened in 1874, acclaimed all over the world as an engineering and architectural wonder—but alas, not a financial triumph! For the railroads on either side made no efforts to use the bridge and incur toll charges. And in the economic depression of the 1870's, the bridge company slipped towards bankruptcy.

Eads was an engineer, not a financier. Before the spans of his bridge were closed he was off on a new adventure vastly more visionary than the bridge. This was a project to open the mouth of the Mississippi, which had become increasingly choked by mud and silt, to the great distress of New Orleans. Government attempts to dredge the channel were fruitless. Then Eads put forward the amazing suggestion that the river current would scour and deepen the channel itself if properly concentrated by a series of jetties. As Congress hesitated over the idea, Eads took the daring step of offering to do the job himself, with the government to pay him for the job only when he had demonstrated its success. In 1875, he set out to work on South Pass where the channel was constricted with a bar only eight feet below the surface. His plan was audaciously simple; parallel rows of pine boards nailed to pilings driven in the mud formed a sort of chute which was then dumped full of willow brush cut on the delta. When this had collected enough sediment from the water to form a solid earth mass, the whole was bolstered at the sides by rubblestone and topped by massive concrete blocks.

Like the bridge, the jetty project was an engineering triumph. The willow walls themselves, without stone, developed enough current to deepen the channel to thirteen feet within eight months of the start. By May 1876, it had reached seventeen feet, and a large ocean vessel had successfully entered through South Pass.

But like the bridge, the jetty project encountered increasing financial difficulties. Eads was enveloped in a campaign of slanders and misrepresentations; most people simply could not believe his idea would work. The government delayed its promised payments, then allowed amounts below those originally stipulated. The jetty company slipped deeper into debt, borrowing from the Bank of the State of Missouri and from other banks in St. Louis, New Orleans, and elsewhere. In 1877, the money ran out and the work continued only because the men were content to accept board and payment in due bills.

In June 1877, the Bank of the State of Missouri closed its doors. It had lost heavily on loans to the bridge and jetty projects, and also on other investments such as the North Missouri Railroad. In December 1878, the great bridge, which had cost $10 million, was sold at auction for $2 million as part of bankruptcy proceedings.

In 1879, the jetty project was completed. As Eads had confidently predicted, the river current had dredged its own channel, which had reached thirty feet in the center. At a cost of slightly more than $5 million, the project had brought results of incalculably greater value.

The largest ships in the world were sailing in and out of South Pass, eight hundred and forty steamers alone during the year of the jetties' completion. In the same period twenty-six times as much export went out through the Mississippi mouth as did in the year that the work was begun. The very same businessmen who had sent their representatives to Washington with desperate prayers that their port be saved from the havoc which the jetties would surely wreak on it, now computed that the saving in freight on a single year's export of cotton would pay the entire jetty cost. Moreover, the shipping of valley grain through New Orleans was trebling—wheat and corn vessels no longer had to sit stranded in Southwest Pass, their cargoes molding in the humid heat, until a freshet came to lift them over the bar. Insurance rates on these perishables had dropped, the price of bread was cheapened over half the earth. Immense land and floating grain elevators were being built at the crescent waterfront. New Orleans, raised from eleventh to second place as the country's export point, was taking its place as a great port. . . .[2]

It is an interesting commentary on American banking historiography that the historian of the Bank of the State of Missouri concluded that "its period of usefulness had ended with its nationalization in 1866." Ultimately, the depositors of the bank were paid in full with interest; most of the losses fell on the stockholders, of whom Eads was one of the largest. Eads died in 1887 while working on his most visionary scheme of all—a railway to haul ocean vessels across Mexico as an alternative to a canal to reach the Pacific. A New Orleans newspaper obituary credited him with having added more than a billion dollars to the wealth of farmers and manufacturers of the Mississippi Valley. Eads was elected to the Hall of Fame in 1920. His bridge still stands, though overshadowed by a recent high-level highway bridge, and his jetty principles have been applied repeatedly to other entries to the Mississippi. American bank credit seldom was put to better use.

Another remarkable chapter in the history of American enterprise is the career of William Chapman Ralston, California banker extraordinary. Ralston came west with the forty-niners as a young man. He functioned initially as a steamboat agent and soon entered private banking in partnership with other prominent steamboat and express leaders.

In 1861, he formed Donohoe, Ralston, and Co., one of the largest private banks in the country. Ralston used his bank as the foundation for increasing involvement in the exciting enterprises of the West. He made investments in railroads, telegraph lines, gold mines. During the war his firm was the largest shipper of gold from the area.

In 1864, Ralston joined with Sacramento banker Darius O. Mills to form the Bank of California, which became an effective vehicle for Ralston's enterprise and imagination. Ralston took over a bankrupt textile plant and reorganized it as the Pacific Woolen Mills. He helped form a construction company to build a large drydock. The Bank of California was an important source of loans for the Central Pacific Railway, as it struggled eastward to meet the Union Pacific. Another railway promoter reported, "Mr. Ralston . . . informs me today that if I, or we, get into a position where we need help, to call on him—*it was his own offer*—he says he feels a personal interest in every rail that is laid on the Pacific Coast." [3]

Ralston became increasingly involved in real estate development, carrying out an elaborate program at Burlingame, as well as a hotel and other developments on South Montgomery Street. He organized the Kimball Manufacturing Company to make railroad cars and equipment, and promoted the West Coast Furniture Co. He backed firms making watches, locks, and silk textiles. Ralston himself had become a millionaire by 1870, and the bank was paying dividends of 1 per cent per month.

Banker Ralston was equally active in civic and philanthropic affairs. He was one of the guiding spirits in the newly founded state university and secured the gift which financed the Lick Observatory. Another offspring was the California Theatre—although a play which Bret Harte had been commissioned to write for its opening never panned out. One of Ralston's family later commented, "You might say truthfully he was the central figure, the man to whom everyone came if they wished to promote some commercial scheme. . . . The most important industries developed on the Pacific Coast originated in backing from the Bank of California." [4]

Ralston's interests were far-ranging. He sponsored an expedition to evaluate the resources and prospects of Alaska; the information it obtained was instrumental in leading to the federal government's decision to acquire the territory in 1867.

Like most enterprising Californians, Ralston was impressed by the riches that had been discovered in the Comstock region of Nevada. Rich strikes had been made in 1859, and miners and prospectors poured into the area during the war years. The silver bonanza brought a mushroom growth of banks in Virginia City, beginning with the local office of Wells Fargo.

Soon after formation of the Bank of California in 1864, it set up an agency for operations in Virginia City. When the silver economy went through a shake-out in 1866 because of floods and financial difficulties, Ralston's bank helped revitalize operations by extensive loans for installing pumps, opening new shafts, and other operations. Ralston, however, was not content to finance other people's profits. By shrewd use of stock purchases and foreclosures, his bank became one of the largest owners of mining properties in the area— one source estimated its investments at $3 million. Soon he promoted a railroad to carry the wealth of Nevada more easily out of the mountains.

Ralston's Nevada enterprises and some of his California schemes were highly profitable, but most of his manufacturing connections were not. He was personally liable for large loans from the bank—$2 million for real estate developments, nearly $600,000 for the Kimball Company, and $1 million for the Pacific Woolen Mills. Although the financial panic of 1873 had no great effect on California, Ralston was hard hit by the rapid decline in silver prices and by difficulties arising from a water-supply promotion, and the Bank of California began to feel pressure from depositor withdrawals. In August 1875, the bank was forced to suspend payment. Ralston died, possibly a suicide, and his death elicited eulogy from Californians which few tycoons of the age of enterprise could hope to equal. The bank soon revived, with the aid of new funds from the stockholders. It disposed of most of its mining properties, and became increasingly active in financing trans-Pacific trade and the fresh opportunities offered by the Pacific Northwest—lumbering, fishing, ranching. By mergers, the Bank of California acquired offices in Washington and Oregon. In 1910, it became a national bank with a special dispensation to retain these branches, and it still functions as one of the country's few truly interstate banks.

While Ralston was having his troubles in the 1870's, another group of Comstockers was on the rise. In 1873, the "Irish quartet" of John Mackay, James Fair, James Flood, and William O'Brien opened rich new veins in Nevada and breached the entrenched position of the Ralston interests. The newcomers capped their success by organizing a bank of their own on the coast—the Nevada Bank of San Francisco. Significantly, when Mackay agreed to join the scheme, he said, "Just see to it you don't loan money on mining securities." [5] The Nevada Bank, which for a time employed a muscular young man named Jim Corbett as a clearing-house messenger, was absorbed by Wells Fargo in 1905.

The great resources of the West also attracted the energies of a very different type of organization—the Mormon Church. By 1860, the Mormons had developed a gracious and prosperous community on the edge of Great Salt Lake. The economic role of the church leadership was large; Mormon economic life combined a stress on the Puritan virtues of hard work and thrift with a powerful strain of collective responsibility and power which contrasted with the individualism so characteristic of the country as a whole.

Church leadership undertook a variety of enterprises, including stores and other distribution facilities. To aid these, they sponsored a bank, first formed in 1868, which became in 1871 the Bank of Deseret. Brigham Young was its president, and in 1872 it took a national charter. The following year church leadership formed a sister institution, Zion's Savings Bank and Trust Co., of which Young was also president. Its principal objective was to encourage savings, and the 10 per cent interest it offered may well have had this effect.

These banks made important contributions to the economic development of the area. During its first twenty-five years, Zion's Savings "made loans to Utah canal companies, railroads, real estate developments, salt companies, sugar companies, power companies, and, indeed, to the Mormon Church itself, on such security as stocks, bonds, and mortgages." [6] The Deseret National passed out of existence through merger in the 1930's; Zion's Savings and Trust, after long operation as a church-controlled institution, merged in 1957 into Zions First National Bank.

The missionary zeal of the Mormons had brought to Utah during the Civil War a poverty-stricken Scottish family which was to write a distinguished chapter in the annals of American banking. Their spark plug was David Eccles, only fourteen when they arrived, who soon converted his driving energy and physical strength into a profitable lumber business. Subsequently he entered other developing fields, such as beet-sugar refining. The latter caught his interest after he had helped the church obtain a loan from the Wells Fargo bank to start a pioneering refinery. When David Eccles died in 1912, he was a millionaire.

His son Marriner applied the same intelligence and enterprise to the family business interests. The holding company through which the family enterprises were owned became, by various circumstances, interested in several banks. By the time he was thirty, Marriner Eccles was president of the largest bank in Ogden. Purchase of stocks in small banks continued to appear a promising investment, and he soon conceived the idea of a special bank holding company through which these banks could be managed with maximum efficiency and safety. The result was First Security Corporation, still a leader in the area. Eccles went on to a distinguished career as chairman of the Federal Reserve Board and one of the most outspoken advocates of aggressive federal action to dispel the depression of the 1930's.[7]

Salt Lake City was also headquarters for the Walker brothers, who developed a private banking business out of their mercantile activities in the 1860's. This evolved into the present Walker Bank and Trust Co. They were particularly active in financing the many mining opportunities opening up—gold and silver, coal and iron. In 1875, they employed a genial young Irishman named Marcus Daly to investigate some silver mining prospects in Montana. These turned out productive and profitable, and helped launch Daly on a dramatic career—but in copper, not silver.

The first man to capitalize on the opportunities of Montana copper was himself a merchant and banker named William A. Clark. After drifting into Montana during the Civil War, Clark employed the profits and opportunities offered by a comfortable trade in supplies to engage in private banking. Lending to silver miners and storekeepers was remunerative, but Clark acquired some claims himself and set his sights on bigger things. He took a year off to study at Columbia University School of Mines, then returned to Butte to put his knowledge to work. Soon he had opened rich veins of copper, and in 1879, when he added a smelter to his facilities, the trickle of Montana copper production became a flood. Soon Clark was the richest man in the state.

Marcus Daly was not far behind. After his initial modest successes in silver properties, in 1881 he also struck a rich vein of copper—the legendary Anaconda. Soon Daly was also a millionaire—and found banking an attractive outlet for his wealth. In 1883, he founded the town of Anaconda as the location for a giant smelter, and there helped organize the firm of Hoge, Daly and Company, Bankers. In Butte itself, Daly and associates formed the private banking firm of Hoge, Brownlee and Company in 1882, and Daly founded the Ravalli County Bank in Hamilton in 1895.

A bitter rivalry developed between Daly and Clark that extended from mining to banking all the way into politics. Clark eventually achieved election to the Senate, but Daly fought him every inch of the way and led a successful campaign to have Clark unseated on charges of electoral bribery.

Both Daly and his banking partner, Hoge, died in 1900, and for a short time Mrs. Daly continued as private proprietor of the banks. Soon, however, they took on corporate status. The bank in Anaconda became the Daly Bank and Trust Company, and the Butte bank, after operating under a similar name, ultimately became the Metals Bank and Trust Company. These two and the Ravalli County Bank are all still thriving; and to cap it all, in 1928, the Metals Bank bought out the remaining business of W. A. Clark and Brothers, Bankers, thus becoming the legatee of both great rivals! [8]

The end of the century witnessed yet another important way of drawing wealth from the natural resources of the country. In the 1880's, Charles M. Hall developed the first commercially feasible method of refining aluminum. He and a couple of former steel men formed the Pittsburgh Reduction Company. Hat in hand, they went forth seeking funds, without much success in the East. They found their backing in Pittsburgh, however, where young Andrew Mellon had just taken over the management of his father's bank, T. Mellon and Sons. Mellon staked them to $250,000 in exchange for a controlling block of stock. Combining the genius of Hall, effective patent litigation against competitors, and a vigorous selling campaign to create markets for the new metal, the firm was fabulously successful, particularly after it took its present name, the Aluminum Company of America.

The Mellon bank, opened in 1869, made numerous other notable contributions to financing industrial development. Mellon loans assisted the rise of Henry Clay Frick as "king of coke." In alliance with Frick, Andrew Mellon financed creation of the Union Steel Corporation, an integrated operation subsequently bought by United States Steel. Mellon developed the Standard Steel Car Company and other important steel fabricators. Mellon loans and underwriting services promoted glass factories, coal mines, rail lines, and utilities; and Mellon funds financed the tanks and pipelines that harnessed the flow of oil from the fabulous Spindletop gusher. Investments such as these brought Andrew Mellon fame—he served as Secretary of the Treasury in the 1920's —and fortune.

However, the Mellon bank (now the Mellon National Bank and Trust Company) was also receptive to less spectacular needs for credit. One of the beneficiaries described his experience as follows:

I came to Pittsburgh a young boy, without friends, or acquaintances, and went to work in one of the first advertising agencies. After I had saved enough money to buy some second-hand office furniture and to pay the month's rent of a small office, I set up for myself. One of my first accounts, small at first, gradually increased, but as it was always promptly paid, no question rose in my mind of the danger of its non-payment until, one month, the check did not appear at the usual time.

Aroused to my danger, I went into the bank of T. Mellon and Sons and asked for Mr. Mellon. When I was asked, "Which Mr. Mellon?" I said, "Any one." I knew none of the Mellons; had no account there; had no business connections with them, but I was so distracted that it was any port in the storm for me. I was directed to Mr. Andrew W. Mellon who was sitting in a little glass-caged room near the entrance.

I told Mr. Mellon my story . . . that I had no property and no one as an endorser but that I felt my business would, in time, enable me to pay the loan I asked for. He listened intently, without comment, and said, "Whom have you done work for? Would it hurt your standing if I made inquiries of them?" And then he said, "Come in this afternoon. I may be able to help you, but I cannot, of course, guarantee that." When I returned in the afternoon, he saw me enter, beckoned me into his glass-room with his finger, and said, "See Mr. Mitchell. He will fix you up." I saw Mr. Walter S. Mitchell, the cashier, signed and endorsed a note, and was saved. Do you wonder that I shall never forget the Mellons? [9]

The spirit of enterprise that carried the American economy rapidly ahead is well illustrated by Rockefeller and Mellon, Eads and Ralston. Each one was enabled to carry out his projects more fully because of access to bank credit. Mellon and Ralston were bankers, but played a large personal role in developing the enterprises in which credit was used. Eads was primarily an engineering genius whose banking role was secondary to his construction enterprises. Rockefeller and Standard Oil progressed from borrowers to suppliers of funds as the firm's profitability grew.

These personal illustrations show also the contributions of different types of banks. Rockefeller and Eads were most closely connected with national banks. The Bank of California was a state bank during the Ralston era, while T. Mellon and Sons remained a private bank until 1902.

Ultimately, the enterprise shown by such men, and their ability to obtain capital funds to back it up, contributed to increasing the economic welfare of millions of Americans through new and improved products and through increased efficiency of production. Yet these cases also remind us that even in backing highly desirable developments with their credit, banks ran the risk that their monetary responsibilities to depositors might be undermined. The National Bank of the State of Missouri failed because of its involvement in the Eads enterprises, and Ralston's promotions forced the Bank of California into a temporary suspension. A banking system dedicated solely to "safety first" might well have denied credit to the sort of men and projects described in this chapter.

The episodes described in the chapter, however, were only one facet of economic and financial development. The great majority of American banks during the half century following Appomattox were primarily concerned with the more prosaic operations related to feeding, clothing, and housing the country's rapidly growing population. Production, processing, and distribution of farm products constituted one of the foundations of the nation's growth, and to this the next chapter is devoted.

CHAPTER

5

BANKING IN THE COUNTRYSIDE,

1865-1929

In the years following the civil war, millions of Americans poured into the vast open spaces west of the Mississippi. Some came seeking the mineral riches of California, the Comstock, or Montana; others came to build railroads or to trade; but most of the newcomers came to farm. The Homestead Act stimulated visions of fertile land available for the taking. The government had also granted vast tracts of land to the Pacific railroads. The railroads, eager to raise money and to develop a clientele of farm customers along the rights-of-way, became supersalesmen. Their agents were active in the East and in Europe as well, and thousands of immigrants came to the country in response to their promotional zeal.

New farms by the thousands appeared in the great plains area, in Iowa and Nebraska, the Dakotas, Kansas, and east Texas. Farther west, cattle ranching flourished. On the Pacific coast, many a man who came looking for gold found

[88]

better prospects in the fertile soil and amicable climate of California.

By 1890, one-fourth of the people in the country lived west of the Mississippi. Production of wheat, corn, and livestock soared in response to the efforts of the newcomers. However, farm acreage also increased in the older areas of settlement.

Side by side with the spread of farming was the spread of small towns. The farmers needed a place to trade, and in the days of buggies and muddy roads, the area a town could serve was very limited. Between 1860 and 1900, the number of towns with populations between 2,500 and 10,000 grew in number from 300 to 1,300. The number with populations less than 2,500 nearly doubled between 1890 and 1910.

Typically, the small town was a service area for the nearby farms. Spread along Main Street were the stores where they could buy dry goods, farm implements, feed and seed, kerosene, and furniture. There were doctors, lawyers, a newspaper or two. The town also offered marketing facilities for the farmers' crops—grain elevators, livestock dealers, etc. And there was a bank—or more likely, two or three.

By 1900 banks were operating in more than 7,000 American communities—three-fourths of them small towns with less than 2,500 people. In Iowa alone, nearly 700 separate communities had banks, and Illinois was close behind.

Often the banker was one of the original promoters or early boosters through whose efforts the town took root and, with its surrounding farms, grew. The historian Lewis Atherton, whose book *Main Street on the Middle Border* gives a rounded picture of small-town life in its heyday, identifies a number of such men. Ambrose Call was one of the founders (in the 1850's) and leading citizens of Algona, Iowa, where he was long president of the First National Bank. He combined real estate and finance with an interest in literature and the arts, founded the town's newspaper, and ultimately furnished the town with an opera house.

Banker Jason Easton came to Minnesota just before the Civil War and played a major role in the founding and early development of Chatfield and Winnebago City, Minnesota. The Root River Bank, which he founded, is still operating in Chatfield.[1]

Often the first banks in new towns arose more or less spontaneously to meet the need for deposit facilities. Often a storekeeper or merchant became a recipient of funds left for safekeeping—particularly if he owned the only safe in town. The mercantile and freighting firm of F. Groos and Co. of San Antonio kept the cash arising from its private banking operations stored in large wooden dry-goods boxes, and often transported coin hidden inside the large wooden axles of freight wagons. In time, the firm concentrated increasingly on banking and ultimately became the present-day Groos National Bank.

Banks originating in this manner often had no more office than the corner of a store, and at least one consisted chiefly of a money belt around the owner's waist. A great number of private banks sprang up from such origins. By 1909, there were at least fifteen hundred of them, mostly operating on a small scale. If a bank's operations grew, however, it usually became incorporated to spread ownership and limit liability. An impressive number of today's incorporated banks started out as private banks.

The bankers and other leaders in thousands of American small towns were carried along by great expectations. Most of them were familiar with the rapid growth of older communities such as Chicago—and with the enormous profits available to original landowners is such a situation. Often the banker was a land speculator, as well, like Jason Easton. But his speculative interests, if any, were likely to make him more eager to attract more settlers to the town and surrounding farm country, to promote the establishment and growth of local enterprises.

Great expectations and the spirit of enterprise were nowhere better evidenced than in the rapid growth in the number of banks, most of which occurred in the small towns. In the 1860's, the country contained roughly two thousand commercial banks. By 1910, the number had shot up over twenty thousand. In the process, banks appeared in many a tiny crossroads hamlet—like Exchange, Pennsylvania, which had a population of eighty in 1915 when a local historian wrote, "It seems strange to see a fine banking house near a corner of the two main streets of a tiny village, with a stretch of forest on one hand. . . ." [2]

In the larger towns, the spirit of the booster often meant a proliferation of banks. Perhaps this coincided with political divisions, as William Allen White describes the situation in Emporia, Kansas, in the 1890's. In larger communities, banks multiplied to serve different nationality groups. In many cases, the impetus came from a group of dissatisfied borrowers, or simply from prosperous business men with money to invest. Still, nothing but great expectations can account for the formation of eight separate banks in Meade, Kansas, in 1886-1887—a town which mustered a population of 457 in the census of 1890.[3]

National banks shared in the expansion of small town banking—by 1910 there were about seven thousand of them. National banks enjoyed the privilege of note issue, although this was not very profitable after the 1870's. They also enjoyed considerable confidence among depositors. But this had its cost: The very regulations which contributed to safety inhibited the bankers' ability to meet the needs for credit arising from small-town and rural growth.

To begin with, before 1900, national banks could not operate unless they could raise at least $50,000 in stockholder capital. National banks were long prohibited from making mortgage loans—but these were often the type of credit most in demand for financing both town and farm properties.

As a result, the bulk of banking expansion in the half

century following Appomattox came through the formation of state-chartered banks. The key factor in their revival after the Civil War was the gradual acceptance of bank deposits as money. The federal tax on state bank-note issues came close to eliminating state-chartered banks in the late 1860's, but their numbers soon began to grow.

By 1900, the number of state-chartered banks was roughly twice the number of national banks. In some areas, the popular form was the stockholder-owned savings bank, offering checking as well as savings deposit services. Toward the turn of the century there was a strong upsurge in the number of trust companies, which in many states could accept deposits and perform banking functions without much supervision and control. Outside big cities, their trust services proper might be rather slight—for instance, Maine trust companies in 1900 held banking assets one hundred times as large as their trust account assets! [4]

Whatever the form they took, state-chartered banks (and private banks as well) found their credit opportunities in the limitations imposed on national banks. In 1909, half of all the non-national banks in the country had capital accounts under $25,000 each, and one-fourth of non-national bank assets consisted of mortgage loans.

Thus the pendulum was swinging in the direction of more abundant facilities for meeting the credit needs of the countryside. Beginning in 1900, the national-banking restrictions were progressively eased, so that the banking system as a whole could share in the process.

Inevitably, there were risks involved in this trend. The success of a small bank in a small town often depended heavily on the prosperity of surrounding farms or local industries. William Allen White, the sage of Emporia, Kansas, describes in his autobiography the collapse of one such bank which lost heavily on its loans to cattlemen and "boom enterprises—a big barn of a hotel in Cascade, Colorado, an electric light company in Salina, stock in an interurban railway, mortgage bonds, and little jerkwater railways that were never built." [5] The cashier committed suicide when the bank failed.

Another tragic case involved Franklin H. Whitney, of Atlantic, Iowa, who had founded both the town and its first bank, but whose bank was dragged under by the farm collapse of the 1890's. His son devoted fifteen years to paying off its debts and ultimately became established as a successful banker in his own right.[6]

The risks were the inevitable concomitant of the sort of banking system which could play a major role in financing the production and distribution of farm products under conditions of rapid development and change.

Just as farming was the activity around which the small town's economy revolved, so it was the focal point for small-town banking. The bank's loans went either to the farmers themselves, or to the merchants supplying the farmers, or to the dealers and processors who took charge of the produce after it left the farm.

More often than not, the farmer needed credit to buy his farm. Even if he was able to buy on time from a railroad or speculator, or found a good homestead tract, he needed funds for stock and equipment, for breaking the land and fencing it, for seed, and for enough supplies to keep the family alive until a crop was in. His first credit resource was likely to be a mortgage loan.

Until 1880, at least, the commercial banks were not a major source of farm mortgage credit. The national banks were prohibited from lending on mortgage, and the spectacular expansion of non-national banks was just beginning to get under way. Instead, the local banks tended to take on an important role as middlemen. Often acting in their individual capacities, local bankers became agents for eastern investors—savings banks, insurance companies, or wealthy individuals. For a commission, the western bankers would handle the paper work of making the loan, and then would service it during its lifetime. John and Ira Davenport of Bath, New York, loaned over $5 million on western farm mortgages between 1868 and 1904, operations which have been described in detail by Allan G. Bogue. A large portion of their loans in Iowa were handled through John Weare, private banker of Cedar Rapids. In Kansas, they worked through various officials of the First National Banks of Ottawa and Paola. Nebraska loans were made through the First National Bank of Lincoln and A. P. Hopkins, private banker, of Fremont. (The latter's operations became the present-day Fremont National Bank in 1882.)[7] Sometimes the initiative came from the East; in other cases, a western banker with some capital of his own would initiate loans and then try to resell them in the East.

By the 1870's, there developed a group of firms specializing in farm mortgage business. A notable example was the J. B. Watkins Land Mortgage Company, which started operations in Kansas and spread into other neighboring states. Initially, the firm concentrated on resale of mortgage paper itself; later the mortgages themselves were placed in trust with the Farmers Loan and Trust Company in New York, and served as backing for debentures issued to investors—an arrangement that had the appeal of lower risk.

Typical mortgage loans negotiated by the Watkins firm in the 1870's involved sums of $300 to $500 on property assessed at more than twice that level, running for three to five years and costing the borrower, in interest and commissions, from 10 to 15 per cent a year. Such high rates resulted from the scarcity of local funds and from the terrific demand for loans. When times were good, there was little complaint about interest charges, and after the mid-1880's rates declined as the supply of capital caught up with demand—but when a year of drought and depression came, complaints about the debt burden were ubiquitous.

The Watkins Company had a number of close banking connections. Bank loans secured by the debenture bonds

were obtained in the East and in England. J. B. Watkins
himself was one of the founders of the Merchants National
Bank in Lawrence, Kansas; and in 1887, he founded banks
bearing his own name there and in New Orleans. The mortgage company obtained loans from Watkins's own banks and
at various times from Brown Brothers, the United States
Trust Company, and the National Bank of Commerce in
New York, as well as Armour Brothers Banking Company
in Kansas City, Missouri. In 1894, the Watkins firm had
over $100,000 in bank loans outstanding.[8]

High interest rates and a relatively good record of payments made the western mortgages increasingly popular
with investors, and in the 1880's mortgage loan funds
poured in at flood tempo. The number of loan companies
rose into hundreds, and funds were pressed on borrowers
until the area was plastered with mortgage debt. Then
came the crash; years of drought and grasshoppers were
followed by the depression of the 1890's. Most of the mortgage companies collapsed, including the Watkins firm. In
the years following, the commercial banks took over a bigger role in supplying farm mortgage funds. But as late as
1910, about three-fourths of farm mortgages were held by
individual investors. Of course many of these were loans
originated and serviced by the banks. The Merchants Savings, Loan, and Trust Company of Chicago marketed a
large volume of farm mortgages to investors about this time,
using country banks as agents.

Commercial banks were more directly involved in making
short-term production loans to farmers. These might go
for actual production expenses or merely to cover the
farmer's living costs during the growing season; they might
be secured by a chattel mortgage on livestock or equipment,
or by the endorsement of a co-signer, or simply unsecured,
in cases of well-known farmers of good character.

In the Southwest, banks experimented with cattle loans
with mixed success. Banks in Kansas City and Wichita

loaned heavily on cattle in the years following 1865, but suffered in the depression of the 1870's. Leadership in cattle loans then passed to the commission houses whose principal function was buying cattle to ship and resell to packers. Like the mortgage loan companies, these often drew on bank credit to finance their own loans. The crisis years between 1888 and 1896 brought disaster to many cattle lenders: The banking slogan "never lend on anything that eats grass or drinks water" probably originated in the drought years.

By this time, the pattern had developed whereby cattle were bred and raised on the ranges of Texas, Colorado, or Wyoming, and then moved eastward into the corn belt to be fattened. A corresponding division of financing developed with the aid of cattle loan companies sponsored by the big meat packing firms, or in some cases, by commercial banks. "Most of the cattle credit in the corn-feeding belts was furnished by local banks, while the cattle loan companies took care of the range. The local commercial banks found feeder loans very attractive because of their high degree of liquidity and growing security value." [9]

The banks also furnished feeder loans for sheep. Loans for raising hogs, which generally did not travel around so much, were almost entirely handled by banks, as were loans for the increasingly important diary farming operations. In the South and Southwest, cotton farming drew on bank credit directly, or through bank loans to cotton factors who in turn financed the farmers.

While the process of bringing vacant territories under cultivation was the most dramatic aspect of postwar agricultural development, another important trend was developing. The industrial revolution was beginning to show its influence on the farm. Cyrus McCormick's reaper had already demonstrated its utility before 1860, and the shortage of farm manpower greatly spurred its adoption during the war. Soon it was complemented with the threshing machine, and in the later years of the century, more daring farmers used steam engines to drive their equipment and sometimes to pull it—great lumbering monsters which looked like undersized locomotives. Investing in equipment took capital funds, which often came from banks.

All in all, by 1900, commercial bank loans direct to farmers amounted to slightly over $600 million and were about 12 per cent of the banks' loans. Of course the proportion was much higher for the smaller country banks.

Besides farm loans, the typical small-town bank extended considerable credit to the local merchants, most of it going to finance inventories or credit to customers. Indeed, much bank credit passed indirectly to farmers in this fashion, for they relied heavily on store credit in many areas. This was particularly true in the South, where the merchant typically advanced food and supplies to the small farmers on crop lien security and took charge of marketing the crop when harvested.

By the turn of the century, there were plenty of other local claimants for bank credit. As William Allen White described it from his own experience:

Machinery everywhere in the last quarter of the old century was multiplying, making new social, economic, and political patterns, all based on the need of capital. The teamster, the shoemaker, the cabinetmaker, the wheelwright, the tanner, the saddler, all lined up beside the printer at the note counter of the bank to borrow the money to buy the new expensive tools needed to practice their trades as master mechanics in a new, shiny world! [10]

Many a town by 1900 had a local factory or two which was on its way to greatness, and of course there were always land schemes and ventures.

But the other great outlet for bank loans in the countryside—and in most of the cities, too—was in financing the movement of goods once produced. Come harvest time, and a flood of produce would hit the market. Someone had to hold it over the remainder of the year, to parcel out the supply at a relatively even rate to meet the sustained demand. This was the job of the grain and cotton merchants, the millers, the canners, the meat packers, and many others. At the grass roots, there would be commission merchants and grain elevators needing funds for the seasonal bulge. Then the financial burden would move to the dealers in the cities and to the processors, until ultimately the products would wind up in the inventories of a million local storekeepers—or be shipped off to the four corners of the earth.

Traditionally, the merchant or middleman bought produce for cash from the farmers and sold it on credit to storekeepers, wholesalers, or processors, receiving from the latter their IOU's in the form of bills of exchange. These he would ordinarily use as the basis for bank loans. Banks would commonly "discount" such notes—that is, buy them at a price less than face value to allow for interest—and considered them top-grade paper. Such IOU's were low in risk: The buyer would most likely pay, since he had the goods and would usually sell them at a markup over cost; but if he defaulted, the seller was liable for the note.

To many bankers (and quite a few economists from Adam Smith on down) such commercial loans seemed the epitome of good banking. They were safe, short-term, and liquid, and they meshed closely with the essential operations of production and distribution. A terminology grew up reflecting this attitude—such bills of exchange were said to be *bona fide* (as if other promissory notes could not be executed in good faith), relating to *legitimate* transactions —as if there were something immoral or illegal about buying land or operating a factory.

Loans of this type were a staple item for most of the early national banks—Comptroller Hulburd boasted in 1870 that "the bills and notes discounted are, to a remarkable extent, based upon *bona fide* transactions. . . ." Loans outstanding at national banks in 1867 had an average maturity of about seventy days.

The importance of this sort of bank credit is amply demonstrated in a detailed case study of the Daniel Shaw Lumber Company. The lumber business underwent a tremendous boom in the last third of the nineteenth century, with the opening of vast timberlands and the great demands for lumber for houses and other construction. The Shaw firm operated in Wisconsin from 1856 to 1912. Its operations were large and diversified, and the firm was chronically short of capital. Consequently, it discounted the commercial paper received for lumber sales, borrowed on its own notes, and purchased on credit when possible.

Bank credit was obtained from widely scattered sources. In its early years, the firm borrowed in the East, obtaining some funds in the 1870's from the Gardiner National Bank in Maine, a locale where the firm's owners had family connections.

At least two of the Eau Claire banks extended the Shaw company credit lines averaging twenty thousand dollars each, and the lumber company borrowed extensively from banks in the nearby communities of Hudson and Chippewa Falls, Wisconsin.

Banks in the neighboring metropolitan centers of Minneapolis, St. Paul, and especially Milwaukee, provided much of the operating capital. During the 1870's and early 1880's Minneapolis and St. Paul banks discounted, at rates ranging up to 10 per cent, many Shaw notes and also several thousand dollars each month of "good business paper" collected by the lumber company. Of the several neighboring metropolitan banks which provided extensive credit for the Shaw company, the First National Bank of Milwaukee played by far the leading role.

The financial needs of the Shaw company caused it to look to more distant metropolitan centers than those just reviewed. Detroit, Boston, and Chicago banks, with their greater capital accumulations, were in a position to extend credit to the frontier lumber concern. During the 1870's and the early 1880's the lumber company drew upon a small credit line at the People's Savings Bank of Detroit, Michigan. As long as the Shaw company maintained a flour mill and shipped flour to eastern seaboard markets, an account was kept with the Market National Bank of Boston. Commercial paper secured from sales of flour often was discounted at this bank. From time to time, when discounts were especially difficult to obtain in the West, commercial paper secured from Mississippi Valley lumber customers as well as promissory notes of the Daniel Shaw Lumber Company were sent to this institution for discount. Various Chicago banks also provided a large share of Shaw loans and discounts [including the Commercial National and First National.]

The Shaw company shipped considerable lumber to wholesalers down the Mississippi River, and found it convenient to discount their promissory notes with banks in the customers' localities. Once banking connections were built up, however, the same banks were called on to discount the Shaw company's own IOU's. After 1890, the firm was able to meet its credit needs from the banks in Eau Claire and Milwaukee.[11]

Loans to finance the movement and processing of farm products, lumber, and other raw materials continued to be a large element in bank loans, but around the turn of the century the emphasis was shifting to borrowing by purchasers, often on loans secured by warehouse receipts on the goods themselves. Commodity dealers, meat packers, millers, and wholesalers had become big firms, with strong credit ratings; they could easily obtain loans and pay their suppliers (often small producers or dealers) in cash.

Improvements in the legal status of warehouse receipts (particularly the development of collateral trust receipts) made them a preferred form of collateral. The development of commodity futures markets made it possible to hedge inventories of cotton, grains, and other storable staples so that risks arising from price fluctuation could be minimized. Describing commodity loans on the "great staples"—wheat, cotton, meat—one bank-sponsored publication remarked

that "So well-nigh perfect is this type of loan in its operation that by changing the collateral successively from bills
of lading to trust receipts and from either of these to warehouse receipts, it is often the case that practically the same
loan covers the progress of raw material from the primary
market through the mill and in the retail market. . . ." [12] By
1917, national banks held more than $300 million of loans
secured by warehouse receipts, more than half covering
cotton.

As firms handling and processing commodities became
large, many of them turned to the issue of open-market commercial paper to meet their short-term credit needs. They
issued notes in standard round amounts (often multiples of
$2,500) which were sold through notebrokers to final in-
vestors. Though unsecured, such paper was (and still is)
generally issued only by large firms with first-class credit
ratings. Banks were usually eager to acquire such notes, although one of them warned against the risks that might be
encountered from producers of "wines, pianos, or period
furniture." [13]

One of the most noteworthy developments in food processing after 1865 was the rise of the giant meat-packing
firms centered in Chicago. These firms achieved great efficiency through large-scale operations, including the use of
what one might call a "dis-assembly line." Another source
of their growth and power was the use of refrigerated shipments, pioneered by Gustavus Swift in the 1870's. Swift and
Company, incorporated in 1885, was one of the most dynamic and expansionist of the packers and relied heavily on
bank loans in the process of growth. According to one member of the family, "there was hardly a bank east of Ohio and
north of Virginia which did not have a Swift note or two
—whether it was a large bank with five hundred thousand
dollars or a small bank with fifteen hundred." [14] By 1893,
the firm owed $10 million in bank loans. It was pressed hard
to pay up during the panic period, but its biggest creditor,

Chicago's First National Bank, fortunately made additional funds available.[15] Not so fortunate was the Boston packing house of John P. Squire and Company, which failed in 1899 and dragged down the Broadway National Bank of that city, which had made large loans to it.[16]

The shift to bank borrowing by packers, millers, and others tended to mean a shift to financing by city banks—the Chicago banks, for instance, loaned heavily on the vast inventories of grain, meat, and lumber which passed through that outstanding entrepôt. This often left the country banks with surplus loan funds after the harvest, and encouraged many of them to accept semi-permanent loans to local enterprises, or to send off funds to city correspondents for re-investment, or even to follow the rainbow into speculations of one sort or another.

Although a great portion of bank lending was oriented towards farmers, their suppliers, and their customers in the late nineteenth century, the farmers were thoroughly discontented with their credit facilities in particular and the monetary situation in general. Their complaints were symptomatic of the poor inter-regional mobility of credit—a problem to which interstate loan companies like the J. B. Watkins Land Company addressed themselves. The railroads also came in for denunciation because of their rates, their land operators, and their financial irregularities. As one country editor put it, "There are three great crops raised in Nebraska. One is a crop of corn, one a crop of freight rates, and one a crop of interest. One is produced by farmers who by sweat and toil farm the land. The other two are produced by men who sit in their offices and farm the farmers." [17]

Farm discontent was particularly sensitive to variations in farm prices. When prices began to slide after the Civil War, farmers who had gone into debt to buy land or machinery at peak prices felt the pinch. The situation became more critical after the country as a whole was swept by a major economic depression beginning in 1873.

The farmers' complaints found expression through a variety of organizations, beginning with the National Grange (correctly, the Patrons of Husbandry). Political pressure from the farmers led to government regulation of railroads and grain elevators. The Grangers also sponsored cooperatives for purchasing and marketing farm products, and in a number of localities they formed their own banks, chiefly to help farmers to hold their crops off the market when prices seemed unduly low. Among these was the Patrons Cooperative Bank of Olathe, Kansas, which is still operating. The bank was formed in 1883 following the great growth and success of the Johnson County Cooperative Association organized by the Grange at Olathe.

The eagerness of local Grange organizations to improve the farmer's access to high-quality consumer goods at moderate price was fortuitously met by the eagerness of a young Chicago merchant to accommodate them. Montgomery Ward had already dealt personally with farmers as a salesman and store clerk in several communities; he knew the Grange first hand. As Stewart Holbrook tells it:

By 1871, Ward had accumulated a modest stake and with it set out to open what he called a mail-order house. The great fire of October swept away his small stock of goods. A year later, largely on eight hundred dollars' capital from a bank, he rented the hayloft of a livery stable on Kinzie Street in Chicago and said that Montgomery Ward & Company was open for business. No heed was paid to city trade. In a one-page "catalog" he said that the firm was founded expressly to "meet the wants of the Patrons of Husbandry." It was perhaps the first store to open to so circumscribed a group of customers. . . .

The Grangers were quick to patronize Montgomery Ward. Four years later the Ward catalogue required 150 closely printed pages to describe the Ward merchandise. As an extra service, Ward was selling grain for farmers at the startlingly modest commission of one cent a bushel. . . . The rest of the Ward story is one of the great legends. Ward had started a trend. His success spawned a host of mail-order houses both great and small.[18]

In national politics, farm discontent focused primarily on money and monetary policy. Some farmers supported the Greenback Party in its efforts to enlarge the circulation of paper currency. Soon a more appealing campaign issue opened up—free silver. Prior to the Civil War, the mint had coined silver dollars without limit for anyone bringing in the metal, but this practice had been terminated. As the enlarged output of the new western mines drove down the market price of silver, the producers clamored to restore the old policy of "free and unlimited coinage." Coming in the midst of depression, this demand, with its implication of an enlargement of the money supply, found widespread support among farmers and business men. In 1878, Congress did authorize the Treasury to purchase and coin a limited amount of silver. Then came a sharp upturn in the economy, sparked by a bountiful harvest sold abroad at high prices. Prosperity and radicalism seldom mix, and the farm agitation quieted down.

In place of depression, the plains states were soon caught up in an unprecedented boom, in which credit was, if anything, too easy. The mortgage companies were hard put to use all the funds pouring in from the East. According to one description:

agents in Kansas with a plethora of money on their hands drove about the country in buggies, soliciting patronage and freely placing loans on real estate up to its full valuation, pointing in justification to the steadily mounting price of land. . . . Farmers could rarely resist the funds proferred them. With bumper crops, high prices, and rising land values, it appeared, indeed, the part of wisdom to borrow money for enlarging holdings, improving breeds of stock, and purchasing the latest and best machinery.[19]

The ensuing crash was all the more painful for the heights previously reached. Searing droughts struck the plains states in the late 1880's, and shortly thereafter, the farmers were hit by the depression of the 1890's. Farm prices dropped further and further, with scarcity of currency taking the blame. There were many other grievances, however—high tariffs, the continued troubles with the railroads, and the rise of industrial trusts in farm machinery, kerosene, meat packing, and other items of vital concern to the farmers. In the late 1880's and early 1890's, farmers were flocking to a new organization—the Farmers Alliance. And in 1892, under Alliance leadership, a new political party was formed, the People's Party, or Populists, as it was generally termed. The new party campaigned vigorously in the presidential election of 1892, and rolled up more than a million votes for its candidate, General James Weaver.

The events of the next four years were hardly such as to quiet the ferment of agrarian unrest. Financial panic in 1893 gave way to a long period of depression, with farm prices falling to unprecedented low levels, and the farmers were not happy to see President Grover Cleveland employ the services of J. P. Morgan, August Belmont, and other Wall Street tycoons in an effort to preserve the gold standard through loans and foreign-exchange operations.

In 1896, the Democratic Party departed from the conservatism of Cleveland and accepted leadership in the farmers' protest. Behind William Jennings Bryan, the "silver-tongued orator of the Platte," the party based its national campaign heavily on demand for free silver. However, a fortuitous upturn of farm prices in the autumn of 1896 helped chill the ardor of revolt in many sections of the country, and Bryan went down to defeat before McKinley and the gold standard.

The price reversal marked the end of a long deflationary price trend. Gold production from South Africa had increased rapidly, and from this stemmed increases in money and prices throughout the world. The next quarter century witnessed an era of farm prosperity without equal in American history; this meant, understandably, a reduction of rampant agrarian radicalism, although not its total elimination by any means.

Whatever one may think of the proposed remedies, the farmers certainly had some legitimate gripes. In particular, their complaints called attention to the need to do something about the violent instability of incomes and prices. Facilities for getting credit into areas of greatest demand could also have been improved, but one should not overlook the fact that existing facilities for farm credit made possible truly remarkable opportunities for individuals to establish themselves in farming with virtually no capital to start with except the strength of their bodies. Consider the situation described by a newspaper in 1884:

A farmer with only a few dollars in his pocket comes out here and takes a claim. It only costs $15 for the preliminary fees, and he has six months to make his improvements. These improvements usually consist of a sod shanty, a well four feet deep, and from five to twenty acres of breaking. When he has done this much he can mortgage his farm for sufficient money to prove up and buy a horse or two. When he is known to be in possession of this amount of property, his credit is good for a plow and he obtains his seed by giving a mortgage on his crop in advance. Then he goes in debt for the necessary machinery to harvest his crop, and by the time his grain is ready to sell he is pretty well buried under a pile of debts.[20]

The Populists stressed the burden of the debts, and certainly in years of drought and depression they hurt. The other side of the coin was the opportunities opened up by the credit system, opportunities which set up thousands of farm families free, clear, and prosperous in the years between 1865 and 1880. It was the great opportunities offered by the productivity of soil and labor that pushed up interest rates on farm loans, and it would be hard to prove that the lenders gained more from them than did the borrowers. The image of the miserly money lender, eager to draw the poor but honest yeoman into a web of debt in order to foreclose on his property at the first opportunity, is a grossly inaccurate caricature. Most mortgage lenders tried to avoid foreclosures if they possibly could. When land reverted, it was usually because the borrowers had packed up and left. The land was worthless when withdrawn from production, and the lenders tried their utmost to keep families on it, granting extensions, forgiving interest, scaling down principal.

The prosperity which followed 1896 put an end to the free-silver agitation, but not to the pressure for reforms in farm credit. In 1900, Congress reduced the minimum capital required to establish national banks in small towns from $50,000 to $25,000. A swarm of new national banks formed in the next twenty years, but the total number of non-national banks grew even more. From just over 12,000 in 1900, the total number of commercial banks mushroomed to 30,-000 in 1920. The vast majority of these were small banks in small towns. In 1920, more than 19,000 banks had earning assets of less than $500,000, and 7,000 held less than $150,-000 each. Two-thirds of all the commercial banks were in towns with 2,500 population or less, and 8,700 were in communities with 500 people or less. This enormous growth of small banks in small towns was particularly evident in the western grain states, from Illinois west through the Dakotas. By 1920, these held 9,000 banks, averaging one for every 1,400 people.

Farms and their banks alike were buoyed up by the rising tide of prosperity and inflation with which the new century opened. The upsurge was gentle at first, but accelerated when Europe plunged into war in 1914. American farm products met a seemingly insatiable demand. When this country entered the war in 1917, the pace quickened still further, and continued on past the end of the war when the needs of stricken war-torn areas remained urgent. Between 1900 and 1920, farm output increased by one-fourth, but prices received by farmers tripled in that period. The sustained boom stimulated the demand for farm loans to buy more land, more equipment, more livestock, fertilizer, seed, etc. Land values skyrocketed, adding a speculative influence to credit expansion.

The banks, new and old, expanded their farm loans right in step. Additional modifications in national banking laws permitted limited mortgage lending after 1914, and made certain farm IOU's eligible for rediscount with the Federal Reserve System. Total farm debt shot up from less than $3 billion at the turn of the century to $18 billion in 1920. Commercial banks furnished $4.6 billion of the increase—much more than all other financial institutions combined. Farm loans outstanding in 1920 accounted for 18 per cent of all commercial bank loans by volume, as contrasted with 12 per cent in 1900. The role of farm loans was most impressive in the grain states where so many of the new banks took root—in South Dakota, 78 per cent of commercial bank credit went to farmers; in North Dakota, 77 per cent, while Kansas and Iowa were just under 70 per cent.[21]

During the same period, pressure from farm groups brought about numerous other banking and credit changes. Between 1907 and 1918 eight states—seven of them west of the Mississippi—put through programs for insurance of bank deposits. In 1910, Congress established a postal savings system, whereby post offices would accept savings deposits and pay interest on them. In 1916, the federal government established its first farm credit institutions, the Federal Land Banks, which were authorized to make farm mortgage loans. These were slow to become a major source of mortgage funds, but did step up competition with the banks in many areas. The law also authorized the formation of private Joint Stock Land Banks under favorable terms, and quite a few of these were established under the sponsorship of commercial banks.

Farm pressure was also successful in getting several state governments to undertake farm mortgage loan operations. The most notable experiment of this sort occurred in North Dakota. Beginning about 1915, the state had been subjected to a new wave of agrarian radicalism in the form of the Non-Partisan League, leaders of which were swept into political power in the elections of 1916. They proceeded in 1917 to establish the Bank of North Dakota, completely owned and managed by the state government. Drawing on proceeds of bond sales and aided by a loan from Chicago's Merchants Loan and Trust Company, the bank in turn served to help finance other state enterprises, particularly a mill and elevator at Grand Forks, for which it advanced over a million dollars. The bank was also designed to help carry out reforms of the commercial banking system, which included compulsory par clearance and deposit insurance, but its major objective was to extend mortgage loans to farmers.

Unfortunately, the zeal of the radical leaders for rapid action exceeded their management skills. The bank became involved with some unsavory private ventures of the League; its loans to the state enterprises were slow, if not lost, and many of the initial mortgage loans were unduly large relative to the value of borrowers' property. In 1921, the radicals were voted out of office and a conservative management took over the state bank. The volume of new loans was cut back sharply and the experiments in general banking control largely abandoned. The timing of the change was unfortunate, for it coincided with a sharp economic recession in which additional loans would have been most desirable. But the changes preserved the solvency of the bank, which is still very much in operation.[22]

In the summer of 1920, the long period of farm prosperity

and inflation came to a crashing halt. An unhealthy speculative build-up of inventories reversed, and the existing supplies were dumped on a rapidly glutted market. Within a year, prices of many farm products fell by 40 per cent. Gross farm income, which topped $15 billion in 1920, was only $10 billion the following year. Some recovery took place in subsequent years, when the economy as a whole revived, but things were never again as good as they had been before 1920.

The impact of the farm depression on the thousands of tiny country banks was devastating. The number of bank failures, which had been trivial during the previous twenty years, skyrocketed. In 1921-1929 inclusive, 5,400 banks suspended, 4,500 permanently—an average of 500 a year. Thousands of others found their capital so impaired by losses that they closed voluntarily without loss to creditors, or underwent "shotgun marriages" by absorption into larger and stronger institutions. Nearly 4,000 banks disappeared through merger during the 1920's.

Thus the structure of what one observer called "filling station banks" began to melt away—a process of erosion which accelerated in the depression of the 1930's. Too many of the tiny banks had committed themselves almost wholly to the local farm economy. Some were caught up in land speculation, or were ineptly managed. Many were simply inadequately diversified and illiquid. Yet they had brought loan and deposit facilities to the grass roots, to people who could not, before the triumph of the Model T, easily reach them otherwise. If some were victims of greed and speculation, others fell because they were simply too generous to their borrowers. A collection of reports of bank examiners on banks which subsequently failed contains some poignant entries.

A report of 1920 noted that "because of a long hard winter and the high price of feed, it has been necessary to strain credits in order to assist some of [the bank's] customers to carry live stock through the winter in order to avoid serious losses. . . ."

Of another bank, the examiner wrote "There are too many tenant farmers owing the bank, and credit has been too liberally extended to this class." At least two other banks were cited for the same generosity. A 1927 report said of the president of another bank, "He tries to help people and concerns who don't even do business with the bank, and anyone can take up his time whenever they desire."

In another case, the examiner noted that "The directors of this institution are all farmers, each being actively engaged in farming operations. They have gone upon the idea that the farmers in their vicinity are entitled to the credit which they have received, rather than upon the strict business standpoint. . . ." [23]

Such cases proved that generosity to borrowers, with insufficient attention paid to discipline, can be detrimental to both borrowers and lenders in the long run. The conventional bank insistence that borrowers limit their debts in relation to their ownership capital, maintain liquidity, and make systematic reduction of debts, imposes standards which, however unpopular they may be with some borrowers, operate to protect them as well as the lenders.

The sad wave of failures among the little banks set many observers to wondering if the countryside could not have been as well served had there been fewer banks, but more branches. Possibly the legislation of 1900, permitting small national banks, had been a step in the wrong direction. In any event, the desire to save impaired banks by consolidations led to liberalizations of the branch banking rules, and the number of branches operating increased greatly during the 1920's.

By 1930, the number of commercial banks had receded from its peak of thirty thousand to less than twenty-four thousand. The reduction was heavily concentrated on the small-size, small-town banks. And worse things were in store after 1929.

If farming was not profitable after 1920, it was still highly productive, and commercial banks continued to provide much of the credit required for the production process.

The constructive side of the picture is well displayed by the extensive farm-loan operations of A. P. Giannini's Bank of Italy (now the Bank of America) in the productive and highly diversified California farm areas. The bank, which commenced operations in 1904, acquired its first "country" branch in 1910, but in 1916-1918 established or purchased a large number in farm areas. As Mr. and Mrs. James described the situation:

> The regions into which the Bank of Italy took its branches were among the most highly specialized in California. Prospective clients were business-minded farmers who regarded agriculture as a commercial pursuit rather than a means of subsistence. They had to be, for they worked lands requiring much capital. Deserts were changed into orchards and vineyards by expensive irrigation plants; wasteland and sloughs were converted into truck gardens by costly filling operations; large sums of operating cash were required to support great numbers of seasonal laborers.[24]

Although the bank's entry coincided with the rise in credit demands, its branches frequently cut interest rates from their previous levels. In Modesto, the bank worked closely with the Borden company to administer a program of cattle loans to dairy farmers, with the creamery withholding funds to service the loans. The bank expanded loans to small orchards and vineyards around Stockton; at the same time, its great lending capacity enabled it to meet the big peak demands of canners and packers around Santa Clara and San Jose. It loaned extensively to cooperative marketing organizations, which were rapidly springing up among fruit and other crop producers.

Although California farmers were not so hard hit as some, they did suffer from the collapse of prices in 1919 and after. A $3 million line of credit to the prune and apricot co-op helped them ease their crop on to the market in 1919, and in the fall, the Bean Growers Association was similarly aided by a $1.5 million line of credit. At the same time, the bank extended an additional half million in loans on the lima bean crop elsewhere in the state. "More than half of the $74,737,000 that the Bank of Italy loaned in 1919 in the ordinary course of business went to farmers, packers, and canners." [25] The bank loaned $80,000 to a supplier of farm tools, $100,000 to a cattle loan company, and $250,000 toward building a plant to make farm equipment in Stockton. In the same year, the bank sponsored the California Joint Stock Land Bank and purchased a considerable amount of its bonds.

In the 1920's, the bank greatly extended its branch operations and farm loans in the rural areas. By the end of the twenties, Bank of Italy had mortgage loans outstanding on over 12,000 farms. These included 600 citrus groves, over 1,200 vineyards, 3,000 orchards, and more than 5,000 in cereals, field crops, alfalfa, or pasture. Large loans were outstanding to ranchers in the Salinas valley.

The bank was also occupied during a good part of the 1920's with the struggles of the California Associated Raisin Company, a cooperative marketing under the Sun-Maid trade name. When the raisin market broke in 1922, the organization owed over $8 million to banks. The Mercantile Trust and First National Bank of Los Angeles joined with Bank of Italy to reorganize the group and extend additional credits while it tried to get back on its feet—an endeavor which was not very successful through 1929. In 1930, a government program for the producers took over the burden, with nearly $6 million in loans from San Francisco's Anglo-California Bank, the Security-First National of Los Angeles, and Giannini's bank helping to get it under way.

By 1929, the Bank of Italy and other California banks had also extended abundant credits to help the development of cotton production and dairy farming in the state. Bank of Italy cotton loans in 1929 came to $10 million and financed half the state's crop. A newly formed subsidiary, the Bankitaly Agricultural Credit Corporation, had extended more than $15 million in livestock loans, chiefly on dairy cattle, by 1929.

We have devoted this amount of attention to the Bank of Italy because it has furnished about as full an account of its operations as any bank in the country. Almost every action we have described, however, could probably be matched by illustrations from other banks. In California itself the Giannini giant often merely continued the extensive farm lending operations of former unit banks, or worked cooperatively with other banks of the state (as noted in some of the illustrations given).

The year 1920 marked a turning point in American farming from a long-run standpoint as well as a short. After 1920, the number of people engaged in farming began a very gradual decline that has continued ever since. This has meant an even more pronounced reduction in the share of agriculture in national output and employment. But the growth in other sectors was facilitated by rising farm productivity, since fewer and fewer people were required to meet the food and fiber needs of the increased numbers of non-farmers. The share of bank credit going to farmers has naturally declined with the shift in the structure of the economy, but farm credit by banks continues to play a large and productive role in the economy, as Chapter 10 will demonstrate.

In retrospect, the period between 1865 and 1920 saw the filling up of the great open spaces of the American land. The number, acreage, and output of American farms increased enormously. The period was also the heyday of small-town America. The growth of farms and small towns had a profound influence on the growth of American banks. The number of banks rose nearly fifteen fold in half a century through the multiplication of small institutions in small communities. Numerically, state-chartered and private banks provided most of the growth. Credit limitations imposed on national banks provided the opportunities on which the emergence of a "dual" banking system depended.

Commercial banks in turn contributed to the development of farms and small towns through their credit facilities. From their initial stress on financing the movement of products by discounting bills of exchange, the banks became increasingly involved in farm-mortgage and production loans and in commercial-paper financing of large commodity dealers and processors.

Between 1896 and 1920, American farming enjoyed its golden age, based on a steady uptrend of farm prices. The postwar deflation which started in 1920 brought an end to farm prosperity, and marked the end of the filling-up process as well. The center of gravity of the economy shifted away from the small town. Farm depression cut heavily into the numbers of rural banks, but the coming of the Model T and better roads would have doomed many of them to extinction, as trade in the countryside became increasingly oriented around a smaller number of larger communities.

In the thirty years that followed the Civil War, farmers directed a flood of complaints against the banking system, principally at the restrictive influence of the national banking regulations. Farm discontent had its real roots, however, in economic instability and deflation of prices. Increasingly, the banking system became what the farmers wanted, and in the first twenty years of the twentieth century it bestowed abundant credit on them. Then instability and deflation turned debt into an incubus on the farmers, while the banks in turn were pulled under in many cases because they had met farm credit needs so abundantly. Ultimately the crash of 1929-1933 wiped out thousands more of the rural banks. It was a painful finish, but to a great degree they had finished their task.

CHAPTER

THE AGE OF THE RAILROADS,

1865-1914

THE MOST DRAMATIC AND COLORFUL of American enterprises
in the post-bellum era was the construction of the country's vast network of railroads. To be sure, there was considerable railroad mileage in place by 1860; indeed, many
analysts of the Civil War have given credit to the railway
network of the North as a source of economic superiority.
In the South, of course, the prewar railroad system was in
ruins by 1865; Sherman and his men had literally tied a
good bit of track in knots during their march to the sea.
West of the Mississippi, where the gold of California mines
and Iowa wheat both beckoned, only a few tentative lines
had been built. Even in the Northeast the existing rail facilities were rudimentary: rails were lightweight and iron;
roadbeds were shallowly ballasted; double tracking was
virtually nonexistent; and rolling stock was primitive. Moreover, the railways had not yet formed a *system,* which required consolidations and joint action to establish through

routes, to pool cars, to set common standards of gauge.

In the half century that followed 1865, the surface of the continent was thoroughly girded with steel. The dramatic rush to span the continent, which culminated in the golden spike of Promontory Point, the scandals and adventures of Jay Gould and Jim Fisk, the struggle for power between Hill and Harriman in the Northwest—these and many other episodes filled the press and captured the public's imagination. The development of the nation's rail system made possible the tidal wave of migration into the West; indeed, the land-grant railroads themselves directly brought about much of it. Without the railroads it would have been impossible for the nation's output of wheat, corn, and meat to move hundreds or thousands of miles to market—or, as industrialization proceeded, for giant factories to gain the benefits of high specialization aimed at a nationwide market.

In a dozen ways, the building of the railroads set the tone of American life for a half century. The railroad kings shaped the pattern of the industrial tycoon—fearless and ruthless, ingenious and original both in creating transportation innovations and in devising opportunities for separating the public from its cash. Railroad construction set the pace for the business cycle and stimulated the growth of steel production and other vital industries. Railroad corporations were *the* big business firms of the country before 1900; their securities completely dominated the nation's stock exchanges, and their finances nurtured and shaped the financial structure of the country. The rise of the great powers of Wall Street was a product of railroad finance, with its insatiable need for the services of investment bankers and trust companies.

Over the half century following 1865, the railroads absorbed nearly $10 billion of capital funds. Commercial banks provided about $1 billion of this sum by purchasing railroad bonds, and also made short-term loans to the railroad companies. Indirectly, much more bank credit passed into railroads through bank loans to brokers or individual investors on collateral of railroad stocks and bonds, and the banks performed the bulk of the work in getting stocks and bonds into the hands of non-bank investors, many of them residents of foreign countries. Individual bankers became promoters and managers of railroads; successful railroad men went into banking. The titans of railway organization and management relied on bank loans to extend their stock ownership for control. Next to farming and the marketing of farm products, railroad finance was the major outlet for the energies and funds of the nation's banks in the half century following the Civil War.

The enterprises which fired the imagination in the 1860's were those to span the continent and connect the long-isolated Pacific Coast with the rest of the country. The Civil War Congresses which created the national banking system and passed the Homestead Act also granted charters and generous aid in the form of land grants and loans for a route across the Rockies. The Union Pacific built west from Omaha, while the Central Pacific was working its way east from California. Despite government aid, the railroads found it difficult to raise cash by securities sales. Union Pacific, which at least had a long stretch of easy construction, struggled along with the assistance of loans from New York's National Bank of Commerce, Manhattan Company, and Phoenix Bank, until improved prospects for success buoyed the market for its securities in 1867. Construction of the Central Pacific, under the direction of bulldozing Charley Crocker, was also financially hard-pressed. It took four years to build through the Sierras, and such a tortuous process brought in little in land-grant revenues or government aid. Loans from the Bank of California helped to keep operations going. Finally, in 1869, the two roads made their historic connection at Promontory Point in Utah.

The Central Pacific soon became the Southern Pacific and the greatest power, for good or ill, in California. Charley

Crocker remained influential in its affairs, but also branched out into irrigation projects, coal developments, and cattle. He also bought a controlling interest in the private bank of R. C. Woolworth in San Francisco, chiefly for his son. The family name is preserved in its successor, the Crocker-Anglo National Bank.

Numerous projects were also afoot to extend lines into the rich lands southwest of St. Louis, and, hopefully, link up with a through-route to the west coast. Even before 1860, the Pacific Railroad of Missouri (forerunner of the Missouri Pacific) had started in that direction, and it was vigorously extended after the war. The Boatmen's Bank of St. Louis was an active promoter of this line. "Before 1860 Hudson E. Bridge, James H. Lucas, and John M. Wimer, directors of the bank, had served as presidents of the railroad company. Of the first $200,000 of its stock subscribed, $80,000 came from Boatmen's directors. . . . In 1864 [the bank] bought $500,000 Pacific Railroad Construction Bonds, and in 1869 $321,000 of its Real Estate Bonds. In 1865 it bought from the Pacific $687,000 St. Louis County Bonds which the railroad had received from the county in payment for stock."[1] During the 1860's, the bank also took $100,000 St. Louis and Cedar Rapids bonds, $200,000 bonds of the Northern Missouri Railroad, and $50,000 of Union Pacific bonds. The bank held some rail securities for investment, but functioned chiefly to resell them to investors.

The siren lure of railroad finance brought the downfall of the nation's leading private banker—Jay Cooke. At the end of the war, his firm maintained large private banking establishments in New York, Philadelphia, and Washington, each closely associated with a national bank. A few years later, he established an office in London run by Hugh McCulloch, after the latter resigned from the Treasury. The private bank offices did a large business in brokerage and exchange, and furnished checking account facilities. Although the firm did not make ordinary commercial loans, it commonly made ad-

vances to firms whose securities it was marketing, and these
were made by creating checking deposits in their favor.

Cooke and his establishment participated in a variety of
railroad and related enterprises in the 1860's—an anthracite
coal property in Schuylkill County, Pennsylvania, a railroad, land development, and mining complex near Carlisle,
Pennsylvania, a mining and land development in upstate
New York, and the Sterling Iron and Railway Company,
which constructed a feeder rail line from its mining properties in Orange County, New York, to a connection with the
Erie. He was also involved with the Warren and Franklin
Railroad Company, built to connect the new Pennsylvania
oil fields with trunk lines.[2]

About 1866, Cooke became increasingly interested in the
prospects for opening up the Northwest. He invested heavily in Minnesota lands, especially in Duluth, and became a
leading promoter of the Lake Superior and Mississippi railroad which was expected to tap the rich resources of the
Superior region. In 1869, he marketed some $4 million of
bonds for the road, many of them taken by his clients among
Pennsylvania country bankers. From this start he was rapidly
drawn into the vast enterprise of the Northern Pacific, which
was to prove his undoing.

Congress had chartered the Northern Pacific in 1864 and
offered a contingent land grant for the road from Lake
Superior west to Puget Sound, but the enterprise languished
for several years. In 1869, impressed by the reports of the
prospective agricultural and mineral wealth of the region
along the projected right-of-way, Cooke took on the financing of a revitalized firm. He organized an initial "pool" of
$5 million to start construction from a connection with his
Lake Superior road—and Cooke advanced the funds for
some of the subscribers to buy their shares in this. Soon
construction was vigorously under way, and the problems
of selling lands and bonds were tackled.

Although the initial planning of the road was well done,

and the country to be traversed was in fact about as good as anticipated, it soon became apparent that the timing of the project could not have been worse. Markets were becoming increasingly glutted with railroad securities, and each road, good or bad, was being shamelessly touted in a manner which made it impossible for investors to tell good from bad. Congress was unwilling to give cash assistance to the projected Northern Pacific, and efforts to market bonds in Europe failed, in part because of the Franco-Prussian war.

Domestic bond sales commenced in 1871, Cooke relying again on the extensive network of agents and ceaseless publicity as in his government-bond campaigns. Some of the exuberant sales talk about the region led scoffers to dub it "Jay Cooke's banana belt." In 1871 and 1872, some $16 million of bonds were sold. Although troubled by inefficient management, the railroad put down over four hundred miles of good track and reached Bismarck, North Dakota in May 1873, having founded along the way the towns of Fargo and Moorhead, named in honor of two of the bankers associated with the enterprise. Construction had also proceeded on the Pacific coast. But the gap between expenditures and bond sales was widening, held together tenuously by increasing advances from Jay Cooke and Co., some of which in turn represented lines of credit from the allied national banks. By the end of 1872, the advances stood close to $2 million. The general financial stringency of 1873 closed the net tighter, and in September 1873, Jay Cooke and Co., Bankers, suspended payment. The First National Bank of Washington, which had made large advances to Cooke, closed at the same time. Cooke's failures set off the violent phase of the panic of 1873, which augured the coming of a long and deep depression.

At the time of its failure, Jay Cooke and Co. held about $16 million of loans and securities. Among these were $4.5 million of loans to the Northern Pacific, and an additional

$2.5 million of other railroad securities. Their value dropped so fast that Cooke's personal fortune was completely exhausted in paying creditors, and even then full payment was not made. The First National Bank of Washington paid its creditors in full within three years, although they received no interest for the delay.

The Northern Pacific itself was soon in bankruptcy as well, and not until ten years later were its eastern and western sections finally connected. But by then the rapid settlement of the great wheat region at its eastern end had put the road well on its way to becoming one of the nation's most useful.

Among Mr. Cooke's customers was the Farmers National Bank of Annapolis, which bought $25,000 of Northern Pacific bonds. When the railroad went bankrupt, the bank accepted a large tract of Dakota land in exchange for $10,000 of them. This was not entirely disposed of until 1906, but ultimately yielded more than the cost of the bonds.[3]

The last third of the nineteenth century witnessed the activities of a host of colorful and enterprising railroad leaders. Cornelius Vanderbilt, the rugged former steamboater, brought the New York Central into New York City and made it one of the nation's finest roads in quality of performance as well as territorial scope. In the Southwest, C. C. Huntington, not content with one connection to the East, built the Southern Pacific route across the desolate expanse of Arizona and New Mexico. In the Midwest, Jay Gould, after leaving the Erie in 1872, carried on a bewildering array of operations which at various times gave him control of the Union Pacific, the Wabash, and the Missouri Pacific. Although Gould was widely denounced for his stock-market maneuvers, his lines built an enormous amount of track—4,000 miles in one feverish period 1879-1882—and were usually a vigorous and undisciplined source of competition which helped bring permanently lower freight rates for the vital shipments to and from the country's heartland. Edwin H. Harriman, after starting out as a stockbroker, achieved brilliant success in revitalizing the Union Pacific. James J. Hill built the vast Great Northern system west near the Canadian border, and in 1901 engaged in a dramatic contest with Harriman for control of the Northern Pacific.

There is not space to describe in detail the operations of the great railroad magnates, except to note that in addition to laying a lot of track, they all contributed to the development of coordinated *systems* out of the early disorder of railroad building. While their individual contributions differed, their aggregate effect was to create, within a half century, an extraordinarily complete network on which rapid technological improvements were put into effect.

For our purpose, it is important to stress that the rail giants almost without exception relied extensively on bank loans to buy or hold the securities essential for control of rail properties. Gould borrowed substantial sums from the Mercantile Trust of New York, of which he was a stockholder and director. (He also directed the trust business of his rail companies largely to this institution.) In the early 1880's, he also borrowed from New York's big Fourth National. One estimate places his debts around $20 million in 1884. Vanderbilt was a heavy bank borrower during his tussles with Gould in the 1860's, and presumably other times as well. Of Huntington, Professor Julius Grodinsky concluded that "by personal credit and by transferring loans from bank to bank and from person to person he succeeded in financing the only single major railroad construction program in the depression of the seventies." [4] Harriman made connections with several New York banks during his early days as a stockbroker, and later came into association with Stillman, National City Bank, and the Standard Oil crowd. Hill maintained close connections with the First National Bank of St. Paul beginning in 1880. In 1912, he bought both it and the Second National and merged them to form one of the major banks of the Northwest—the present First National.

The needs and opportunities for creating stability and order out of the railroad chaos of the era also opened the way, after Jay Cooke's failure, for a new financial giant—J. Pierpont Morgan. His father, Junius Morgan, born on a Massachusetts farm, had become by 1865 an important international banker in London. The younger Morgan, after a brief apprenticeship, opened his own banking house in New York, dealing largely in foreign exchange, gold, and securities. In 1871, he entered a partnership with Anthony Drexel of Philadelphia. With his advantageous foreign connections, he soon became prominent in underwriting securities issues.

In 1879, he took on an important responsibility—helping William H. Vanderbilt dispose of a large portion of his enormous holdings of New York Central stock. Morgan found English buyers for them; moreover, he became their representative on the Central's board. From this developed Morgan's role for the next thirty years—using his ability to raise funds and market securities as a lever to bring about stability, order, and profit in the business world, while using his reputation as a stabilizer to enhance the confidence of investors in the securities he sold. Morgan's opportunities arose from the kind of environment in which Jay Gould thrived. Speculative rail building had created excess capacity in many areas; numerous small lines urgently needed to have their operations (if not their ownership) consolidated, and cutthroat competition and securities frauds seemed endemic. The prospective economic benefits from a degree of consolidation and stabilization were substantial. For one thing, the railroads still needed vast amounts of additional capital to improve their lines and rolling stock, and anything which built up investor confidence, particularly in Europe, would help them obtain it. Second, the railway system, to function efficiently, required a high degree of cooperation among adjoining lines. The danger of such action, however, was that it inevitably shaded over into monopoly.

Morgan's opportunities arose particularly from the numerous bankruptcies into which American railroads were thrown during the late nineteenth century. His firm became the chief expert in financial reorganization, a channel by which fresh funds, usually so desperately needed, could be injected into a prostrate firm. The price was usually commensurate with the need: a substantial portion of the new securities to the House of Morgan as commission, and sufficient representation on the board of directors to see that the interests of investors were protected.

Such activities reached a peak in the depressed years of the 1890's when Morgan's firm managed or shared in the reorganization of such roads as the Erie, the Reading, the Norfolk and Western, the Northern Pacific, and the Baltimore and Ohio. The firm handled millions of dollars of securities issues for new construction and equipment, and for consolidations like that which produced the Southern Railway. Morgan's influence with the railway community was immense, and it was strongly exerted in the direction of keeping out adventurers and securing a relatively high standard of gentlemanly conduct.

In 1894, after the death of Anthony Drexel, Morgan's firm was reorganized. In New York it now became J. P. Morgan and Company, while the Philadelphia office was known as Drexel and Company. Although the specialty of the firm was investment banking, securities transactions, and, we might say, management consulting, it remained a commercial bank as well, and, indeed, one of the largest in the country. It maintained checking accounts for its corporate clients and wealthy individuals, dealt in foreign exchange, and commonly made advances to corporations on securities that were in the process of sale to the public.

The twenty-year period from the reorganization of the

firm until Morgan's death saw the firm at the height of its relative power and prestige. Three outstanding episodes punctuated this era. In 1893, the United States Treasury found itself confronted with a first-class monetary crisis— a run on the gold reserve, largely motivated by fear that free-silver legislation would end the gold standard and cause a depreciation of the dollar. Morgan volunteered his services to the reluctant Grover Cleveland and organized a syndicate to help the government out of its plight. The syndicate marketed new issues of government bonds to replenish the gold reserve and devoted its fullest efforts to prevent further gold from leaving the country.

In 1901, Morgan was one of the key figures in the formation of the largest business corporation in the world—the billion-dollar United States Steel Corporation. In 1907, when Wall Street was swept by a financial panic which threatened to pull down many of the banks, Morgan assumed the role of a "one-man Federal Reserve bank," as Frederick Lewis Allen put it.[5] He called together the heads of the city's leading banks and half-forced, half-cajoled them into putting up enough cash to prevent suspensions of payment by the weaker banks, realizing that such suspensions would only lead to worse runs on the others.

In 1912, J. P. Morgan and Company held $162 million in deposit liabilities, which ranked it among the largest banks in the country. Half of this sum represented the accounts of seventy-eight corporate clients. In the previous ten years, the firm had handled the marketing of some $2 billion worth of securities issues. The House of Morgan also was influential in such other prominent Wall Street institutions as Bankers Trust, National Bank of Commerce, and Guaranty Trust. Through subsequent mergers, the Morgan firm has evolved into the present Morgan Guaranty Trust Company.

Besides such prominent figures as Cooke, Gould, and Morgan, there are innumerable other cases of close ties between banking and railroad development. Erastus Corning, president of the City Bank of Albany, was one of the important forces that brought about the formation of the New York Central system by consolidation in the 1850's; Corning was president of the Central until 1864.[6] William C. Ralston's Bank of California built considerable railroad mileage in connection with its development of Comstock mining properties. Moses Taylor, long president of New York's National City Bank, was a heavy investor in railroads—the Michigan Central for one, the oddly named International Great Northern (in Texas!) for another. Taylor also owned a large interest in the Farmers Loan and Trust Co. and used his influence on the railroads to throw profitable trust business to it. Grenville Dodge, who directed the construction of the Union Pacific, was a partner in a private banking firm in Council Bluffs, Iowa, predecessor of today's Council Bluffs Savings Bank.

The Philadelphia (National) Bank invested over half a million dollars in railroads during the Civil War years, chiefly in the Pennsylvania, the Reading, and the Lehigh Valley. The Central National Bank, founded in 1864 by industrialists of the Philadelphia area, loaned $75,000 to the Pennsylvania Railroad in 1865. Its loan customers soon included such related firms as Baldwin Locomotive Works (also a regular borrower from Philadelphia National), Lehigh Coal and Navigation Co., Pencoyd Rolling Mills, Cambria Iron Co., and other rail suppliers.[7]

In a massive study of New England railroad development, Professor Kirkland found that, of one hundred prominent railroad capitalists, "sixty-nine were officers of New England banks. Without enumerating a few assorted cashiers and treasurers, the sixty-nine held one hundred and four bank directorships or trusteeships and fifty bank presidencies."[8] Prominent names linking banks with railroads in the region were Franklin Haven, president of Merchants' Bank of Boston, private bankers Joseph W. Clark and Nathaniel Thayer, and Chester W. Chapin, president of the Boston and Albany from 1866 to 1878, whose family controlled the Chapin (National) Bank and Trust Company of Springfield, Massachusetts. Since banks, railroads, and land were the three great investment attractions of the period, it is not surprising that many wealthy persons were involved in all three.

Reconstruction of the southern railway system after the Civil War was helped along by the survival of two unusual firms established in Georgia before the war—railroad companies with banking powers. The Georgia Railroad and Banking Company, and the Central Railroad and Banking Company of Georgia both controlled considerable rail mileage before the war. Their banks survived the war by the foresighted accumulation of foreign-exchange assets in London, and both were able to play an important role in postwar reconstruction by credit creation and by new issues of securities. The Central ultimately failed in the 1890's, but the other firm eventually separated its banking operations from railroading. It is still successfully operating as the Georgia Railroad Bank and Trust Company of Augusta.

Incorporated banks performed a considerable amount of securities marketing during the initial postwar railway boom. The panic of 1873 caught a good many of them with substantial advances outstanding and currently uncollectable, and they left the business to the private bankers for many years thereafter. Besides the House of Morgan, these included Kuhn, Loeb, in New York, Lee Higginson, in Boston, and N. W. Harris, predecessor of today's Harris Trust, in Chicago.

For a long time, incorporated banks participated in rail finance chiefly by buying securities or by making collateral loans on stock. As an illustration, the Maverick National Bank of Boston at the end of 1890 held about $474,000 of rail bonds, including $135,000 Santa Fe, $150,000 Atlantic and Pacific, and $164,000 Richmond West Point Terminal. The bank also had extended about $225,000 of collateral loans on rail stocks: $56,000 on Boston and Maine, $38,000 on New York and New England, $33,000 on Cleveland and Canton, $24,000 on Burlington, $23,000 on Santa Fe, and lesser amounts on stocks of fourteen other lines.[9]

The rising tide of railroad finance contributed to the development of the great trust companies in the post-Civil War era. Bond issues and reorganizations created profitable trust opportunities and fiscal agency relationships; the trust company could expect not only trustee fees but also large deposits from corporate customers. At the same time, an increasing number of families were becoming wealthy enough to use personal trust services—particularly as the first-generation tycoons began to age or die. In addition to such prewar firms as New York's Farmers, Philadelphia's Girard, and Chicago's Merchants, the field was soon entered by Guaranty Trust (1864), Rhode Island Hospital Trust (Providence, 1867), Illinois Trust and Savings (Chicago, 1873), and an increasing number of others. By the 1890's, many of these were active in securities marketing.[10]

National banks were not permitted to exercise trust powers, a restriction which became quite galling by the turn of the century. One reaction was that a number of them formed or acquired trust affiliates—separately incorporated but linked by stock ownership and possible interlocking management. Chicago's First National Bank created the First Trust and Savings in this fashion in 1903. In that same year, a group of New York banks and bankers sponsored the formation of Bankers Trust Company.

The high level of securities issues and company promotions around the turn of the century brought the incorporated commercial banks increasingly back into the securities business. The First National Banks of New York and Chicago, and New York's National City Bank, among others, began to participate in investment banking on a large scale, and they were large investors in bonds, whether for resale or permanent retention. National City's bond portfolio in

1912 included holdings of twenty-six rail firms totaling about
$18 million, and including million-plus holdings of Santa
Fe, Chesapeake and Ohio, Detroit Terminal, Florida East
Coast, Illinois Central, New York Central, and Seaboard
Air Line.[11] In 1907-1914, Chicago's First Trust and Savings
handled $77 million of securities issues, including $14 million of rail securities representing thirty-six companies.[12]
When the national banking authorities began to criticize
securities transactions, national banks created securities affiliates—New York's First National in 1908, National City in
1911.

By 1912, the commercial banks held about $900 million
in railroad bonds. Bank loans on collateral of rail securities
were about the same magnitude, and bank-administered
trust funds held perhaps $500 million in rail securities. In
the aggregate, these sources furnished more than $2 bil-
lion to the enormous capital needs of the railroads. Between
1865 and 1912, commercial banks directly and indirectly
furnished about 15 per cent of railroad capital. Additional
bank contributions came through the marketing of securities and the direct personal investments of wealthy bankers
in rail lines.[13]

The first decade of the new century marks the turning
point in the role of the railroads. By 1915, the country's
rail network was laid out, and further financing needs for
equipment and improvements never bulked anywhere near
as important as the initial construction. But the social and
economic repercussions of the railroad age were felt long
after. The railroads opened up the West, settled it, and
carried its products to the East, many of them to be exported. Crop exports and capital imports for railroad building enlarged the international economic role of the United
States after 1865, a move which became more pronounced
after the acquisition of the Philippines. American banks
increased their international role by stages. In the 1870's
and 1880's, they dealt in foreign exchange; gradually they

increased the extension of credit on exports. Foreign banks maintained branches in such American cities as San Francisco and Chicago; after 1900, a counter movement began when New York's National City and Boston's First National set up foreign branches. The Federal Reserve Act of 1913 stimulated financing of international trade by use of bankers' acceptances, and by that date a few of the bigger banks were also buying and selling foreign bond issues. World War I hastened the rise; J. P. Morgan became a major fundraiser for the Allied Powers, and the American banks and other investors held foreign bonds in quantity through the 1920's.

The age of the railroads had major repercussions on their suppliers, as well. The enormous demand for rails and rolling stock stimulated iron and steel production, which had already received a powerful push from the Civil War. Young Andrew Carnegie, working for the Pennsylvania Railroad, was impressed by the opportunities offered in supplying the railroads. As he describes it in his autobiography, he was riding on a train one day when

a farmer-looking man approached me. He carried a small green bag in his hand. He said the brakeman had informed him I was connected with the Pennsylvania Railroad. He wished to show me the model of a car which he had invented for night traveling. He took a small model out of the bag, which showed a section of a sleeping-car.

This was the celebrated T. T. Woodruff, the inventor of that now indispensable adjunct of civilization—the sleeping car. Its importance flashed upon me. I asked him if he would come to Altoona if I sent for him, and I promised to lay the matter before Mr. Scott at once upon my return. I could not get that sleeping-car idea out of my mind, and was most anxious to return to Altoona that I might press my views upon Mr. Scott. When I did so, he thought I was taking time by the forelock, but was quite receptive and said I might telegraph for the patentee. He came and contracted to place two of his cars upon the line as soon as they could be built. After this, Mr. Woodruff, greatly to my surprise, asked me if I would not join him in his new enterprise and offered me an eighth interest in the venture.

I promptly accepted his offer, trusting to be able to make payments somehow or another. The two cars were to be paid for by monthly installments after delivery. When the time came for making the first payment, my portion was two hundred and seventeen and a half dollars. I boldly decided to apply to the local banker, Mr. Lloyd, for a loan of that sum. I explained the matter to him, and I remember that he put his great arm . . . around me, saying, "Why, of course I will lend it. You are all right, Andy."

And here I made my first note, and actually got a banker to take it. A proud moment in a young man's career! The sleeping-cars were a great success and their monthly receipts paid the monthly installments. The first considerable sum I made was from this source.[14]

By 1863, Carnegie's sleeping-car investment was paying him $5,000 a year, and a few years later he maneuvered it into a merger with Pullman which was extremely profitable. He also struck it rich in some investments in Pennsylvania oil properties.

Aided by these financial successes, Carnegie blossomed into entrepreneurship during the Civil War years. In rapid succession, he founded a firm to build iron railroad bridges (it furnished most of the members for the Eads bridge), a rail mill, and a locomotive works. In each Carnegie displayed his ability to choose the right men to put in charge and to elicit top performance from them, so that the enterprises prospered despite his own lack of technological brilliance. By 1870, he extended his operations from fabrication and had a furnace to make his own pig iron.

Carnegie's multifarious enterprises drew on as much credit as they could get from the Pittsburgh banks, the burden of negotiation usually falling on his partner, Henry Phipps. Jokesters argued that his chief utility was the way he could "keep a check in the air for several days" and that his horse could not pass a bank without stopping. Before long, however, Carnegie's enterprises were able to meet their credit needs without difficulty. In the early 1870's, they were substantial borrowers from the Exchange National Bank of Pittsburgh.

During the 1860's, the iron trade was increasingly stirred by the reports of Henry Bessemer's remarkable process for mass-producing steel. Some of the older American iron makers experimented with the process, but without success. Carnegie took no great interest in it; indeed, he spent a good part of his time during the boom years between 1865 and 1872 selling railroad securities abroad. In 1872, however, he met Bessemer and was captivated by watching his process in operation. Carnegie rushed home and organized a new company to make steel and roll it into rails, selling off most of his outside investments to raise cash.

Just then, the panic of 1873 engulfed the country. Carnegie's firms were hard pressed; at one point he had to pay a premium of $2,400 for currency to meet a $100,000 payroll and had to secure extensions on some bank loans. But the troubles were temporary. Carnegie and his associates were distinctly solvent, and in 1874, they fired up their new mill at Braddock—the J. Edgar Thomson steel plant, named in honor of the president of the Pennsylvania railroad, but shrewdly placed with access to the B and O as well! Aggressive price cutting soon gave them a big share of the market for steel rails, and what was to become the Carnegie Brothers steel company was on its way to leadership in the industry.

Carnegie soon joined forces with another remarkable man —Henry Clay Frick, the "king of coke." While still in his teens and working in Grandfather Overholt's distillery, Frick had started buying or leasing coal properties and setting up coke ovens. In 1871, at the ripe old age of twenty-two, he applied to the Mellon bank and asked to borrow

$10,000 to build fifty coke ovens. Judge Mellon was impressed, and made the loan. In a short time, Frick asked for $10,000 more for additional ovens. Mellon sent an investigator, who reported adversely. Frick had too many irons in the fire, he observed; besides, he spent part of his time looking at pictures. Mellon sent another man, this time a coal man. He was impressed with Frick's competence and enterprise, and the additional funds were granted.

The panic of 1873 found Frick, like Carnegie, strong enough financially to take advantage of the low prices of properties and extend his operations enormously. In 1881, Carnegie brought Frick into his firm, and eventually the coke magnate became the operating head of Carnegie's steel empire, while the master spent most of his time gadding about the world. Despite the enormous size of the firm, however, it remained a limited partnership, and thus did not rely on public securities issues to finance expansion. Reinvested profits supplemented by bank credit provided the needed capital.

Carnegie had plenty of competition in steel-making. Firms with such familiar names as Bethlehem and Jones and Laughlin were prominent in iron-making even before 1860. As the turn of the century approached, many newcomers entered various phases of the industry. Like Carnegie, these began to see virtue in integrating—bringing successive processes under single ownership. During the 1890's, the industry was swept by a fever of consolidation, spurred by the ease with which securities issues could be sold to the investing public. Security issues also financed much of the expansion of productive facilities, with banks participating in marketing the securities and buying some for themselves or trust accounts.

By 1900, a large part of the industry had coalesced into three giant "interest groups," of which Carnegie's was one. An outbreak of furious competition among them seemed ahead—but Carnegie, long the principal boat-rocker of the industry, was known to be eager to retire. Other leaders of the industry joined with J. P. Morgan to help Carnegie on his way and to serve their own interests at the same time. They engineered the most colossal of all industrial combinations, the United States Steel Corporation, with a nominal capitalization well over $1 billion, into which were brought productive properties representing about two-thirds of the steel capacity of the country. The corporation's share of the market, however, declined from that point on. The industry was soon joined by a formidable competitor when Charles Schwab, formerly of the corporation, built an integrated industrial complex around the old and respected name of Bethlehem Steel. The firm soon made a permanent impact on the architecture of the world when it built the first plant devoted to producing the structural steel beams invented by Henry Grey. Loans from banks in Philadelphia and Bethlehem were important in financing the plant, which was soon swamped with orders from the builders of sky-scrapers in many cities.

Further repercussions of railroad and steel developments rested heavily on bank credit. Loans from the Bank of New York to the Tredegar Iron Works in Richmond helped the former "Arsenal of the Confederacy" expand its pro-duction of freight cars in the 1870's, until by 1880 the firm was making two thousand a year. Cleveland banker Dan Eells also entered the business of railroad equipment, but he soon turned his firm into production of steam shovels and other construction machinery. Aided by large loans from the First National Bank of Milwaukee, the Commercial Na-tional Bank of Cleveland, and the South Milwaukee Na-tional Bank, the firm weathered the depression of the 1890's, prospered as a leading supplier of equipment for digging the Panama Canal, and functions today as the Bucyrus-Erie Company, whose name is commonly found on the fasci-nating monsters reconstructing the American highway sys-tem. Lake Superior iron ore greatly stimulated the growth of the lake shipping industry, and one transport company named vessels after the presidents of the Bank of Pittsburgh and the Keystone National Bank to honor their financial assistance. Earl Oglebay and David Norton both came from banking backgrounds to form Oglebay, Norton, and Company, which remains after seventy years one of the leading firms in mining, transport, and distribution of iron ore.[15]

Just as the coming of the railroad made possible the enormous expansion of American farm acreage and output, it also made possible the rise of the great cities. Without railroads, the size of cities would have been limited by their need to draw food supplies from the nearby areas. Development of cheap, rapid long-distance transportation also made it possible for large-scale manufacturing enterprises to develop in areas such as Pittsburgh, drawing raw materials and sending finished products over considerable distances.

In 1860, less than 10 per cent of the population lived in the nine cities with over one hundred thousand population. By 1890, New York had passed the two and a half million mark, and Philadelphia and Chicago both exceeded a million. In 1910, no fewer than fifty cities were above one hundred thousand, and they contained some twenty million people— more than one-fifth of the population.

As the cities grew, there grew with them requirements for such public facilities as streets, schools, water supply, and sewage disposal. Usually bond issues were made to finance these projects. Commercial banks helped market these bonds, besides buying substantial amounts for themselves and their trust clients. By 1900, state and local governments had about $1.7 billion of bonds outstanding. Of this, commercial banks held about 10 per cent for their own accounts and a nearly equal amount for trust funds. In the years 1901-1912 inclusive, state and local governments issued an additional $2.4 billion, of which banks and their trust accounts combined purchased nearly one-fourth.[16]

The city also made great demands for the services of public utilities. In the years right after the Civil War, the important forms were street railways with horse-drawn vehicles and the production and distribution of gas for cooking and illumination. The whole picture changed radically with the important developments in electric lighting, generation, and transmission that began in the 1870's. The rapid rise of electric generating and distribution companies was closely followed by the spread of telephone service. Electricity spawned the trolley car, and, a little later, the metropolitan subway.

These utilities, developed almost entirely at first by private companies, were heavily bond-financed, and again the commercial banking system played an important role in marketing and buying these securities. J. P. Morgan was a strong backer of Thomas A. Edison in the 1870's and was one of the first New Yorkers to install electric lighting, in 1882. By 1909, commercial banks had invested $400 million in bonds of "public service" companies of this type. National City Bank of New York's bond portfolio in 1912 included nearly $8 million of such issues, led by $4.5 million of Consolidated Gas of New York, and including Chicago Elevated, Metropolitan Street Railway, Pacific Light and Power, Toledo Traction, and Washington Light and Electric Co. Chicago's Illinois Trust and Savings was a large factor in telephone securities; a list of securities bought for investment or resale in 1907-1912 includes five different "tel and tel" firms bearing such diverse regional designations as Western, Southern Bell, New York, Cumberland, and Pacific. The bank also took $932,000 of Western Electric bonds.[17] For the period 1901-1912, American utilities issued about $3.7 billion of bonds, of which the banks bought about $400 million for themselves and $200 million for trust funds.[18]

For a long time, cities grew by spreading out, but with

the development of steel girders and electric elevators, they began about 1900 to grow vertically as well. The erection of larger and larger buildings soon began to transform the character of central city areas—and began also to take substantial amounts of bank credit, chiefly through mortgage loans. Construction of a new store for R. H. Macy and Company in 1902 gives us a good illustration.

Macy's had been operating for nearly half a century, and had already made its mark as one of the country's outstanding low-price mass distributors who, like Ward's and Sears', were helping to spread the benefits of industrial productivity among the people. By 1902, it was doing $10 million of business a year, and decided to move into a large new building farther uptown—the one it still occupies. As Ralph Hower describes it:

Today we are so accustomed to large buildings and astronomical figures that it is difficult to appreciate the impression which the new building made upon contemporary New York. It was not particularly tall even for 1902, being only nine stories high, but it occupied a large area. In addition to Koster & Bial's Theater, 32 buildings had been razed to make way for it, and the completed structure contained 23½ acres of floor space. To provide both a basement and a sub-basement contractors had been obliged to remove earth and rock to a depth of 30 feet below street level, and the resulting excavation was the largest in the city. . . .

Contemporary newspaper accounts described the new Macy store as the largest and best-equipped department store in the world, and the best information available confirms this view. . . .

The new building, together with the ground leases involved, cost slightly more the $4,800,000, in addition to which there was a substantial sum invested in fixtures. In point of fact, the whole project was done in the name of L. Straus & Sons, who in turn leased the premises to R. H. Macy and Co. To finance the project Isidor Straus borrowed $4,200,000 from the National City Bank, the Farmers' Loan and Trust Co., and the United States Trust Co.; all this was obtained at five per cent without collateral, an arrangement which gives ample testimony to the credit standing of the Strauses as well as to contemporary banking opinion of Macy's prospects. All these loans were repaid in full by 1906.[19]

The coming of the skyscraper age opened even more intriguing prospects for banks. A big bank should have a big building; it could occupy the lower floors and rent the rest profitably. There was one snag—banking laws generally limited the amount of funds that could be invested in real estate. The answer was, as in many other cases, to form a subsidiary. So one after another, big city banks began to put up impressive structures in which they were, nominally, tenants, paying rent like the rest to the owner corporation. But the last-named was, of course, owned by the bank or by its stockholders, and of course this technique channeled more bank credit into skyscraper construction.

By 1914, it is safe to say, the uses of bank credit in the United States were as diverse as the productive enterprises of the country. From the stress on commerce and agriculture which characterized much of the nineteenth century, the banks were drawn increasingly into financing mining, transportation, industrial production, and capital-using public services. Bank credits played an important part in the continued expansion of the textile and furniture industries, particularly in the South.

Diversity is evident in the records of individual banks. Important borrowers from the Union Savings Bank and Trust Company of Steubenville, Ohio included a number of clay and pottery factories, glassmakers, and wool factories, as well as steelmakers and fabricators which have become so important in that area. A list of firms borrowing from the Keystone National Bank of Philadelphia in 1890-1891 includes the prominent mercantile firm of Wanamaker and Brown, and such typical small business names as Penn Roofing Co., Excelsior Hosiery Co., Cleverly Electrical Works, Wayne Stone Co., Dairyman's Supply Co., March

Brownback Stove Co., Herder Cutlery Co., and Schwacher Piano Co.[20] By the turn of the century, larger firms were likely to incorporate and sell bonds. National City Bank's portfolio in 1912 included holdings of Associated Simmons Hardware, Armour and Company, Consolidated Coal, National Distillers, National Enamel and Stamping Company, and Union Bag and Paper.[21]

The great increase in national output that occurred during the half century following the Civil War was an indication of the benefit which the country derived from the increase in capital goods, used in combination with abundant natural resources, advancing technology, and a population of increasing numbers and improving skills. The increased capital in turn resulted from saving. Much of this saving was turned directly into investment by the owners of the business firms themselves—this has always been one of the great advantages of a society with a large number of small, privately-owned firms. Much saving also came through personal acquisitions of stocks and bonds, a process which occurred on a relatively large scale because of the concentration of income and wealth. The third channel for saving (and my guess is that the three named were of roughly equal magnitude) came through financial institutions, of which the commercial banks were the most important. Commercial bank credit outstanding to business in 1900 was about $4.9 billion (including security loans), with an added $1.5 billion from bank-administered trust funds. By comparison, mutual savings banks and insurance companies, the other major financial intermediaries, accounted in combination for about $1.9 billion of business credit (mostly through securities holdings).

By 1900, American business firms were using real capital goods, such as machinery, buildings, and inventories, valued at about $25 billion. Even excluding trust funds, bank credit to business equaled one-fourth of this sum. Non-financial businesses had net indebtedness of about $13 billion. About 30 per cent of this represented funds obtained directly from banks. This comparison gives some idea of the important contribution of the banks to economic growth—a contribution further enhanced by trust funds and trust services, by marketing of securities, and by checking-deposit services.[22]

There is no denying that this period of economic enterprise and growth was also an age of rough-and-tumble pursuit of wealth and power, in which productivity and the public interest were not invariably served. It was the Age of the Moguls, the Robber Barons, the Lords of Creation, in which the enormously attractive opportunities for gain could be undertaken under a minimum of restraints. The banking system, although more carefully regulated than most sectors of the economy, shared this crude vitality. Regulation was not always effective, even for national banks, and was often nominal or nonexistent for state or private institutions. Because new banks could be started easily, and because banking regulations were relatively mild in many areas, the banking system was highly sensitive and responsive to evolving credit needs. Bank credit continued to provide a resource whereby the man of enterprise could convert aspiration into achievement. For the same reasons, the banking system was vulnerable to abuse, through fraud or incompetent management, through participation in speculative ventures of questionable character.

Public concern over the performance of the financial system produced the showy but relatively inconclusive "Money Trust" investigation in 1912. Alarm over the apparent increase in the concentration of ownership and control of industry produced new antitrust legislation in 1914—although recent statistical investigations indicate that relative increases in the degree of industrial concentration had come to an end before that date.

Of greater long-run importance was the widespread dissatisfaction with the performance of the banking and financial system over the business cycle—dissatisfaction which ultimately led to the creation of the Federal Reserve System in 1914. To trace this development, the next chapter shifts emphasis away from the relation of banks to credit, capital, and enterprise, and focuses instead on banks and money.

CHAPTER

7

BANKS AND THE MONEY SUPPLY,

1865-1925

BESIDES THE VITAL CONTRIBUTIONS that bank credit made
to the financing of capital and enterprise, the commercial
banks also supplied most of the expansion in the money supply needed by the economy. Monetary expansion was
needed to finance a rising trend of total expenditures, enabling the demand for goods and services to keep up with
the rapid rise in the productive capacity of the economy.
And as a national transportation system coalesced, the economy became unified into a great nationwide pattern of
specialization and exchange, in which money and the price
system played a vital coordinating role.

Between 1865 and 1914, the quantity of money in the
United States increased about ten fold. That this was not
an excessive amount is evidenced by the fact that prices in
1914 were lower than in 1865. Commercial banks supplied
about 90 per cent of the expansion in money. This striking
performance was possible because of the rapid increase in

the relative monetary importance of checks and bank deposits. Whereas deposits made up about half the money supply in the 1860's, by 1914 they accounted for 85 per cent of the total.

Before the Civil War, observers had found it noteworthy that most business firms kept checking accounts. By 1914, checks constituted about 90 per cent of the flow of business payments, and were becoming increasingly common for personal finance as well. In 1909, there were about eleven million checking deposit accounts in the country. Eight million of these had balances of less than $500 each, and represented mostly personal and farm accounts. A study of funds deposited on a typical business day in 1909 showed that checks made up almost three-fourths of retailers' deposits. About 30 per cent of payrolls were found to involve check payments in that year. The director of these investigations concluded that "the retail trade of the country shows that the habit of paying by check has probably reached down in some measure to all economic classes of the community whose income is $1,000 or more, provided they are other than what is classified as manual laborers." [1]

What brought about this great increase in the use of deposits? Among individuals, rising real incomes and increased urbanization were certainly important. Among business firms, one factor was the great increase in the volume of business transacted over a broad geographic area. Also, with the development of large firms, systematic business procedures became increasingly important—procedures in which the advantages of deposits and checks for record-keeping and receipts were apparent. Finally, there were business firms who simply had more funds to handle than could prudently be kept in the form of currency. Restrictions on bank-note issue led banks to encourage the use of deposits, even to the extent of paying interest on demand deposits.

Many city banks were reluctant to accept personal accounts, fearing they would be called upon to lend to the depositors. The Bank of New York, for instance, for many years would not accept a new account unless sponsored by someone who was already a customer. But most banks—and especially the new ones—were eager for deposits, large or small. This led to complications when depositors were illiterate. The Boatmen's Bank of St. Louis identified by appearance those depositors whose signatures were represented by a scrawled "X," giving rise to such succinct characterizations as: "James F____. A redfaced Mick with whiskers around his face. Works in the Lindell car barns and smells like a horse." [2]

The banks, of course, also issued a portion of the nation's currency in the form of national bank notes. Originally, these notes had been subject to a rigid limitation of total issue, but this was removed in 1875. In 1900, national banks were permitted to issue notes up to the full value of Treasury bonds held as security, instead of the previous limit of 90 per cent. Despite these measures, bank notes were fading from importance relative to deposits. By 1914, national bank notes had slightly more than doubled their volume of the 1860's—but bank deposits had increased thirteen fold in the same period.

The growth of money and expenditures was far from a smooth and orderly process. Instead, the economy was subjected to repeated alternations of boom and depression. Banks and money received much of the blame for this instability. Periodic economic depressions and declining farm prices provided a fertile ground for the seeds of monetary controversy.

Controversy broke out almost as soon as the war was over. It was concerned with the relative status and merits of the greenbacks—the legal tender United States notes issued by the Treasury—*versus* the national bank notes. "The national banking system was intended . . . to furnish the people with a permanent paper circulation," said righteous Hugh McCulloch, who had moved up from Comptroller of the Currency to Secretary of the Treasury. "The United States notes were intended to meet a temporary emergency, and to be retired when the emergency had passed." [3]

Certainly a lot of people had regarded the greenbacks as temporary when they were first authorized, but when the time came to get rid of them, it was another story. When the Civil War ended, Treasury surpluses drew some of them out of circulation, and McCulloch asked for authority to issue bonds in order to mop up more of them. He was particularly offended by the fact that both greenbacks and national bank notes were "off the gold standard," and that gold and silver were selling at high premiums above par. "By common consent of the nations," said he, "gold and silver are the only true measure of value. They are the necessary regulators of trade. I have myself no more doubt that these metals were prepared by the Almighty for this very purpose, than I have that iron and coal were prepared for the purposes for which they are being used." [4]

There were others, however, who did not share the Secretary's version of divinely revealed truth—notably crusty old Thaddeus Stevens and a goodly number of his Pennsylvania constituents engaged in the iron and steel business. Their war orders finished, these gentlemen found themselves faced with deteriorating markets—and they had plenty of company in other industries and areas. Sound money was fine when you had it, they might concede, but drawing all that currency out of the economy was a mighty painful way to achieve it.

McCulloch and his Treasury staff had no use for a permanent issue of government currency. "Such a currency possesses no inherent qualities which adapt it to the wants of trade," complained Comptroller Hulburd in 1867. "It does not contract during seasons of inactivity, nor expand to meet the demands of active business." By contrast, he felt that a convertible bank-note currency would "exert a most wholesome influence by contracting and expanding as the seasons of inactivity and demand should vary." [5] He would have been dismayed had he foreseen that his own arguments would be used against the national bank notes forty years later!

Morality and virtue to the contrary notwithstanding, Congress soon put a stop to McCulloch's policy of trying to reduce the volume of greenbacks in circulation. Indeed, there were vociferous demands that the national bank notes should be abolished. Let the government replace them with an equal amount of added legal tenders and save the interest costs on all those bonds. According to Representative Fred Pike of Maine, "there is not a man in this country . . . that prefers the bank note to the 'greenback.' All of them . . . are content with the money to which they have become accustomed and which costs the Government nothing but the expense of making." [6]

Those who advocated restoring the currency to convertibility into gold at par tended to be critics of the greenbacks and defenders of the national bank notes. Support for the greenbacks, on the other hand, generally came from those who opposed currency contraction, or even favored a further increase in the money supply. The balance among these forces was such that contraction was halted, and return to full convertibility was postponed until 1879.

What McCulloch could not accomplish, Salmon Chase almost did. After his presidential intriguing became intolerable, Chase was forced out of the Cabinet in 1864, but Lincoln charitably appointed him Chief Justice of the Supreme Court. There Chase found himself in the unusual position of passing on the constitutionality of the major monetary legislation of the war. When the Veazie Bank of Bangor had the temerity to challenge the punitive tax on bank notes, he upheld its propriety with ringing tones. A year later, however, when the legal-tender issues were contested, he delivered the majority opinion of a closely divided court that the legal-tender provision was unconstitutional if applied to previous contracts, and took the occasion to denounce "the long train of evils which flow from the use of irredeemable paper money." The government's embarrassment at this shaft was short-lived, however; two additional justices shortly took their seats on the high bench and proceeded to reinstate the bearers of Mr. Chase's campaign portrait to their former legal-tender status.

For eight years after Appomattox, the nation's economy grew and prospered. Rapid expansion of railroad mileage furnished the principal stimulus. Then in 1873, Jay Cooke's failure set off a major financial panic, and the country slipped into a state of economic depression which did not really lift until 1879.

The alternation of boom and depression was repeated in subsequent decades. Financial crises broke out in 1884, 1890, and 1893. The last of these led into the most serious industrial depression yet encountered.

To these cyclical variations was added another theme— trouble on the farm. Farm prices were falling, year after year, with very little respite. They fell faster during business depressions, but throughout their trend was strongly downward. By 1886, farm prices were 60 per cent below their peak of 1864, and by 1896 they were 20 per cent below 1886. Wheat, which brought nearly $3.00 a bushel in 1866, fell below $1.00 in 1884 and went for $0.56 in 1894, while cotton dropped from over $0.40 a pound to $0.07 in the same period.

Money and the banking system figured prominently in both the common explanations and the proposed remedies for cyclical depression and secular farm deflation. The depression of the 1870's received its most noticeable opening shock from the banking panic. This unpleasant episode showed up a number of structural defects in the national banking system. The great majority of "country" banks were required to hold reserves equal to 15 per cent of their notes and deposit liabilities, but three-fifths of this reserve could take the form of funds deposited with banks in major cities. These banks could in turn keep part of their reserves with banks in New York. The latter might have said "the buck stops here"—but not quite. For the New York banks were required to maintain only 25 per cent reserves of cash in vault, even against the "reserve" funds they were holding for country banks. These reserve funds were very large, and they were the bread and butter of a number of New York banks who competed vigorously to obtain them by paying interest to the out-of-town banks. Having paid for them, they naturally wanted to earn income on them, and generally regarded call loans to stock brokers as the use that best seemed to combine income with liquidity. Such loans were, after all, repayable on demand, so the banks could collect whenever they needed the money—at least in theory.

The entire structure had an element of make-believe about it. Banks throughout the country were making believe that they held substantial cash reserves, payable on demand. But it could easily happen that two or three banks were counting the *same* cash, and that if they all wanted funds at once, they would soon discover their illusion. Similarly, the New York banks treasured the confidence that call loans were payable on call—a confidence more often kept than broken, but liable to break if too many demands for payment came at once. And the system was all linked together, so that demands for cash starting at one point were transmitted through it.

However, the fictitious quality of bank liquidity was far from the worst feature of the reserve pattern. If the banks were faced with demands for cash, either from the public or from other banks, and if the cash was not in the vaults, the banks were likely to try to get more by calling in loans. When the New York banks called their brokers' loans, stock usually had to be sold to raise the cash, and the market might panic. When banks in general called loans, it meant less spendable funds for business, and that was serious.

In the bad old days before 1863, bank panics arose mainly from demands to convert bank notes into coin. After 1863, this problem never arose again. The public had no qualms about holding national bank notes. The trouble came from depositors, who were likely to get a bit uneasy if trouble seemed to be brewing, and often the trouble started because of the "inelasticity" of Mr. McCulloch's favorite currency. Over the seasons of the year, there were wide variations in the public's desire for currency. The big rise came with "crop-moving season"—usually about the first of September. Farmers wanted to be paid in currency, and a lot more was needed for shipping and processing transactions.

When currency flowed into the banks during the slack period of spring and summer, however, the banks did not let it accumulate in their vaults. Instead, they shipped it off to their city correspondents, to earn interest, and the city banks in turn increased their stock-market loans.

Every fall, when the system tried to reverse the pump, stress and strain were evident. In 1873, the financial system was vulnerable. Many firms had reduced their liquidity unduly to carry large holdings of stocks or commodities, and much credit of dubious quality had been extended by banks and other lenders. When the autumn pinch came, the pressure was too great. The usual tightening of loans found borrowers who could not pay, and who failed. Publicity created a panic atmosphere among depositors, intensifying the demand for cash. This in turn increased the pressure on the banks to curtail loans, which increased the likelihood of further difficulties among borrowers, and so on. In the process, bank loans and the money supply were contracted sharply, and short-term interest rates shot up.

Such was, with minor variations, the typical pattern of the crises of the period between 1863 and 1913. In those after 1880, things were frequently complicated by movements of gold out of the country—this particularly in 1890 and 1893.

The tendency to blame the banks for business depressions has pervaded American history. It was fostered in the period we are considering by widespread adherence to the quantity theory of money, by the disproportionate amount of publicity given to developments in money, credit, and finance, and by its inevitable moral overtones. Economist Richard Bernhart has written that "there are always some who feel that depressions after periods of prosperity are somehow right and just, or that they are good and beneficial. For them, prosperity is sin. In the depression, mistakes are rectified, the bill for the good times is paid, sins are atoned for, the economic purge is taken, and after this a new start can be made." [7]

For those who maintained such a "Sodom-and-Gomorrah" theory of depressions, banking and finance provided good scapegoats. The prevailing remnants of Puritanism taught millions of people to look with horror on credit, profit-seeking, and most of all, speculation. Speculation has a horrid fascination for moralists and intellectuals, who attribute to it a marvelous capacity for doing harm.

Now there was certainly plenty of the spirit of speculation in America's age of enterprise, and the corporation development of the period was marred by practices of dubious morality. But this provides us with no understanding of the mechanism of economic behavior.

Several significant facts need to be incorporated before we can get a clear view of the role of banks in business depressions prior to 1914. First of all, American business fluctuations showed a fairly close correspondence with those of European countries, suggesting some causal connection. European prosperity tended to be transmitted to the United States through stronger demand for American exports and greater willingness to supply the investment funds which were so important to many capital projects, such as railway construction. It is also true, of course, that conditions in the United States affected the European economy, particularly through purchases of European products. But no one has ever suggested that the European economies were purely passive reactors to American conditions; the American economy did not yet set the tone of world business cycles as it later came to do.

Second, the rapidly growing American economy was making heavy investments in railroad, industrial, and housing capital—all types of investment spending subject to wide fluctuations. In general, these fluctuations were not so much brought about by monetary and credit conditions as they were by changes in technology, by variations in current and prospective demand or in the intensity of competition.

The reason the depressions of the 1870's and 1890's were severe was that fixed-capital expenditures fell off so greatly. Financial panics helped set off the downswings, but could do so only because existing investment opportunities had largely been used up. By contrast, in 1907, the country had one of its worst banking panics—so well publicized and annoying that it led to drastic changes through the establishment of the Federal Reserve System—yet the economy suffered only a momentary setback, because economic conditions abroad and profit expectations for fixed-capital investment at home were not substantially adverse.

Besides instability in fixed-capital expenditures, the economy was subject to fluctuations arising from variations in crop output from year to year. With a large proportion of grain, meat, and cotton being exported, variations in commodity output and prices tended to show up in fluctuations in the country's receipts from abroad.

The banking system was simply one unstable element among a considerable number. The banks tended to worsen fluctuations in the economy by reducing loans during periods of economic downswing and by over-expansion of credit during boom periods. But curing the ills of the monetary system would have left strong disturbing forces operating elsewhere in the system. It is worth noting that bank *failures* were not a major factor in the depressions which followed 1873 and 1884; and even though they were more of a problem in the 1890's, they did not at any time between 1865 and 1920 approach the relative magnitudes reached prior to 1865 and after 1920.

Every period of business depression was livened by monetary controversy. During the depression of the 1870's, there was great agitation to increase the supply of greenback currency. From what we know now about the behavior of the money supply at that time, an increase from some source would probably have been beneficial to the economy. In 1874, Congress voted to increase the volume of currency in circulation, but President Grant vetoed the bill on grounds that it would delay a return to currency convertibility. Congress then turned around in the following year and voted to make the currency convertible into gold as of 1879, instructing the Treasury to accumulate a gold reserve in the meantime. Restoration of convertibility went off on schedule. As a sop to the expansionists. Congress removed the $300 million ceiling on the circulation of national bank notes, but this did not prevent the circulation from declining in response to reductions in the national debt and low interest rates on bonds.

By 1879, however, the agitation had changed character. The great decline in the price of silver bullion brought demands from silver producers that the government resume coinage of silver dollars, which it had ceased in 1873 to mint. Moreover, they were able to enlist the aid of many discontented farmers and business men who wanted more money, but who distrusted inconvertible paper. More money would mean more spending, an end to falling prices, a return to prosperity—or so the silverites argued. And their case won much support during the particularly bitter depression years of 1877-1878. In 1878, Congress authorized a limited amount of silver purchases and coinage by the Treasury.

During the relatively more prosperous 1880's, monetary agitation was less common, but when serious depression returned in the 1890's, the free-silver agitation reached its peak. Under the Sherman Silver Act of 1890, Treasury purchases were increased, and the government issued currency for which the holder could obtain either gold or silver at his choice. This did not satisfy the silver advocates, who wanted all limits to coinage removed. Their discontent contributed to the strong showing of the Populist Party in the elections of 1892.

The new legislation alarmed many foreign holders of American securities who sold out and took their funds in gold. The Treasury gold reserve dipped alarmingly, bank reserves were depleted, and credit became stringent. In the emergency, President Grover Cleveland accepted the aid of J. P. Morgan and a group of prominent international bankers, who agreed to supply the Treasury with gold in exchange for bonds and to try to stem the outflow by foreign-exchange operations. The offending silver legislation was repealed; and after a series of adventures, the gold crisis ended in 1895, and the gold standard was preserved. It was a costly victory, however, for the government's policies tended to reduce the quantity of money in the economy at a time of severe industrial depression. And most galling to many people was the sight of the government working with the mighty Morgan and his fellow capitalists, who were not exactly heroes in the hinterlands.

The political showdown came in 1896, when William Jennings Bryan, the "silver-tongued orator," became the Democratic candidate for President primarily on the basis of the free-silver issue. The Republicans in turn defended "sound money" and the gold standard, while denouncing the Democratic proposal as wicked and immoral. Bray Hammond casts a nostalgic reminiscence over the campaign:

There has been none like it since—when I was nine years old and my breast was covered with badges attesting to the gold standard. My father, a country banker in Iowa, on occasion wore a waistcoat of golden yellow to the same purpose; he was a young man of great ardency, and as a member of the McKinley and Hobart glee club he sang derisive songs about greenbacks and the free and unlimited coinage of silver at the ratio of 16 to 1.[8]

Bryan was defeated in a close race, but the long tide of deflation miraculously ended. The great increase in African gold output began to draw the world price level upward. The thirty years of deflation were followed by nearly twenty-five years of what gold-standard advocates regarded as "soundly-based prosperity," but we would call it inflation. At any rate, it made the farmers happy and quieted the silver controversy.

The prosperity of the new century was rudely shattered by another banking panic in 1907. The banking difficulties in the 1890's had been largely obscured by the silver agitation, but now they were out in the open. The public was outraged at the panic itself, which seemed to have no justification. Adding an aggravating note was the prominent role played by J. P. Morgan and other Wall Street leaders in parceling out cash among banks threatened by a run—something the Federal Reserve System would do today.

There was more than Populism to the criticism of the panic, however. Conservative business men were getting fed up with the frequent interruptions to cash payments and loans, and many bankers longed for a better way of doing things. Soon after the panic, Congress established a National Monetary Commission, which conducted an extensive investigation into money and credit in the United States and abroad.

The major problem, as conceived by contemporary authorities, was how to avoid banking panics. Emphasis was placed on the need for an "elastic" currency—a paper money which would increase in volume when the demand for it increased. It should be capable of adapting, for instance, to the seasonal variations in demand for currency which plagued the financial system, and there should be some way of enlarging the currency circulation to meet panic demands for cash.

To put it another way, the authorities were concerned with the liquidity of the banks—their ability to pay cash on demand. Under the national banking system this problem supposedly was dealt with by the required cash reserves, but no one was satisfied with the way they worked. Cash reserves scattered around the country were not very satisfactory; no bank held enough cash in its own vaults to meet a run. What was needed, prevailing opinion agreed, was some sort of central warehouse where all the reserves could be stored, available in large volume for the individual banks suffering heavy demands. There was also dissatisfaction with the use of interbank deposits as reserves. They gave a sense of fictitious liquidity, helped transmit panics from one bank to another, and worst of all, they concentrated reserve funds in New York where they were used for—whisper the word—*speculation*.

Compare the situation with that of a half century previous. In the 1860's, the pressing objective was reform of the bank-note currency. The first goal was to make the currency itself safe and suitable for nationwide circulation. This was accomplished with complete success (if not universal satisfaction) by giving national bank notes a hundred per cent (and a little more) backing in government bonds; even more significant, perhaps, it was made fully known that the faith of the government stood behind the notes.

By 1913, checking deposits had become the predominant form of money in the country, and the problem was to improve the monetary functions of the banks as purveyors of deposits. The stress on elastic *currency* should not divert our attention from the fact that it was convertibility of deposits into currency that was really at issue. Reformers also hoped to improve the monetary functioning of checking deposits by providing facilities for rapid collection of checks at their full value.

Although there was much dispute about the details, most discussions recognized the need for some sort of reserve institution or association to hold cash on behalf of the banks and pay it out when needed. The bankers wanted it to be something like the existing clearing-house associations in many cities, owned and controlled by bankers. Bryan and company wanted a government institution to keep Wall Street under a watchful and unsympathetic eye and to issue government currency (and the more, the better). The result was a peculiar compromise called the Federal Reserve System. Enacted into law in December 1913, the Federal Reserve Act was the most important and revolutionary modification of the country's system of money and banks since the national banking legislation of half a century before.

The law created twelve regional Federal Reserve banks, each of which was expected to be relatively autonomous. Bankers were to be represented on the boards of the Federal Reserve banks, but the entire system was to be supervised and coordinated by a Federal Reserve Board in Washington, whose members were to be appointed by the President. All national banks were required to become member banks of the system. As members they would be obliged to keep a portion of their required reserves on deposit with a Federal Reserve bank. These reserve deposits would furnish a medium through which check clearings could be centrally managed, by bookkeeping additions and subtractions. Each member bank would also be entitled to borrow from its Federal Reserve bank, under conditions to be noted.

But what about all those state banks and loan and trust companies? The Federal Reserve Act, like the National Currency Act of 1863, did not make it obligatory that all banks join the system, but they were cordially invited to come in. A more immediate problem, however, was to make sure of keeping the ones already in, since national charter status was something a bank could easily discard. So the Federal Reserve Act added a number of features designed to improve the competitive status of national banks. They were given authority to make real-estate loans and to do an acceptance business (that is, to act as guarantors or endorsers of certain customers' IOU's). The law provided opportunities for national banks to exercise trust powers. In the next few years, further concessions included a substantial reduction in reserve requirements in 1917, and a series of measures to permit a limited amount of branch banking by national banks.

The Federal Reserve banks were to be mainly bankers' banks. They were not intended to do a loan and deposit business with the general public, as had the First and Second Banks of the United States. Their deposit liabilities were to be chiefly the reserve accounts of the commercial banks. In addition, they would hold Treasury deposits, and perform fiscal agency services to the government which had not been available before; and they would issue Federal Reserve notes, a new kind of paper currency.

The creators of the system expected that the Federal Reserve would issue its notes like the commercial banks of old—that is, it would lend them. And much as the founders of the national banking system had attempted to safeguard national bank notes by linking them to one type of asset, so the Federal Reserve notes were closely linked to one particular type of loan—the promissory notes of private business men, "arising out of actual commercial transactions" and having not more than ninety days to maturity. These IOU's would come first into the commercial banks through normal loan procedures. The member banks could then, if they wished, "rediscount" these notes—in effect, sell them to the Federal Reserve banks at a price slightly discounted to reflect an interest charge. The law required that Federal Reserve notes be backed one hundred per cent by such commercial IOU's (or by loans on farm commodities); in addition, the notes were to have a 40 per cent gold reserve and be convertible into gold on demand.

To the fathers of the Federal Reserve System—Congressman Carter Glass, economist H. Parker Willis, and others —the provision to link Federal Reserve note currency to the volume of commercial loans was the key to achieving an "elastic" currency. When business expanded and more money was needed, the volume of commercial loans by banks would naturally increase. The banks in turn could meet the demand for currency by rediscounting some of their paper with the Federal Reserve. During slack times, currency would return to the banks, and loans would be paid off. Should a panic demand for currency arise, the banks could meet it by selling more commercial paper to the Federal Reserve.

This was certainly well designed to meet two of the undesirable inelasticities of existing currency. It would adapt much better to seasonal variations, and could keep up with secular growth in demand for currency. But elasticity also created certain possibilities that were less desirable. It created a tendency for currency and credit to expand during business booms and to contract during recessions—not a pattern well designed to smooth out fluctuations. And although the chief single purpose of the system was to make sure that currency was available in a panic situation, there was no assurance that banks would have the necessary "eligible paper" to rediscount in a crisis.

The founders of the Federal Reserve System thought of it as a great warehouse arrangement, where the monetary reserves of the country were stored. They did not realize, nor did the officials of the system itself for a decade, that they had really invented an institution with the power to *create* bank reserves as well as currency. When member banks borrowed from the Federal Reserve banks, they did not always take their loans in currency, but often had the proceeds credited to their reserve accounts. This made the cyclical tendency of the commercial-loan arrangement even more dangerous. For member-bank reserves, then as now, were high-powered money, able to support loans and deposits equal to a multiple of the reserve balance.

The agitation to do something about bank panics produced another important development—the establishment by individual states of programs for the insurance of bank deposits. The idea was supported largely by Granger-Populist forces, who succeeded in having it first instituted in Oklahoma in 1907. It spread to a number of other farm-belt states, until by 1918 eight states had such programs. Proposals for a federal program had been heard in Congress as early as 1886, and in his unsuccessful campaign for the presidency in 1908, Bryan had whipped up considerable support for the idea. Deposit insurance was included in the Senate version of the original Federal Reserve Act, but was struck out by the House.

Deposit insurance proved a potent factor in attracting accounts to insured banks in the states where it was tried. When national banks were sternly forbidden to participate, many of them gave up their national charters rather than sustain the loss of deposits. The programs were generally denounced by banking leaders, who feared that insurance would make depositors indifferent to the safety and competence with which individual banks were managed. They also anticipated that the strong and conservative banks would end up footing the bill to pay off depositor claims.

These misgivings proved to be well founded. The state systems, set up during the flush times before 1920, ran into difficulty from the farm troubles of the 1920's. The claims from failed banks soon used up accumulated reserves and assessment authority, and one after another the systems folded up. In general, the state experiments with deposit insurance did not make sufficient provision for controlling entry into banking or for maintaining strict quality standards over bank assets and operations. Established in a period when bank failures were rare, they operated on the theory that small premiums would cover losses and did little or nothing to try to prevent bank failures in the first place.

Would a federal system have done better, if established in 1913? Quite possibly it would, if supported by the credit of the government, to permit payment of claims beyond assets accumulated in a reserve fund. It is doubtful, however, whether a federal program, if initiated in 1913, could have achieved the universality and high standards later attained by the FDIC.

The Federal Reserve banks were still undergoing their initial organizing phase when the economy began to feel the repercussions of war in Europe in 1914. The first reaction was a financial crisis in the United States, but this phase was short-lived. Soon the inflationary backwash of war became increasingly evident. Sales of munitions and foodstuffs began to pick up, financed in part by foreign sales of gold and other assets in the United States, in part by loans from American banks and private investors. Soon the economy was booming, unemployment was at a minimum, and prices moved steadily upward. Between autumn of 1915 and spring of 1917, wholesale commodity prices in New York rose more than 50 per cent—a sizeable inflation for a country nominally at peace with the world.

Expansion of bank credit contributed force to the inflation. Commercial bank loans and securities increased from $17 billion in mid-1914 to $24 billion in mid-1917, a process which increased the money supply by 36 per cent within three years. The Federal Reserve Act, which had substantially reduced reserve requirements for national banks, was partly to blame. Federal Reserve officials, though disturbed at the trend, had no means for curbing credit expansion. They had no authority to raise reserve requirements, and no portfolio of securities to sell.

Entry of the United States into the war in 1917 accelerated the inflationary trend. Federal expenditures, which had averaged less than $1 billion a year, expanded more than ten fold. Despite increased tax rates, nearly three-fourths of expenditures were financed by borrowing. To promote bond sales, the Federal Reserve banks discounted liberally for member banks at low rates of interest. This provided member banks with abundant reserves, which they utilized to buy securities themselves or to extend credit to individual buyers. Commercial banks were able to buy $4 billion of securities for themselves and to extend their loans by $6 billion.

Despite the reduction of federal spending after the end of hostilities in 1918, the inflationary increase of money and credit continued, taking on an increasingly speculative character as business firms built up inventories in hopes of selling at still higher prices. By 1920, the money supply was double what it had been in 1914, and the price level had risen even more than that. Federal Reserve policy was an active engine of inflation, its prime goal being to keep credit easy so that the Treasury could borrow at low rates of interest. This policy was continued through 1919, to assist the Treasury in refunding a large mass of short-term obligations. Thus the unwholesome speculative expansion was allowed to run unchecked. Indeed, Federal Reserve credit expanded by more than a billion dollars in the two years following the Armistice.

Beginning late in 1919, however, Reserve officials began to move their discount rates upward, though not sufficiently to halt the rise in the volume of member-bank borrowing for several months. The bubble burst in mid-1920, and gave way to a sharp downswing. The inventories that had been speculatively accumulated were now dumped on the market, and prices fell precipitously, with particularly devastating effects on farmers. Federal Reserve policy made no hasty efforts to stop the decline. High discount rates were maintained until May 1921, and the volume of member-bank borrowing was allowed to decline, reducing bank reserves in the process. Fortunately, business incentives to invest in fixed capital were not impaired, and the depression ended when businesses started adding to their inventories instead of reducing them.

Much favorable comment was bestowed on the Federal Reserve banks for their aid to government finance during the war. The Reserve System had made it easier to borrow and had greatly improved the efficiency with which government funds were handled. Favorable comment resulted, too, from the fact that there had been no banking panic during the sharp downswing of 1920-1921.

Nevertheless, there is much evidence that the establishment of the Federal Reserve System, and its operations in its first decade, aggravated rather than alleviated the instability of the economy. The Federal Reserve banks greatly facilitated Treasury finance during the war, but in the process made an inflationary financial policy even more inflationary. The maintenance of easy credit conditions after the war worsened the distortions and maladjustments that came with inflation. In particular, the farm sector was permanently harmed when price collapse greatly enlarged the burden of heavy debts incurred to buy high-priced land to produce high-priced products.

Fortunately, the depression was short; moreover, it brought prices to consumers back down substantially from their inflated levels of 1920. As a result, the complaints of the farmers found no substantial echo elsewhere in the economy.

Reserve bank officials were themselves not well satisfied with the record, and during the 1920's, their conception of the system and its operations improved greatly. It became apparent that a passive adaption to the "needs of trade" or to movements of the gold reserve would not automatically produce good policies. Instead, Federal Reserve doctrine accepted the need to offset disturbances by raising discount rates and selling securities during boom periods, and by opposite measures during slumps. Such measures were followed during the minor fluctuations of the 1920's, with apparent success.

At the time, the period of the 1920's seemed one in which the favorable state of current conditions was dimmed only by comparison with the improvements to come. In retrospect, it is apparent that the financial system contained dangerous weaknesses that would be exposed in a crisis. How these developed will be the subject of a subsequent chapter.

By the 1920's, the monetary predominance of bank deposits was far advanced indeed. Coin and currency, which had furnished about 26 per cent of the money supply in 1896, constituted only 14 per cent in 1929. The great increase in country-bank facilities, which we noted in Chapter 5, did much to promote this trend. In 1896, farmers' holdings of coin and currency were twice their demand deposits; whereas by 1929, the proportion was reversed.[9]

The number of checking accounts increased from eleven million in 1909 to more than twenty-three million in 1920.[10] Much of this increase represented an increased number of small accounts. A study of nine country banks in Minnesota in 1930 disclosed that half the accounts had balances of less than $50 each.[11]

During the 1920's, demand deposits averaged more than $20 billion, a level far above any previous period. This reflected the monetary inflation of the war. The volume of check transactions reached record levels, especially as the stock market picked up speed. In 1928 and 1929, bank debits (roughly, check payments) exceeded $1 trillion annually, and at the 1929 peak, every dollar of checking deposits was being spent, on the average, once a week! Such high velocity has never been matched before or since.

In sum, the half century following the Civil War saw the commercial banks become the dominant suppliers of money needed for rising expenditures and a broadening market economy. The national banking legislation lavished care on the safety of the bank-note currency, with considerable success, only to have bank deposits rise to eclipse currency as a medium of payments. Their capacity to expand deposits "by a stroke of the pen" was the source of lending power that enabled the banks to supply the expanding need for credit in the age of enterprise.

Against a background of rapid growth in production, the nation's economy was buffeted by financial panics and economic depressions, as well as a long downswing in prices which bore heavily on the farmers between 1865 and 1896. Out of these arose agitation for fundamental changes in the monetary and banking system which culminated in the Federal Reserve Act of 1913. Its objective was to improve the liquidity of the banks—to enable them to meet demands for currency and to avoid panics, seasonal stringency, or long-run monetary deficiency.

Unlike the national monetary legislation of the 1860's, the Federal Reserve Act and its subsequent amendments did not attempt substantially to curtail the amount or types of credit extended by the banks. True, positive encouragement was extended to commercial lending by making such loans eligible for rediscount, but on the whole, the trend was toward a relaxation in previous restraints on national bank activities. This was done to make Federal Reserve membership attractive, so that the essentially voluntary character of the system would not deprive it of scope to act.

In its first decade, however, the Federal Reserve System probably augmented the instability of the economy. It fed the fires of inflationary credit expansion during and after World War I, then tolerated (if it did not actually encourage) a painful though short-lived postwar depression. During the 1920's, its command of circumstances appeared to improve, but ultimately this appearance proved false.

The narrative will return to the financial problems which

ended the balmy economic climate of the 1920's. But first it is desirable to take note of some important changes in the patterns of consumption, production, and finance—changes associated in one way or another with the rise of the automobile.

CHAPTER

8

THE AUTOMOBILE AGE, 1900-1930

As the coming of the railroad had vastly altered the character of American life in the nineteenth century, so the rise of the automobile brought about or symbolized far-reaching changes in the twentieth. More than any other product, the automobile exemplified the rise of living standards for a large proportion of Americans to a level beyond the requirements of physical subsistence. During the period of almost unbroken full employment between 1896 and 1929, increased productivity doubled real income per person.

Automobile production demonstrated the enormous benefits possible through mass production, based on massive capital formation and technological progress. The policies of the Ford Motor Company showed dramatically that rising productivity could expand job opportunities and raise wages for industrial workers, while at the same time benefiting consumers through a cheaper and better product. Bank credit helped underwrite the capital growth in automobile production and supporting industries which made these developments possible.

The automobile age also gave rise to a new trend in commercial banking itself. Banks became increasingly oriented toward consumer loan and deposit business. This trend, already apparent in the 1920's, was carried much further during the 1930's and set the stage for the emergence of the highly diversified pattern of credit associated with the banking system of today.

In the 1890's, when the railroads dominated the corporate and financial picture, the automobile "industry" consisted of a lot of tiny machine shops where dedicated and occasionally crack-brained mechanics tinkered, experimented, and assembled component elements which were almost entirely made for them by someone else. "Automobiles were being made by almost every large machine shop in New England," declared one contemporary. Total auto production in 1899 was not quite three thousand vehicles, but even this was a creditable showing less than a decade after the Duryea brothers had run their pioneer creation on the roads.

Mechanical improvements by men like Ransom Olds, and vigorous promotions through spectacular races or endurance runs brought a rapid rise in production. By 1910, auto output was nearly 200,000, produced by more than fifty firms. Unlike the modern auto industry, these early firms did not require much capital. "Manufacturing amounted to designing and assembling. An idea for an automobile could be drawn up, and orders for engines, bodies, and all of the other parts placed with the many machine shops and carriage works then in existence. An enthusiastic promoter could secure parts on 30 to 90-day terms, and contract with prospective customers or dealers to take the finished autos for cash. The assembly operation was often done in rented quarters, so that the capital requirements were actually small." [1]

The financial stratagems of the early auto makers were a matter of necessity as well as convenience, for the financial community did not leap at the opportunity to supply funds. Wall Street was diverted by the boom in inter-urban trolley-car lines, which absorbed vastly more capital than the auto industry in the decade before Sarajevo. The chaotic conditions and uneven standards among the producers confirmed the reluctance of investors and lenders. In his notable biography of Henry Ford, Allan Nevins points out that "Capitalists were very wary because so many shoestring enterprises and flamboyant promotions had failed. Some crooks sold stock and disappeared. Some reputable men, to avoid bankruptcy, used desperate expedients. They even loaded freight cars with junk; issued bills of lading, and drew sight drafts on distant retailers, cashing them at the bank; and then, when the consignees complained, loaded another car—if they were able—with the missing machines." [2]

Some bankers were willing to take a chance—particularly in the Detroit area. In later years, one of Ransom Olds' early associates, Roy Chapin, stated that this drew auto producers to that area in the early years of the new century. "There was a great deal of prejudice in other parts of the country on the part of bankers, particularly in the East. They lacked the business sense that was needed. The Detroit bankers had it and were not afraid of our sight drafts." [3]

In 1903, Henry Ford incorporated the Ford Motor Company with a capital of $100,000, most of which represented stock issued in exchange for patents, machinery, or supplies. However, important cash capital came from John S. Gray, the Scottish president of the German-American Bank in Detroit. Indeed, Gray's contribution was so important that he became the first president of the Ford company. Another initial cash investor, Horace Rackham, borrowed the funds for investment from the Michigan Savings Bank. [4] But from the start Ford and James Couzens were the men who ran the show.

The firm's cash capital pulled it through initial production expenses just by a whisker. Once sales commenced, the firm was able to obtain bank discounts on drafts drawn against purchasers. Profits rolled in—the firm cleared $100,000 in its first ten months—and were reinvested in further expansion. This policy was to be a fundamental of Ford finance from then on, to such an extent that minority stockholders ultimately sued to get a share in profits. Soon the firm expanded beyond mere design and assembly and began manufacturing its own components. In 1909, Ford made his momentous decision to concentrate production on a single model, to be a low-cost utility car for mass consumption, rather than a luxury car like most of these being produced. Such standardization soon paved the way for a degree of specialization in production which was to make Detroit world famous.

Ford, one of the great individualists of American history, fought the efforts of other firms to form collusive price-fixing agreements. As efficiency lowered his production costs, he made the Model T cheaper and cheaper—by 1927, it sold for less than $300 new. His great empire was built on retained earnings, and all his life he took pleasure in public disparagement of "the bankers." However, this did not prevent him from relying on $75 million of credit from a group including Chase National Bank and Boston's Old Colony Trust Company in 1919 to buy out minority stock interests in the firm.

The other prominent firms of the early era were more conventionally financed. After the shakeout of the industry during the panic of 1907, stable firms such as Packard found it easier to obtain funds through securities issues, and some auto company bonds began to make their way into bank portfolios. Inevitably, the industry was swept by the fever for consolidation so prevalent elsewhere. The leader was William C. Durant, hitherto one of the leading architects of Buick's success. In 1908, he formed the General Motors Corporation, and rapidly added to Buick such well-known firms as Oldsmobile and Cadillac.

Durant was a visionary promoter who perceived the virtues of diversified product line and periodic model changes, but his financial creation, though profitable, was sloppily put together and desperately short of cash. Cadillac was within hours of shutting down when temporary loans from the First National and Old National Banks of Detroit were obtained. Seeking more permanent assistance, Durant approached J. P. Morgan, but without success. With the aid of the First National Bank of Boston, to which Buick owed $7 million, Durant was able to make arrangements with a syndicate including Lee Higginson, J. and W. Seligman and Company, and the Central Trust Company of New York to float a large bond issue.[5] The bankers received a substantial chunk of stock and set up a voting trust arrangement to control the company. Durant was removed from active management. Though many critics have regarded this step as typical Wall Street arrogance, a recent study concludes that without the bankers' intervention, "General Motors would have died in infancy." [6] The reorganized firm was healthy, profitable, and growing.

Before long, Durant was back on the scene, this time as guiding spirit in the newly formed Chevrolet company which had arisen to contest with Ford for the mass market. Chevrolet drew important financial aid from L. G. Kaufman, president of New York's Chatham Phenix Bank, who served as an officer of Chevrolet for many years. The remarkable success of Chevrolet enabled Durant to regain control of General Motors by exchanging one stock for the other and by open-market purchases on bank credit. In 1915, Durant was in command again. The du Pont chemical company was willing to make a substantial investment in General Motors, an arrangement which became a major bone of contention with antitrust authorities forty years later.

Spurred by continued high profits, Durant continued to

expand, bringing major producers of bodies and parts within the corporation and commencing expensive construction programs. When depression struck in 1920, the firm was again strapped for cash. However, du Pont and the House of Morgan were now prepared to market a stock issue for G.M. In an effort to get them to take it at a good price, Durant had borrowed heavily to buy shares in the falling market; his debt to bankers and brokers was estimated at $35 million. To keep his shares off the market, the Morgan group bought him out and once again he left the firm—this time permanently. Needless to add, the firm survived, and weathered its future crises with equanimity.

It was about this time that other banking interests took over the moribund Maxwell Corporation and were foresighted enough to back Walter Chrysler's new ideas, which formed the basis for the emergence of the third of the modern "big three" after 1925. And General Motors had funds aplenty for its successful campaign to wrest leadership from Ford by quality and design improvements in the late 1920's. Auto company securities were bought by banks themselves and by their trust accounts, or served as the basis for margin loans.

The emergence of the auto industry coincided with the opening up of vast new petroleum resources far from the original Pennsylvania sources. The biggest splash came when James Guffey and his partners brought in the first great gusher at Spindletop, Texas, in 1901—100,000 barrels a day. Guffey enlisted the aid of the Mellons, who quickly put up $3 million to bring the flow under control and construct tanks and pipelines. Soon the Mellons sponsored a $5 million bond issue, half taken by their own bank and another $1.5 million going to Boston's Old Colony Trust. Rebuffed by Standard Oil in a feeler toward consolidation, they turned their company into a fully integrated organization to refine and market its product. We know it today as Gulf Oil. Other leases in the same area started the Texas

Company, and soon important wells were opened in Oklahoma as well. In 1910, a group of independent oilmen, including Harry F. Sinclair, sponsored the formation of the Exchange National Bank, intended from the start to be an oilmen's bank. Twenty years later it held assets of more than $100 million, and its present-day successor, the $300 million National Bank of Tulsa, still calls itself "The Oil Bank of America."

Humble Oil, starting out in 1917, found its expansion requirements consistently straining its resources. The company borrowed $100,000 from various Texas banks; in 1918, it obtained $250,000 from the Liberty National Bank in New York and soon after a similar sum from Guaranty Trust. The company finally broke its financial bottleneck by selling a large stock interest to Standard.

The nation's output of petroleum, less than 100 million barrels a year in 1900, expanded to meet the new demand. By 1910, it passed the 200 million mark, and in 1929 went over one billion. The first impact of the vast new resources of the Southwest was to bring prices down, but they went skyrocketing during the war. At the peak of the boom, in 1920, oil sold at the well for $3 a barrel—a level never matched since. Overproduction and the postwar depression dropped the price nearly 50 per cent in the next year, causing much distress among producers and many failures among boomtown banks in the oil states. From that date, it was consumers, rather than producers, who were the primary beneficiaries of the vigorous explorations and the increased competition in the industry.

Automobile development also spurred the development of the rubber and glass industries. Many tire firms relied heavily on bank loans. Harvey Firestone drew credit from numerous banks in Akron, Massillon, and small neighboring Ohio towns during the early years of the century. The firm was still in the struggling stage when it made a fortunate connection with the First National Bank of Chicago which eased the way for obtaining more funds. By 1920, the firm had $43 million in bank obligations—a high point from which it subsequently retreated.[7] Libbey Glass Company weathered rough times in the 1890's with the aid of a Toledo bank and thus survived to benefit from the automobile boom.[8]

The internal combustion engines which powered the automobile were also well adapted to trucks and tractors, which soon became essential capital assets for millions of America's farmers—often with the aid of bank credit. Motor truck lines came into existence, most of them small. Bank loans, direct or through finance companies, were an important resource permitting many truck drivers to set up in business for themselves. Increased use of autos and trucks soon prodded government into an expanded program of highway construction. The banks were, then as now, an important channel through which bonds were issued for highway construction, and bought a considerable quantity for their own investments.

It is not these aspects of the automobile age with which we are most concerned here, however, but with the gradual transformation of banking itself. In the process, the rise of the automobile was partly cause and partly symbol.

In 1906, a university president named Woodrow Wilson had denounced the automobile for giving "a picture of the arrogance of wealth" and claimed that "nothing has spread socialistic feeling in this country more than the automobile." Ten years later, auto production passed the million-a-year mark, and in 1929, it went over four million. By then the total number of automobiles registered was twenty-three million. From a rich man's toy, the automobile had become the symbol of a broadening middle-class market of mass consumption at a high level. And credit played a vital role in developing this mass market.

At an early stage in the development of the auto industry, the independent dealers became the important channel for distribution. For some years, they sold for cash on delivery

—and sometimes in advance. It was fortunate that they could, since the manufacturers shipped the cars "sight draft with bill of lading"—essentially COD. Once the cream was skimmed off the auto market, however, dealers needed to have a stock of cars on hand for inspection, demonstration, and choice. The important servicing and repair business required inventories of parts and supplies, and it became increasingly evident that extending credit to the buyer would enlarge the market enormously.

Dealers turned to commercial banks for assistance, and for a time were able to handle their needs in this manner. But neither their receivables from buyers nor their inventories quite corresponded with traditional bank standards. Customer credit was uncomfortably long-term by bank standards; besides, the loans were "unproductive." The actual cars in dealer inventories came and went too rapidly for the conventional chattel mortgages.

In 1915, a specialized credit firm styling itself Commercial Credit Company entered the auto finance field. It operated chiefly by purchasing instalment IOU's from dealers, but also advanced funds to finance dealer inventories. The following year it was joined by CIT (Commercial Investment Trust). These two are still the largest firms in the business. CIT early formed an alliance with Studebaker, and gave the other auto companies an illustration of how important credit was in promoting sales. Consequently, in 1919, General Motors sponsored its own finance subsidiary. These sales finance companies were readily able to qualify for bank credit and have always relied on it for a major portion of their total finance.

The finance companies, auto producers, and dealers worked most of the bugs out of auto credit, and were soon making large profits from it. This made the business increasingly attractive to banks. In the 1920's, individual banks experimented with buying instalment paper from dealers, and by the end of the decade some had taken the plunge of lending direct to consumers.

Important as the growth of automobile finance was in directing commercial banks to consumer lending, it was only one element in a broad evolutionary process. In the nineteenth century, commercial banks were strongly oriented towards business, and to a lesser extent, government. Bank loans and investments were directed into these channels, bank deposits were derived from these sources, and other operations, such as underwriting and trust functions, reinforced this orientation. Of course, one must remember that a great many Americans owned and operated unincorporated businesses and farms, and that many of these could obtain bank credit for personal use through their business status.

Consumer credit was not absent from the nineteenth century economy—quite the contrary—but it was extended almost exclusively by sellers of goods. Stores usually offered charge accounts, and some products, such as pianos, were sold on the instalment plan. Bank loans often helped sellers to finance such credit extension, but the scope for consumer borrowing of any duration was quite limited. In a day before automobiles and electrical appliances, most families had little beside furniture that we would consider "consumer durable goods."

There were, however, at least two types of credit which many families sought, in the years before 1900. The first was what we might call "distress loans"—credit to tide a family over some misfortune, such as illness or accident, unemployment, or some other crisis. In those days, very little private or social insurance existed to protect the mass of people against such calamities; nor were their incomes high enough, even in good times, to permit accumulation of very large savings backlogs. Distress credit came first from the store, the doctor, or the landlord—suppliers of services who simply had to wait for payment. After that, cash loans were hard to come by. Pawnshops would lend on pledge of goods; and for families without such resources, loan sharks would usually advance a few dollars—at a crushing cost. There were no important segments of the country's financial system designed to make distress loans, even when the need was clearly temporary and the breadwinner's long-run ability and willingness to repay might be unquestioned.

One of the great obstacles to the creation of "legitimate" small loan firms arose, paradoxically, from state usury laws intended to protect borrowers. Such laws frequently set maximum interest rates on loans as low as 6 to 8 per cent. Now regardless of the ethics of the lender, no one can operate a small-loan business and break even with loans paying only 6 per cent a year. Expenses of credit investigation and loan administration are very high, proportionate to the funds loaned, and risks are substantial. The usury laws had the effect of cutting off small borrowers from banks and other "legitimate" lenders, who could not handle such business without loss. Into the vacuum moved the loan sharks, able to capitalize on need and ignorance to rake off as much as 100 per cent interest per month!

The other use for which families often wanted credit was to buy a house. And this was something which did not necessarily fall outside the scope of commercial bank operations. National banks, however, were long prohibited from making mortgage loans, and many other banks simply did not care to bother with the business. In 1900, commercial banks held only about $150 million of home mortgages, representing about 5 per cent of the total volume outstanding.

However, personal and home-mortgage loans were sometimes extended by one other type of institution, the so-called "immigrant banks" which flourished around the turn of the century. The Commissioner of Immigration in 1910 reported that over 2,600 such institutions were in existence. The typical immigrant "bank" operated in connection with a grocery store or saloon. The proprietor was himself commonly an immigrant and his clients were people from the same nationality and language background—often people who might be illiterate, who could not speak English, and who had little familiarity with American institutions and customs. The "bank," usually unincorporated and often highly informal, would accept deposits of funds for safe-keeping; it handled remittances to the "old country"—a business which reached an impressive volume in the aggregate. These firms were not generally true commercial banks, since they did not furnish checking-account facilities. Sometimes funds deposited were absorbed into the store operations, or redeposited at interest, but in some cases, personal or home-mortgage loans were made, or store credit extended to members of the national group. Subject to little or no formal control, the immigrant banks displayed standards of the most diverse sort. Some were carelessly or fraudulently conducted; others maintained high banking standards. Many failed during periods of financial crisis, and the total number dwindled as state after state subjected private banking to regulation or prohibited it entirely.[9]

There were also full-fledged commercial banks conducted by and appealing to particular nationality groups. The Midwest abounded in institutions with the words "German" or "Scandinavian" in their titles. In port cities, such as New York or San Francisco, there developed, around 1900, numerous small banks catering to families from southern or eastern Europe. From such a humble origin came the bank which has become the largest in the world. As the Bank of Italy, it was founded in 1904 by A. P. Giannini. Today, as the Bank of America, it measures its branches in hundreds, its customers in millions, and its assets in billions. Although it did not neglect business loans, the Bank of Italy set out from the beginning to cultivate home-mortgage borrowers, particularly to aid in the vast reconstruction made necessary by the San Francisco earthquake of 1906.

Bank credit also found its way indirectly to home buyers through enterprising real-estate and construction men like Jesse Jones. After working for his uncle's lumber business in Dallas, Texas, Jones branched into a variety of related enterprises in Houston. As early as 1903, he was building houses and selling them on the basis of amortized mortgages with monthly payments.

Jones's operations utilized bank credit to the utmost, and he was an expert on how to obtain it. Early in his career, he had established a good credit standing with the National Exchange Bank in Dallas in part by borrowing funds, keeping them idle, and repaying them. In 1900, he financed a very profitable acquisition of timber lands with $17,000 borrowed from the bank (a forerunner of the present First National Bank of Dallas). In a few years he broadened his credit facilities by connections with major city banks, including the Hanover Bank in New York. In 1908, he became involved in a project for a new hotel, and from this went on into a notable career as builder and developer in the Houston area. By the mid-1920's, he had built and was managing about thirty commercial buildings.

Jones also became active in Texas banking. He played a prominent role in helping distressed banks to obtain cash during the panic of 1907. During the 1920's, he became president of the National Bank of Commerce, and took the lead in averting bank failures in Houston in 1931. These experiences prepared him to render distinguished public service soon after as head of the Reconstruction Finance Corporation.[10]

Besides these developments in real-estate lending, important innovations were brewing in personal loans as well. During the early years of the century, an accommodating young lawyer named Arthur Morris, of Norfolk, Virginia, found himself increasingly pressed to use his influence and endorsement to help individuals obtain bank credit for personal uses. As Morris later described it:

I began to investigate several of these applicants and found them to have the human need for money. They held steady jobs with fair earning power and were persons of good character. Subsequently, I was able to persuade my bank clients to make some of these loans. Within a period of less than two years, several banks represented by my firm made loans totalling $40,000. I was compelled to guarantee each and every loan. My faith in humanity was well founded, as each and every loan was repaid.[11]

Soon Morris set up separate facilities for his loan business. In 1910, he formed the Fidelity Savings and Trust Company in Norfolk and began to put into operation an ingenious plan for making personal loans. Borrowers were charged a standard 6 per cent per year on the full amount borrowed. However, they were required to make monthly instalment payments into a non-interest-bearing savings account with the lending firm. At maturity, the funds were taken from this account and the loan canceled. In effect, the lender received interest of about 12 per cent on the unpaid balance—a rate which remains standard for instalment credit and which few modern consumer-finance companies can match on personal loans. The device, which made personal loans available about as cheaply as possible, became famous as the Morris Plan, and it rapidly spread throughout the country.

Some of the early Morris Plan banks have developed into full-fledged commercial banks. Notable among these was the Morris Plan Bank of Richmond, which opened on a modest scale in 1922. Soon it developed branch operations in other cities and in 1928 acquired the original Morris unit in Norfolk. In 1932, the bank began to accept demand deposits and in 1942 began making business loans. Today the institution is the Bank of Virginia, one of the largest in the state.[12]

While Attorney Morris was devising a method for getting around the restrictions of usury laws, other forces were at work to modify them. Under the leadership of the Russell Sage Foundation, a campaign was undertaken to allow realistic interest rates on small personal loans, while retaining safeguards for the borrowers. The Foundation promoted the widespread state adoption of a Uniform Small Loan Law. This permitted lenders to charge up to 2 or 3 per cent a month on loans of small amounts, subject to rigorous inspection and licensing of lenders. This legislation opened the way for the growth of consumer-finance companies, and for the entry of banks into the personal-loan business.

Still another influence in the broad trend came from an unusual banking development in the 1920's—the labor banking movement. The first twenty years of the century had brought a considerable development of trade-union strength in such areas of the economy as railroads, building trades, coal mines, and a number of crafts. As individual unions accumulated substantial funds in their treasuries, union leaders began to think of the possibility of using these to establish banks. The motives were varied; they included the desire to provide services to the membership, the prospect of a profitable investment of union funds, the possibility of enhancing the power and prestige of union leaders, and assurance of credit to employers accepting unionization.

The plans matured in 1920 with the establishment of the Brotherhood of Locomotive Engineers Co-operative National Bank in Cleveland. Its capital was raised among the union membership, and it allowed its savings depositors to share to a limited degree in profits. Its lending policies, however, were those of a normal commercial bank. The Engineers found their initial experiment highly successful and soon established or purchased banks in Birmingham, Minneapolis, Spokane and elsewhere. By 1924, at least nine banks had sprung up under their auspices. In addition, the New York State Federation of Labor sponsored the establishment of the Federation Bank in New York in 1923, and in the same year and place, the Amalgamated Clothing

Workers opened the Amalgamated Bank. By 1926, no less than thirty-six banks in the country were identified as labor banks.

At their best, the labor banks performed considerable benefit in extending banking facilities to working-class families who did not formerly use them. This was done not merely by vigorous publicity campaigns, but by paying generous rates on savings, by staying open hours when employees would be able to come in, and by creating a more congenial atmosphere. Some experimented with payroll deductions for savings and with banking by mail. Transmitting funds back to the old country for immigrants was a substantial service for many.

A few of the labor banks made a creditable entry into the small-loan business. The outstanding example is the Amalgamated Bank of New York, which offered loans in sums of $50 and up, secured by co-signatures and repayable in ten monthly instalments, with interest of 6 per cent on the unpaid balance, plus a small fee. During 1928, the bank loaned about $1 million in slightly over 4,000 personal loans.

A survey published in 1929 concluded that perhaps seven or eight labor banks were emphasizing personal loans, while others made them available, but did not do a large volume of business. This study concluded that "Labor banks, and most especially the Amalgamated banks, have made an important contribution in pioneering this new field in city banking. Through their interest in democratic banking and their example, they have been instrumental in arousing old-line bankers to the need of fighting the loan shark in his own territory." [13]

Several of the labor banks provided home-mortgage loans. New York's Amalgamated Bank furnished important financing for construction of a cooperative apartment building for union members.

At worst, some of the labor banks were developed either by remarkably naïve management or were promoters' schemes bearing a resemblance to many of the other get-rich-quick propositions with which the 1920's abounded. Four of the labor banks failed between 1924 and 1928, all badly mismanaged, and two more were pulled down in 1929.

After 1926, the movement as a whole began to wane. The various goals were obviously not consistent with each other. The importance of bank loans to support "fair" employers in collective-bargaining struggles turned out to be slight, although the labor banks did help out in a few cases and their presence may have helped prevent others. The bank system developed by the Locomotive Engineers suffered because it was exploited to promote the power and prestige of certain union leaders and because of a vast number of unsound commitments. Many of the labor banks found that their survival depended on doing a successful commercial business, and severed their labor connections. New York's Federation Bank, which is still successfully operating, followed this course. The depression of the 1930's eliminated most of the remaining labor banks through failure or absorption.

Today the Amalgamated Bank in New York, and its cousin, The Amalgamated Trust and Savings Bank of Chicago, are the only real labor banks left. Both are owned by the clothing workers union and its members—a union which has always been distinguished for its high ideals, honesty, and social consciousness. The banks do a general business, but have consistently offered personal loans at low rates. Both banks make commercial loans, and the New York bank has a substantial volume, much of it with small business firms. It does not lend to firms with which the union has collective-bargaining relationships, but has made numerous loans to garment subcontractors. The New York bank even made a loan to a member of the New York Philharmonic to finance purchase of a Stradivarius violin.[14]

Commercial bank activity in home-mortgage lending expanded more impressively than consumer credit. Mortgage loans were much closer to conventional bank standards and came as a welcome outlet for the funds of many banks in smaller communities where farming was in a slump after 1920. Commercial banks' holdings of home mortgages grew from around $150 million in 1900 to about $2 billion in 1929, a growth which raised their share of the mortgage market from about 6 per cent to more than 10 per cent.

According to estimates by Raymond Goldsmith, bank loans to households, both personal and mortgage, (but excluding loans on securities) were about $300 million in 1900, representing about 6 per cent of bank loan volume. By 1922, they had risen in dollars to about $1.3 billion, but this represented a slightly smaller proportion of bank loans than in 1900. During the remainder of the 1920's, however, loans to households rose more than other bank credit. By 1929, personal and home-mortgage loans had shot up to $3.3 billion and represented more than 9 per cent of bank loans. Symbolic of the change was the establishment in 1928 of a a special instalment-loan department by the National City Bank of New York.

The increased participation of commercial banks in financing individual households was closely related, of course, to the steady rise in real incomes and living standards which had brought into existence a substantial and prosperous middle-class group. By the 1920's the better-paid industrial wage earners had reached a level at which they could become purchasers of homes and automobiles. Home ownership showed a slow but steady rise. From 3.5 million in 1900, the number of owner-occupied homes (other than farms) tripled, reaching 10.5 million in 1930, and the proportion of owner occupancy rose from 37 per cent to 46 per cent. Home loans by banks contributed to this increase.

But here is a remarkable paradox—while rising incomes, steady employment, and the widening of middle-class status helped bring the banks increasingly into lending to households, the depression of the 1930's, which created mass unemployment and reduced job opportunities, accelerated the trend very markedly. The paradox is less surprising when we note that the big rise came after the upturn in the economy starting in 1933. During the recovery period, banks found the demand for business loans very weak, because of existing excess capacity and internal financing. Demand for consumer credit, however, revived sharply, and lender experience with consumer loans had been fairly good during the crisis years—consumers were, by and large, conscientious in meeting their obligations.

Another influential factor was the establishment of the government's program for insuring home loans through the Federal Housing Administration (FHA). Banks were attracted by the low-risk, long-term home mortgages offered. Furthermore, FHA protection was available for shorter-term home-improvement loans, which more closely resembled consumer instalment loans. The high interest rates available on home-improvement loans induced many banks to set up full-fledged instalment loan departments which then entered automobile and other consumer financing as well.

The figures tell the remarkable story of the transition. In 1939, the total dollar volume of commercial bank loans outstanding was less than half what it had been in 1929, falling from $36 billion to $16 billion. Yet the dollar volume of consumer and home-mortgage loans was higher in 1939 than ten years previous! Quality improvements and price reductions in automobiles and electric appliances such as refrigerators made these attractive enough so that many families were willing to incur debt to buy them. The proportion of bank loans going to households rose from 9 per cent in 1929 to over 20 per cent in 1939. From that time to the present, the banks have maintained a major interest in this area, helping to maintain a highly competitive market for consumer loans.

One of the most remarkable bank success stories of recent

times concerns a bank which hitched its wagon wholeheart-
edly to the new trend. The Franklin Square (Long Island)
National Bank started up in the 1920's, and mustered less
than $1 million in assets when young Arthur Roth joined it
in 1934. He immediately set to work to sell banking services; in the process, he put his bank in the limelight, aided
the recovery of the economy, and stimulated the local community to improve itself.

Roth's bank secured one of the first FHA charters and
worked aggressively to spur home building, to the extent of
acquiring promising tracts on its own initiative. The bank
also gave heavy promotion to personal loans, developing an
original plan for financing medical bills on instalments. By
1941, its loans had expanded to four times their 1934 volume, largely by lending to households. It held $1 million
of consumer loans and $2 million of home mortgages, com-
pared with only $549,000 of business loans in 1941.

The bank's aggressive and imaginative policies continued
without letup during and after the war. Most striking was
the way Arthur Roth got his community off on a head start
toward reconversion. As *Readers' Digest* described it:

Roth obtained a photographic panorama of the somewhat dismal stores along the main street. Then he had an architect sketch
the street with every store front done over in a uniform early
American motif. Calling the businessmen together, he showed
them the picture of today, pointing out a lack of paint here, a
torn awning there, narrow shop windows, cramped doors. Sud-
denly, he flashed the panorama of tomorrow, each store modern-
ized and in harmony—white trim, neat, with its name lettered on
the front.

"To make our town look like this," Roth told the merchants,
"will cost $500 for each 15 feet frontage. The bank will lend the
money on a five-year basis. Who will sign up?"

Everybody signed up. So far, so good. But Roth sees things
through. A committee went to the big manufacturers. A glass

company agreed to handle the job as a unit, at low rates. Companies making building materials and store fixtures sent experts to a series of discussions.[15]

Soon the bank itself remodeled, providing in its new quarters display space for much of the merchandise it was prepared to finance—including automobiles and an airplane! Certainly this was carrying department-store banking to its logical extreme.

The combination of Roth's formula and the booming economic development of central Long Island enabled the bank to expand at a remarkable rate after 1945. Changing its name to the Franklin National Bank, it soon developed branches throughout the Island. At the end of 1960, its total assets were $800 million, making it one of the forty largest banks in the country.

But the full account of the momentous changes which followed 1929 demands a chapter of its own. Let us here cast some retrospect over the role of the banks in the economy prior to 1929—a period in which, despite increasing concern for consumption, bank financing was still overwhelmingly directed toward productive capital.

Between 1900 and 1929, the amount of productive capital goods—buildings, equipment, and inventories—in use by American business firms (excluding farms) increased from about $51 billion to about $134 billion, valued in 1929 prices. To make this increase required net capital outlays of about $90 billion (the discrepancy resulting from price level changes). In addition, business firms added substantial amounts to their holdings of cash and other financial assets.

To finance this large increase in assets, businesses obtained about $100 billion through loans and through issues of securities. Through loans to business and through acquisition of business stocks, bonds, and mortgages, commercial banks supplied about $20 billion. Bank loans for purchasing or carrying securities (mostly corporate) added another $7 billion. Combined, these figures indicate that the banks contributed about one-fourth of business financing. By comparison, all other financial institutions combined provided about $16 billion (one-sixth) of business funds.

In addition, the commercial banks continued to play an important role in marketing securities issues. Furthermore, they administered a large flow of personal savings as custodians of personal trust funds, which grew in importance after 1900. By 1929, bank-administered trust funds held about $30 billion of assets.[16]

By 1929, the commercial banks held about one-fifth of the net indebtedness of the non-financial sectors of the economy. Their share was largest for non-corporate business and farms (about 30 per cent), smallest for households (13 per cent).

Despite the rise in bank loans to households, the major business of banks through 1929 was business, which accounted for about 70 per cent of bank credit in 1929. The scope of bank lending to business continued to be widely varied. A survey of national bank loans in 1920 indicated that about one-fourth of the dollar volume went to firms engaged in distribution of goods—wholesalers, retailers, etc. The survey showed 21 per cent going to manufacturers, and 15 per cent to farmers, but less than 2 per cent to railroads and utilities.[17] (These figures do not include bank credit extended through bond purchases.)

Bank credit played an important role in one new industry of this era which expressed its spirit very well—the movies. Motion picture production involves a production cycle of a few months during which most costs—chiefly labor—are incurred. Once the golden financial prospects of the industry developed, bank loans were widely used to cover much of the production cost.

The Bank of America made its first movie loan as early as 1909, to Sol Lesser, but an advance of $50,000 to Famous Players-Lasky in 1918 was its first big commitment. In New

York, the Giannini-affiliated East River National Bank also made loans to industry pioneers who had not yet fled to the West. It made a real splash in 1921 with a loan of $250,000 to First National Distributors. The film was *The Kid*, with Charlie Chaplin, which made so much money the loan was repaid in six weeks. By 1936, Bank of America was lending over $30 million on films. It financed some five hundred features in the following fifteen years, one of the more notable being Walt Disney's *Snow White*.[18] Bank loans helped build the movie theaters, too. And in the spirit of the times, it is only honest to record that more than one bank helped finance the production and distribution of bootleg whiskey.

Capital formation and technological progress created new employment opportunities for the rising population and labor force. Consequently, the number of people with non-farm jobs increased from eighteen million in 1900 to thirty-seven million in 1929. Real income per capita rose from about $367 in 1897 to about $670 in 1929. Wage rates in manufacturing, however, moved up by a smaller proportion (after adjustment for price changes). It was not until after the severe limitations on immigration imposed during the 1920's that the way was opened for wages to rise as rapidly as salaries, profits, and professional incomes. Factory workers did gain substantially through the reduction of the work week from roughly sixty hours in the 1890's to about fifty hours in the 1920's—the equivalent of one full day of added free time.

Higher incomes, more leisure, more jobs, new and improved products—these were the ultimate payoff which the American public derived from credit expansion and capital formation in the age of the automobile.

From 1900 to 1929, the total volume of bank credit expanded from $7 billion to $49 billion. The expansion was made by creating new demand deposits, which rose by $21 billion. A large portion of newly created deposits, however, came to roost in the banks' savings accounts, which grew phenomenally from about $1 billion in 1900 to $19 billion in 1929. This was a period when commercial banks greatly increased their eagerness for savings business, stimulated by the favorable reserve requirements for savings deposits adopted in Federal Reserve legislation. The number of savings accounts reported by commercial banks rose from eight million in 1909 to forty million in 1929.[19]

Thus commercial bank deposit services, as well as loans, became increasingly oriented towards consumer households. Other financial institutions expanded to meet these opportunities as well. Mutual savings banks, though confined mainly to the Northeast and largely static in numbers, competed vigorously for savings and extended a substantial volume of home-mortgage loans. Savings and loan associations, which were numerous but usually very small prior to 1900, offered similar savings and home-mortgage services all over the country, and experienced rapid growth of assets in the years down to 1929.

As for consumer credit, the sales-finance companies (noted previously on page 175) did not usually lend directly to consumers, but the adoption of small-loan legislation favored the growth of consumer-finance companies which did.

Taken together, these developments reflect the fact that an increasing proportion of home-mortgage lending and consumer credit was being handled through financial institutions, with a decreasing proportion handled by non-financial business firms and personal lenders. This was probably a healthy development. It left non-financial firms with greater freedom to concentrate on their primary tasks and diminished the scope for loan sharks to operate.

Personal savings as well as credit became increasingly institutionalized. This development resulted from the increased number of families whose incomes were large enough to provide a margin for saving, but not large enough to warrant acquisition of risky assets such as securities or real estate. Commercial banks, thrift institutions, and life insurance companies became the media with which the savings of the great majority of the population were kept.

The depression of the 1930's provided a temporary setback to the expanded use of bank deposit facilities by individuals. But after the financial reforms of that decade —particularly the insurance of bank deposits—the trend resumed and has continued to the present.

The great depression casts a long shadow on the topics we have treated in this chapter. It is the great watershed in American financial history, the dividing line between the past and the present. Because the banking system played an important role in the onset of depression, and because the depression brought far-reaching changes to the banking system, the next chapter is devoted largely to an examination of its causes and consequences.

TWENTY YEARS OF TURBULENCE,

1925-1945

THE PLEASANT STATE OF THE ECONOMY in the 1920's created for the first time the vision of a state of affairs never before achieved in any part of the world—a condition where there would be well-paying jobs for all, where poverty would be abolished, where high productivity and enterprise would create a level of comfort and well-being which would extend throughout the mass of the population.

Instead, the good times of the twenties gave way to twenty years of unprecedented economic disturbance. The economy plunged into the deepest and longest depression in its history. The banking system suffered its darkest hour. Within the space of four years one-third of the country's banks failed, and many of the others barely survived. The depression led to far-reaching changes in the structure of the banking system, and in the policies of the government. Then, out of a decade of mass unemployment and social tension arose the terrible spectacle of world war, which spun the United States dizzily into a still different set of problems.

Adherents of the Sodom-and-Gomorrah theory of economics have never found any difficulty in explaining depressions—they are the punishment for the wickedness and sin which abound in prosperous times. Certainly there was no shortage of sin in the prosperous twenties. This was the age of prohibition, the bootlegger, and the speakeasy; an age of giantism, ballyhoo, and quackery in infinite variety. It produced the feverish land boom and bust in Florida, and pushed the skyline of Manhattan up into the clouds. The age spawned the professional public-relations man, and harnessed his talents to dozens of schemes to make man healthy, wealthy, and wise—especially wealthy. Company promotions abounded, some based on glamorous new technical developments, such as radio, others on great mergers and consolidations, such as the public-utility holding company empire of Samuel Insull.

The trend toward putting together large diversified organizations was apparent in banking as well. In 1900, only half a dozen banks had more than $50 million of loans and securities; by 1920, more than seventy had passed that mark, and by 1930, the number was more than one hundred. In 1900, New York's National City Bank was the nation's largest with slightly over $150 million of assets. In 1920, it was still the largest, with assets over $700 million. By 1930, National City, Chase National, and Guaranty Trust had all broken the billion dollar mark, and the Bank of America and Chicago's Continental National were close to it. The giant banks extended their operations in many directions. They formed securities affiliates to hold or deal in stocks and bonds, and real-estate affiliates to own and manage office buildings and other properties. Foreign branches and subsidiaries developed. Giant mergers contributed to the expansion of the giant banks; National City absorbed the historic Farmers Loan and Trust Co.; and the National

Bank of Commerce was merged into Guaranty Trust in 1929. In 1926, Chase National absorbed the Mechanics and Metals National Bank, which was itself the successor to such historic banks as the Mechanics Bank (1810), the Leather Manufacturers' Bank, and Jay Cooke's Fourth National.

With growth came the increased participation of the commercial banks in "high finance." Underwriting of new securities issues, which had been largely left to private bankers before 1900, became increasingly popular among the large commercial banks. Banks became owners of stocks and bonds to an increasing degree, and also stepped up the volume of loans to enable private borrowers to purchase or carry securities.

The productive economy of the country appeared to be in a remarkably healthy state in the 1920's. Once recovery was achieved from the sharp but brief postwar depression, total output maintained high and rising levels. Gross national production rose from $75 billion in 1922 to $104 billion in 1929. Unemployment was small, yet there was no unhealthy inflationary pressure, and prices remained stable. There was nothing phony about the production or about the vast productive plant that made it possible. Here was tangible support for the theory that the United States had achieved a "new era" of stable prosperity—even if one did not share Professor Irving Fisher's conviction that it all rested on the higher productivity of the workers caused by Prohibition! Cyclical interruptions of expansion in 1924 and 1927 had been almost imperceptible; if anything went wrong, there was always the Federal Reserve to help keep the engine of prosperity on the right track.

To be sure, the farm sector was not sharing in the general good fortune. Although farm prices revived somewhat from the postwar collapse, they never came close to regaining their peak levels of 1919-1920, and debts incurred at that time remained to plague both debtor and creditor. Rural banks were closing by the hundreds, and already some ingenious plow salesmen had invented the concept of "parity" as a rallying cry for political action.

The state of the international economy also left something to be desired. World War I had wrecked the old international gold standard, and at the war's end many of the European countries had been caught up in runaway inflation. Ultimately, these price spirals were brought under control—Germany's in 1924, France's in 1926—but the underlying financial structure of the new "gold-exchange" standard was flimsy. The gold reserves of individual countries were pitifully small relative to the amounts of currency and deposits nominally convertible into gold. Financiers with sharp eyes and sharp pencils watched tirelessly for signs of weakness, ready to convert their own funds into gold before it became impossible to do so. For the moment, however, the danger of panic was held down by the abundant flow of American loans into Europe. Should these slow down, the high level of American tariffs might make it difficult for Europe to obtain enough funds to keep up payments on reparations, war debts, and other noble devices by which the statesmen of the age achieved immortality.

All the while, the greatest manifestation of the spirit of the twenties was building up in Wall Street—the Big Bull Market. Stock prices rose in the early 1920's for the best of reasons—high profits and dividends. But about 1924, the up-trend developed a momentum of its own. More and more people were buying, not for investment income, but for the capital gains that would result when the price of the stock went higher. It is one of the peculiarities of the seeker of capital gains—the speculator—that he can easily become totally indifferent to the condition of the company whose stock he buys. What is important is what other people think the stock is going to do, and so stock prices can become increasingly divorced from the realities of sales, profits, dividends.

A speculative market thrives on credit. When the price of

a stock is expected to rise by 10, 20, 30 per cent in a few months, the best way to get rich is to borrow all the money one can get and buy it. Interest costs within the normal ranges become insignificant. Credit carried the Big Bull Market to its heights: credit which made it possible for speculators to buy on "margins" as thin as 10 or 20 per cent of the price of the stock. Margin buying in a rising market tends to generate a self-aggravating spiral. As prices rise, one can borrow more on one's existing holdings, and if everyone does this to make more purchases, stock prices rise more.

Beginning late in 1923, stock prices began to move upward at a relatively steady and slightly accelerating rate of increase. They rose about 10 per cent in 1924, 20 per cent in 1925. The pace slackened in 1926, then speeded up rapidly. By the middle of 1928, prices averaged double what they had been at the start of 1925, and they rose more than 50 per cent above mid-1928 by the time the peak was reached in 1929. It is not much wonder that a lot of people decided to try their luck.

The stock boom had a lot of repercussions. For one thing, it made it easy to sell stock. This activity attracted all kinds of people, honest, competent, and otherwise, into the securities business. It encouraged the formation of investment companies, which sold their own stock to the public and used the funds to buy stock of productive enterprises. It spawned great holding companies and other mergers and consolidations through which stock issues could be multiplied, and it encouraged ordinary business firms to issue more stock and expand their productive capacity. The boom also stimulated the use of convertible bonds, which could be exchanged for stock at some set price at the option of the bondholder.

Commercial bank credit was drawn upon heavily to finance stock buying. Bank loans to brokers (which enabled the brokers to extend credit to margin buyers) reached the $1 billion mark in 1922. By 1925, they were running around

$2 billion and at the end of 1927 reached $2.5 billion. Bank loans to brokers then leveled off, but their loans to other borrowers on securities collateral rose to exceed $8 billion by 1929. Such loans had always been regarded as highly safe and liquid, and the interest rates offered by eager borrowers were very tempting—10 per cent and more during the feverish days of 1928 and 1929. These rates attracted loan funds from other lenders too; business firms poured their idle cash balances into stock market loans, some even going so far as to issue stock and lend out the proceeds.

By 1928, some voices of alarm were raised. The members of the Federal Reserve Board were concerned; after all, one of the purposes for establishing the system was to prevent the undue use of bank credit for speculation. But the authorities faced a dilemma. There was no excess of credit and money for the economy as a whole—quite the contrary. If anything, stock-market lending was tending to draw credit away from some other outlets; interest rates were creeping up for business and home-mortgage loans, and the volume of home construction was declining. If the Board were to put on the brakes by tightening credit, this might deprive the productive economy of needed funds and start a depression. And no feasible method was at hand to stop the growth of stock-market credit without such undesirable repercussions. What the authorities needed, and did not have, was direct control of margin lending as such.

Divided and indecisive, the leaders of the Federal Reserve System had no real policy. Mild increases in discount rates were put into effect, but the volume of Federal Reserve credit actually expanded substantially in 1928. This was the natural result of the rediscount system, under which the volume of commercial paper eligible for rediscount always expanded during boom years, (as did the eagerness of banks to rediscount it rather than hold it). Reserve banks did sell government securities, but not enough to offset the increased discount volume.

More troubles were brewing in the banking system, largely in areas beyond the ken of the Federal Reserve. Many rural banks were faced with deterioration of their assets. And commercial banks as a group were rendered increasingly vulnerable to shock by the failure of their capital accounts to keep pace with the rapid growth of assets and deposit liabilities. In 1910, commercial bank capital accounts covered about 19 per cent of assets, while in 1929 they were only 14 per cent. This reduced the amount of asset deterioration the banks could absorb without becoming insolvent.

At the same time, the banks were increasing their holdings of assets which were themselves vulnerable. The heavy loans on securities collateral were of this character. So were many real-estate loans, as the Florida banks had already found out to their sorrow. But some of the worst troubles arose in an unexpected quarter—in the banks' holdings of bonds.

Although the limelight was on stocks, the period of the twenties also gave rise to a substantial boom in bond issues. State and local government issues came on the market in large volume, many of them for improvements related to the coming of the automobile. Suburban developments, made accessible to the cities by auto, were promoted extensively; these involved streets, water and sewage facilities, schools. Between 1913 and 1927, state and local government debt increased from $4 billion to $14 billion. Business firms made bond issues; these included holding-company bonds. Another major source came from abroad—foreign governments and business firms were eager for loans and were prepared to pay high rates for them.

Commercial banks furnished an important market for these issues; in the decade ending 1929, the banks increased their holdings of corporate and foreign bonds by $3 billion and state and local government issues by $1 billion. In the process they financed many worthy capital developments, public and private. They also acquired assets of very uneven quality, including convertible bonds, holding-company bonds, bonds of real-estate developments. Many banks found themselves caught between a slack demand for conventional loans to business and agriculture, on one hand, and intense pressure on earnings arising from high rates of interest paid in a competitive struggle to obtain deposits.

Thus both the stock market and the commercial banks were vulnerable to shock—and the shocks started coming in the latter part of 1929. After a feverish climb, the stock market broke, the climax coming in October. Amid unprecedented panic, stock prices lost one-third of their peak values in the space of two months. The crash, with its strong moral implications and its tragic significance for many individuals, has inevitably become one of the dramatic landmarks of American history. There are very few historical treatments of the crash that do not treat it as the cause of the great depression into which the economy sank as inexorably, one might think, as the Titanic once it had been pierced by the iceberg.

This attitude is unduly fatalistic. It implies that nothing could have been done to halt or reverse the economic decline, whereas in fact the authorities missed numerous opportunities for corrective action.

To treat the stock-market crash as an incurable blight is also analytically unsound. Why should it affect the productive part of the economy? Why need production, employment, and consumption decline? A drop in stock prices might make it hard for firms to raise capital funds. There is no evidence, however, that this happened in the months following the panic. Corporations managed to float $1.5 billion of stock issues in 1930, a total below the 1929 peak but far from negligible. Corporate bond issues in 1930 were much higher than in 1929. Conceivably a drop in stock prices might reduce consumer spending by unsuccessful speculators—but the statistics on aggregate consumer expenditure provide no support for the belief that this happened on any substantial scale.

Two bits of evidence persist in undermining the conviction that the stock-market panic was to blame for it all. The first is the fact that the productive economy had turned downward *before* the market crash: A gentle recessionary movement in production and demand began in mid-summer of 1929. The second is the fact that stock prices reversed their drop at the end of 1929, and proceeded to stage a vigorous recovery for several months. By May 1930, they had recouped almost half of the ground previously lost. When they turned down again, their decline was a symptom of trouble elsewhere—of declining profits and dividends—and not an autonomous force in its own right.

Indeed, the decline in the productive economy can be explained largely in terms of its own inner logic. Reasons why a downturn should have commenced are not hard to find; the most important one is that accumulation of capital goods had been carried in a number of sectors to the point where capacity was well in advance of production and demand. In a growing economy, excess capacity is often a blessing. Today's excess capacity provides the growing room into which tomorrow's expansion of production can take place. If capacity becomes unduly large relative to present and prospective demand, however, the incentive for business firms to make further expenditures for capital goods becomes weakened, and if investment expenditures slacken off, this transmits weakness throughout the system in a manner which can be self-aggravating—cuts in business spending reduce consumers' incomes, their spending falls, etc. If demand begins to fall off, then of course excess capacity appears in many areas—but because there is too little demand, not because there is too much capital.

Professor Robert A. Gordon has presented impressive evidence that residential housing construction in the 1920's attained levels that could not be sustained in the face of existing rates of population growth and family formation.[1] The behavior of housing expenditures indicates that something was wrong, for they began to decline around 1926, although the rest of the economy continued to expand. It is also likely that the demand for automobiles, which had provided a strong expansionary force, was losing strength as the market became relatively saturated.

The mild downturn in business in mid-1929 probably started out as an inventory readjustment comparable to the mild ripples of 1924 and 1927. Once under way, however, it tripped a number of booby traps which speeded its downward pace. The international situation deteriorated rapidly. The flow of American payments to foreign countries fell sharply as loans were curtailed and import purchases reduced. Foreign countries found their receipts from us drastically cut. Their currencies weakened on the foreign-exchange market, and gold withdrawals began to take place. These forces pulled them into the vortex of panic and deflation.

At home, the initial decline in expenditures for business products made existing productive facilities seem more nearly adequate or redundant. Thus business firms reduced their capital outlays still further. Here the stock-market crash may have had some influence. When the economy had faltered in 1924 and 1927, there was no rush by business to cut spending for plant and equipment, for business men were confident that demand would recover and expand. After the market crashed, this implicit faith in expanding sales was weakened, and as business spending fell, it dragged down consumer incomes and expenditures as well.

To this process was added the deterioration of the financial system. The number of bank failures jumped sharply; in 1930, more than thirteen hundred banks suspended. The rapid weakening of farm prices and incomes which accompanied the economic slump was a contributing factor. So was the

deterioration in bond portfolios. A study of the bond holdings of a sample of country banks revealed a decline in
value of 37 per cent from 1928 to 1932. The authors concluded that "the decline in bond prices . . . pursued the
banks like a Mephistopheles. It so impaired their assets that
suspension of payment became inevitable with hundreds of
banks, and the subsequent liquidation of the bond portfolios
of the suspended banks proved a new force that brought
about renewed declines in bond prices." [2]

Deposits in banks which suspended in 1930 totaled $800
million, and although most of these were ultimately recovered by depositors, they were temporarily deprived of the
funds. Depositors in other banks became increasingly uneasy and began to withdraw currency for safety. Many of
the suspended banks had been teetering on the brink of
trouble for years; now with the quality of their assets declining, bank examiners became increasingly hard-boiled.
This was understandable, but also unfortunate. Suspending
banks often meant dumping their securities on the already
weak markets; it meant putting pressure on borrowers to
repay when they desperately needed more credit, not less,
in order to keep going. And it spread distrust of banks
among depositors.

In 1931, the atmosphere of financial panic became in-
tensified. The flimsy structure of European international finance cracked, as a series of banking and foreign-exchange
panics drove one country after another off the gold standard. More than two thousand American banks were forced
to suspend, tying up $1.7 billion in deposits. The solvent
banks, increasingly pressed by depositors, tightened their
lending standards. Unable to borrow, business firms were
forced to liquidate their inventories. The unhappy sequence
of lower incomes and lower demand repeated itself, and the
flow of total expenditures marched steadily down, from $104
billion in 1929 to $76 billion in 1931 to a scant $56 billion in
1933. Business firms cut back on production and laid off

workers, until one worker out of four was out of a job. Bank loans were drastically reduced, and in the process the quantity of money declined from $27 billion in 1929 to $20 billion in 1933.

What was the government doing all this time? Where was the Federal Reserve, which had been created to prevent precisely this sort of crisis? Reserve officials did move to ease credit once the stock-market crash was an accomplished fact. They cut discount rates sharply, and bought government securities on the open market, but the pernicious character of the rediscount system was painfully apparent. As business declined, so did bank holdings of "eligible paper" to rediscount, and the volume of Reserve bank rediscounts fell steadily. Furthermore, the Reserve banks had to have eligible paper to back up Federal Reserve notes; lacking the eligible paper, they were reluctant to undertake measures which would have put more currency into the system. Finally, the Reserve officials were torn by a conflict of objectives. They wanted lower interest rates to slow the economic decline; but when the international financial crisis developed in 1931, higher interest rates seemed necessary to help prevent undue withdrawals of gold from the country.

Federal Reserve inadequacy is best measured by what happened to the bond market. During the height of the pressure in 1931 and 1932, prices of United States Treasury securities fell as much as 10 per cent, as banks and other investors scrambled for cash. This weakness was transmitted to other high-grade bonds as well, while the lower grades were tumbling much more in response to defaults and bankruptcies. The very least the Federal Reserve could have done would have been to buy enough United States government securities to keep their prices from falling, and preferably, enough to raise them somewhat. This would have served two purposes: It would have protected the solvency of banks which were forced to sell bonds, and it would have pumped additional liquidity into the economy as a whole, permitting the banks to meet demands for cash more easily without putting so much pressure on borrowers.

In 1932, Congress liberated the Federal Reserve from some of the perverse restraints on lending to member banks and issuing currency. At the same time, Congress created the Reconstruction Finance Corporation, designed to lend government funds to distressed banks and other business firms. But the RFC legislation contained a barbed provision designed to please those who thought it more important to punish the banks than to revive the economy—a provision requiring disclosure of the names of banks receiving RFC funds. This became a depositor's guide to weak banks, and for some institutions an RFC loan led directly to a run and suspension.

For this and other reasons, the tempo of the banking panic increased during 1932. As currency panic spread from one community to another, governors of individual states imposed "bank holidays," closing their banks in order to protect them and particularly their borrowers. The process culminated in March 1933, when virtually the first act of President Roosevelt after his inauguration was to close all the banks in the nation. Most of them were permitted to reopen in a few days, with an official stamp of approval on their soundness, and with assurance that they had enough currency to meet demands. The panic was over. Currency flowed back into the banks. But what dreadful damage had been done! Some nine thousand banks had been forced to close their doors, involving deposits of nearly $7 billion. Bank loans outstanding had been curtailed from $36 billion in 1929 to a mere $16 billion in 1933. Credit had dried up and money became desperately scarce at the very moment when easier credit and more money were most urgently needed.

The debacle arose because of inherent weaknesses in the economy—over-building, over-speculation on credit, undue vulnerability by the banks. These weaknesses were shown up in part because of the inability or unwillingness of Federal

Reserve authorities to undertake a vigorous policy of credit expansion. In addition, the deterioration of the productive economy was aggravated by inappropriate government policies, particularly a tariff increase in 1930 and an enormous increase in tax rates in 1932.

Once the financial crisis ended in 1933, the bottom of the depression was past, but the process of recovery was a slow and unsatisfactory one. Because consumer spending was weak, business firms had little incentive to add to their capital. Because business capital expenditures did not rise vigorously, the flow of incomes to consumers likewise failed to make a strong comeback. The only effective way of breaking this vicious circle could come through government finance, which could raise the flow of consumer income and spending by tax reductions and expenditure increases. If done on an appropriately large scale, however, such actions would entail large government deficits, a consequence greatly deplored by both Presidents Hoover and Roosevelt. The New Deal program did increase federal expenditures substantially, including such urgently needed measures as relief for the unemployed, but tax rates were greatly increased, thus holding down the rise of consumer incomes and expenditures.

The overly zealous tax program reflected a widespread failure, both in government and out, to interpret the depression as a problem of deficient total expenditure for goods and services. Instead, Mr. Roosevelt and his advisers treated it primarily as a problem of unduly low prices, an emphasis which confused symptoms with cause.

New Deal measures sought to raise prices directly by reducing the gold content of the dollar and abolishing use of gold coins as domestic money, by curtailing output of farm products, and by encouraging the formation of collusive NRA codes of "fair competition" under which competition was to be reduced or eliminated among producers. A similar philosophy underlay the measures to encourage the formation of labor unions and to forbid payment of wage rates below a certain minimum. These measures tended more to reduce the supply of goods and services than to remedy the inadequacy of expenditure.

Despite the misguided character of much of the New Deal program, increased federal expenditures did help push the economy in the right direction. More important, perhaps, President Roosevelt was able to convince the great majority of the people that the government was doing what it could. At a time when extremist political solutions were being adopted in many other countries, political parties advocating Communist or Fascist ideas made no headway in the United States.

The New Deal era also produced an extensive and fundamental reconstruction of the financial system. The Federal Reserve System was reorganized and given many additional powers. Reserve authorities were given the power to raise and lower member-bank reserve requirements. Stock-market credit, which had caused so much woe, was now brought under control by authorizing the Federal Reserve to set minimum margins required. Securities markets, brokers, investment companies, and advisers were all brought under the watchful eye of the newly formed Securities and Exchange Commission. Commercial banks were barred from participating in the marketing of corporate securities and had to cut loose from their securities affiliates. The banks were also prohibited from paying interest on demand deposits.

A program of federal insurance of bank deposits, so long in the air, was finally put into operation, under the newly created Federal Deposit Insurance Corporation. Coverage was optional for state-chartered banks, but after the troubled times just past, few banks wanted to be without insurance. Their eagerness to join made it possible to bring virtually the entire commercial banking system under federal supervision for the first time since the initial phases of the national banking system. The FDIC was more than merely a pool of funds; it put into effect rigorous policies of bank examination which greatly helped to raise standards among non-member banks.

Desire to promote more lending and spending in the interests of recovery led to the creation of a great variety of government lending or loan-guarantee programs, chiefly oriented toward farmers and home owners. Notable was the establishment in 1934 of the program for government guarantee of home-construction and home-repair loans under the Federal Housing Administration. FHA brought about the extensive adoption of the monthly-payment mortgage, far better in protecting both borrower and lender than the single-payment mortgages so common in the 1920's.

The impact of the banking crisis and changes in policy caused a great transformation in the structure and functioning of the banking system. Both state and national banking authorities became more willing to limit the formation of new banks where existing institutions appeared to be doing an adequate job. Branch banking became more prevalent as a substitute for an excessive number of tiny unit banks. The total number of banks declined by 1934 to half what it had been in 1920. Private banks, once so important, virtually all disappeared. Further issues of the historic national bank notes were halted.

Recovery from the depression came at a sluggish and halting pace. Business investment spending recovered somewhat, as firms at least replaced their worn-out facilities and replenished depleted inventories. By 1939, total output had risen above the 1929 peak, but this was far from sufficient to restore full employment. There were still eight million unemployed in 1940—nearly 15 per cent of the labor force.

The role of the commercial banks in the recovery process was a mixed one. After the end of the crisis in 1933, the banks found themselves with abundant reserves, chiefly as a result of the large flow of gold into the United States from abroad. Banks purchased a large portion of the new Treasury securities being issued to cover deficit expenditures, increasing their holdings from about $6 billion in 1932 to $16 billion in 1940. In the process, new demand deposits were created and were pumped into active circulation by the government's expenditures.

The volume of commercial bank loans, however, did not expand to any comparable extent—they were only $1 billion higher in mid-1940 than in 1933.

Between 1929 and 1935, curtailment of the supply of bank loans was certainly an important depressing factor in the economy. In 1935, a government-sponsored study of the availability of credit in the Chicago area reached these conclusions:

1. That there exists a genuine unsatisfied demand for credit on the part of solvent borrowers, many of whom could make economically sound use of working capital.

2. That the total amount of this unsatisfied demand for credit is considerably smaller than is popularly believed, but is large enough to be a significant factor, among many others, in retarding business recovery. . . .

4. That there is a larger unsatisfied demand for long-term working-capital credit than for one-turnover loans.

5. That one of the most serious aspects of this unsatisfied demand is the pressure for liquidation of old working-capital loans, even sound ones.

6. That this pressure is partly due to a determination on the part of the bankers to avoid a recurrence of the errors to which they attribute much of the responsibility for the recent wave of bank failures.

7. That it is also due in large part to the attitude of bank examiners, both state and national.[3]

After 1935, weakness in demand for credit was the chief factor limiting the rise of business loans. As we have already seen, many banks enlarged their consumer and home-mortgage loans to take up the slack. Others experimented with term loans to business: loans scheduled for repayment over a period of years. Like the fully amortized home mortgage, the term loan was a big improvement over the "accommodation loans" of earlier times, which were nominally repayable on short term or demand, but were in practice renewed indefinitely—or until a crisis erupted.

The government's gloomy survey of credit availability showed the bankers at their worst. To see them at their best, let us take a look at the activities of a remarkable western banker. In 1932, Walter Bimson was a successful young executive of a Chicago bank. Partly through experience in administering the relief program there, he had an acute sense of the tragedy of the depression. He saw a great opportunity for banks to meet the existing credit needs and in the process to stimulate recovery for the economy as a whole—which would help reduce the lending risks of which they were then so conscious. At the end of the year, he accepted a top position with the Valley Bank of Phoenix, Arizona. The bank, which had about $9 million of assets at the time, had weathered the shock of depression only with the aid of heroic financial transfusions by the stockholders.

Bimson seized the chance to put his ideas to work for the benefit of the bank and the economy. His New Year's challenge to the bank's staff was in striking contrast to the mood of the financial community as a whole:

Make loans! That is the way to recovery, and I want this period of automatic loan refusal to end and end now. Make loans! The biggest service we can perform today is to put money into people's hands. Especially, let us go into mass-production on small loans. Plain people at this very moment need to borrow for all kinds of useful buying purposes. So great is their need for credit that some of them are paying heavy interest to loan sharks, and this is the bank's fault. This bank's credit capacity isn't what it will be, but we have some capacity, and I want it used. Use it to get buying under way, to get building under way, to get business and farm production under way.[4]

The Valley Bank took a big loan from the RFC to expand its lending power. It bought up several distressed banks to keep facilities open in other communities. It was the first bank in the state to join FDIC. Deposits flowed in—and loans expanded by leaps and bounds. In 1934, the bank was one of the first and most aggressive lenders under the newly created FHA program.

The men and women of the bank rang doorbells, interviewed people, talked about new porches and additional rooms and plumbing repairs, septic tanks and domestic cooling systems. They quickly spread word that these things could be had on a monthly installment basis at 6 per cent. . . . Response was immediate—in one week's time after the Washington announcement [inaugurating the program], 700 Title I loans were set up in Phoenix alone, and on August 30 the first loan was made—to a couple that had a new baby and needed another room. It was one of the first FHA loans made in the nation.

The material dealers and building contractors woke from their long sleep, and this was a time when town dwellings got coats of paint and gas furnaces and duct-cooling systems, while farm houses got modern plumbing and electric lighting plants.[5]

The bank developed extensive lending for home construction as well as improvements. By late 1935, the bank—now the Valley National—had more than three thousand FHA loans and ranked fifth in the nation in volume.

In 1936, the bank initiated a program of automobile instalment loans at rates below those of the finance companies. It took out a small-loan license to broaden its personal-loan business. Commercial and agricultural loans expanded also. By the end of 1940, the Valley National's total assets had grown to $50 million; after allowance for mergers, this represented new credit of more than $30 million over the 1932 level.

Like its eastern counterpart, the Franklin National, Valley National continued its dynamic banking growth through the war and postwar era. The two banks are now very close to each other in total assets, and both rank among the fifty largest banks in the country.

Although the dominant tone of the 1930's was a dark one, the period was one of considerable technological progress and of important innovations in products and ways of doing business. This was the period when commercial air transport gained a firm foothold as a part of the national transportation system. Bank financing was frequently employed by the airlines to finance aircraft purchases, a practice which continues to the present. In 1939, for instance, Pan American obtained $2.5 million from the New York Trust Co. and First National Bank of Boston to buy planes. Pioneering experiments in self-service grocery supermarkets were made during the 1930's, and bank financing contributed to the ability of independents to carry through this innovation, which was neglected by the big chains until much later. Development of quick-frozen foods, which expanded so rapidly during the 1940's, was another innovation pioneered by small business with bank backing.[6]

The depression brought the banks down from the heights of high finance. By law they were excluded from participating in marketing and trading operations in corporate securities, though not from government obligations. Bank holdings of corporate stocks and bonds and bank loans on securities collateral dwindled from $14 billion in 1929 to $5 billion in 1939. This process reduced the proportion of bank earning assets committed to corporate securities finance from 29 per cent to 13 per cent. By the end of 1960, the proportion was below 5 per cent.

In compensation, the banks have extended a development they began in the 1930's—making term loans to finance business fixed-capital investment. Indeed, the increased use of repayment by regular instalments is one of the great changes in banking practice since 1929, covering personal and home-mortgage loans as well as business. The results have been eminently satisfactory for both banks and borrowers. The instalment system seems to have provided a solution to a century-old problem of bank financing of fixed-capital assets.

The outbreak of war in Europe in 1939 brought a quickening of pace in the American economy. Federal defense expenditures were stepped up. Then at the end of 1941 came the blow that drew the United States fully into the conflict. The government's expenditures spiraled upward—more than $50 billion in 1942, over $80 billion in 1943, until at the peak, near the end of the war, they were running at an annual rate of about $100 billion. Tax rates were substantially increased, partly because government officials realized for the first time the importance of tax collections in curtailing the inflationary impact of government expenditure increases. The proportion of expenditures covered by taxes was larger than in any previous major war, but spending went up so much that it would have been economically unwise to try to cover the entire amount by taxes—the effects on productive incentives would have been disastrous. Very large deficits occurred, which had to be financed by borrowing.

Between the end of 1940 and the end of 1945, the national debt was increased by more than $200 billion. Of this increase, $40 billion represented sales of savings bonds to millions of small investors. The Treasury appreciated the importance of a broad sale of bonds to the public as a method of mopping up excess purchasing power and helping restrain inflation. The banks served as distribution agents for savings bonds and other United States securities, and bankers were active in the campaigns to enlist public purchases.

The Treasury was not eager, however, to permit the interest rates on marketable securities to rise much above the low levels they had maintained during the 1930's. (Savings bonds, then as now, were not marketable—that is, they could not be sold from one person to another; they were redeemable on demand, whereas marketable United States securities are not.) Rising interest rates would mean falling prices for the long-term bonds already in existence, and might create unfavorable price expectations among investors, who would become less willing to buy new issues of medium- and long-term securities unless very high interest rates were paid on them.

To keep down interest rates and to prevent bond prices from falling became the task of the Federal Reserve System. The Reserve banks became a sort of price-support agency, buying securities whenever selling pressure threatened to cause price declines. To execute this responsibility, the Federal Reserve banks added $22 billion to their holdings of Treasury securities. This action had far-reaching consequences, for Reserve bank purchases were made with "high-powered dollars" which increased the reserves of the commercial banks, and enabled them to extend credit on a large scale.

This the commercial banks did by purchasing government securities. Their purchases totaled about $75 billion in 1941-1945 inclusive. The banks bought Treasury securities by creating deposit credits on their books in favor of the Treasury. When the Treasury used its bank accounts to pay soldiers, military contractors, manufacturers of red tape, the funds became part of the money supply of the general public.

The sale of bonds to the Federal Reserve and commercial banks was thus a highly inflationary method of finance. It was a complicated and sophisticated method of printing-press finance, with money created in the form of deposits rather than greenbacks. Fortunately, a considerable amount of the demand deposits created was recaptured by further bond sales to the public, or was transferred into time deposits. But the public's holdings of currency and demand deposits increased by some $60 billion during the war, which made them more than double what they had been in 1940.

Commercial banks provided important credits to industries engaged in war production. Many of these were government-guaranteed "V" loans, ranging in size from a few hundred dollars to a billion-dollar loan to General Motors from a pool of four hundred banks. Growth in such loans compensated for the declines in consumer and home-mortgage loans which resulted from reduced availability of consumer durable goods and construction materials. Consumer credit was also held in check by Federal Reserve restrictions imposed under Regulation W. Since the government's financing arrangements with its suppliers frequently relieved them of the need to borrow heavily, the dollar volume of bank loans expanded only slightly in the aggregate during the war. Thus inflationary credit expansion arose primarily from credit created to buy government securities.

The experience of the early years of the war gave a dramatic demonstration of the power of large-scale government deficits to pull the economy out of the depression. The government's own outlays raised the demand for production, and also poured funds into consumer incomes to stimulate private demand as well. Output increased, and unemployment melted away. Total production in 1944 was nearly 50 per cent above the 1941 level, and while production of consumer durable goods and housing was drastically cut, the total amount of consumer non-durable goods and services produced was actually greater than before the war. Millions of people (particularly those previously unemployed) enjoyed higher living standards during the war than they had ever achieved previously. In saying this, there is no intention to minimize the suffering and hardships imposed on millions of families by the war itself, but the financial implications are vitally important. Many observers came to see clearly that major depressions could no longer be regarded as inevitable or incurable; that what was needed was, to paraphrase William James, a "financial equivalent of war."

Increased production and employment were the good aspects of wartime deficits. The bad side was inflation of the price level. As demand began to press increasingly on productive capacity, and as the number of idle men and machines declined, the upward pressure on prices became stronger—by 1942 they were increasing more than 10 per cent a year. To meet this pressure, the government imposed far-reaching direct controls on prices and established a system for rationing certain products among consumers. Commercial banks performed much of the necessary bookkeeping for the rationing program. Price control and rationing were fairly successful in slowing the price rise, although hidden inflation continued in the form of quality deteriorations and shortages of specific desired items. Prices in 1945 were on the average about 40 per cent higher than they had been in 1941.

Price controls, rationing, shortages, savings-bond drives, and other factors combined to reduce sharply the proportion of their incomes that consumers spent. As a result, people accumulated cash, savings bonds, and other savings assets at a rapid rate. To some observers, these were a cushion of potential demand which would help avoid a postwar depression; others saw them as a threat of further inflationary influence. Ultimately both views turned out to be correct.

▪ The generation which was demobilized in 1945-1946 had known little else but instability and disturbance in the economy—and in world affairs generally. They had been given a demonstration of the productive power of the economy, and had been offered during the war a steady diet of rosy predictions of the brave new world to come. There were, indeed, good reasons to hope that the postwar economy would not slump into renewed depression. The financial reforms of the 1930's had greatly strengthened its resistance to shocks. Improved economic understanding of the flow of expenditure and the effects of taxation and government spending had developed in the decade before 1945, and new statistical measurements of national income and expenditures were available to complement theoretical knowledge. In addition, political leaders of all shades of conviction realized the urgency of avoiding another economic shambles like that of the 1930's.

The commercial banks found themselves at the end of the war in the unprecedented position of having 60 per cent of their total assets in the form of government securities. Although the war period had been a relatively prosperous one for the banks, after the hard knocks of the 1930's, most bankers were eager to get back to the sort of world in which their credits went to business firms and consumers to finance beneficial and productive transactions. But few of them could have anticipated just how extensive this process would be—a subject described in the next chapter.

CHAPTER

10

FINANCING THE GROWTH OF

CAPITAL, 1945-1960

THE END OF THE WAR in the summer of 1945 brought tremendous relief and jubilation to the American people. The image of a better world and a better life had been so vigorously presented during the war that everyone was eager to taste the benefits. Yet there were many misgivings. War had brought the economy to unprecedented levels of production and had furnished jobs in superabundance, but could the economy prosper without the artificial stimulus of war? Some ten million Americans would soon be released from military service, eager to find jobs. How could they be absorbed into an economy which had turned in such a disappointing performance in the decade preceding the war?

The much-feared crisis did not materialize. Instead, after a brief grinding of gears, the economy embarked on a spectacular climb. The war's end found a tremendous pent-up demand for goods both at home and abroad. Consumers were eager to enjoy the goods and services they could not afford in the 1930's and could not obtain during the wartime period of limited production and rationing. Business firms had undergone fifteen years of capital starvation and now hastened to expand and modernize their productive facilities. The war-ravaged countries of Europe were even more desperate for the products of American factories and farms, and were enabled to obtain them by generous American financial assistance, both public and private.

These pent-up desires to buy were matched by abundant purchasing power. It came first from the vast amount of cash and liquid assets people had accumulated during the war, and second, from the high incomes generated by the boom itself once it got under way.

The flood tide of consumer spending provided producers with the best of all incentives for high output, and they responded. In particular, output of consumer durables and housing leaped to record levels after virtual extinction during the war. In 1946-1949 annual consumer durable goods output was more than double its average level for the previous fifteen years, and housing production was about three times as high. Production of business capital goods underwent a similar boom. In consequence, no problem of unemployment greeted the returning service men; the economy easily managed the "sixty million jobs" which had been regarded as a utopian demand a few years earlier. The strong underlying demand for capital assets carried the economy forward at a strong pace, from 1945 until 1957, although the tempo of activity varied in reflection of several minor recessions, on one hand, and the pressure of the Korean War in 1950-1952, on the other.

The long postwar boom exacted a penalty in the form of substantial further inflation of prices, so that by 1960 consumer prices were twice their 1941 level. Nevertheless, rising productivity carried living standards to record levels during the same period. Production in 1960 was more than 50 per cent above 1946 levels, and despite a 36 per cent rise in population, real disposable income per person was 20 per cent above 1946 and 50 per cent above 1940.

Much of this increase in productivity and living standards resulted from the large additions made to productive capital. The reproducible real wealth of the economy increased by about 70 per cent from 1945 to 1960. Business firms added about $180 billion to their stock of productive capital goods, measured at 1947-1949 prices. The amount of non-farm housing rose about $100 billion, and the quantity of consumer durable goods in use increased by almost the same amount. Government structures increased about $40 billion.

The big increase in the amount of machinery, buildings, and inventories held by business firms played a vital role in improving the nation's economic welfare. The increase enabled business to equip an expanding labor force, increase the amount of capital per worker, and put into effect many improvements in products and methods of production. Productivity per man-hour in non-agricultural production increased by about 29 per cent between 1948 and 1957.

A large part of the additions to wealth was financed by borrowing. Net public and private debt rose from about $406 billion at the end of 1945 to $882 billion at the end of 1960. Business firms and farms added $270 billion to their debt, households $172 billion, government units $34 billion.

Commercial bank credit was an important source of loan funds for each major sector of the economy. To get a picture of the importance of bank credit in this period, let us look at the uses made of it by business, agriculture, government, and consumers.

Business firms received about $44 billion in bank credit directly and an additional $32 billion through securities purchased by bank-administered trust and pension funds. Combined, these sources accounted for about 40 per cent of business borrowing and security issues (excluding trade credit).[1]

A vast number of firms relied on bank credit in the post-war era. The number of loans reported outstanding at Federal Reserve member banks doubled between 1946 and 1957. By the latter date, commercial banks had more than 1.5 million business loans on their books. One survey reported that 40 per cent of firms were regular bank borrowers and an additional 35 per cent borrowed occasionally.[2]

Among business firms, it is the small and middle-sized firms who constitute the vast majority of borrowers. In 1955, seven-eighths of bank business loans by number went to borrowers with less than $250,000 each of assets. Moreover, small and middle-sized borrowers drew more heavily on bank credit relative to their assets. Bank loans to non-financial businesses with assets of less than $25 million each averaged about 8 per cent of total assets of such firms. For larger firms the proportion was smaller, to the point where bank credit to firms with assets of $100 million or more apiece equaled only about 2 per cent of the assets of such firms.

As a corollary, small and medium-sized firms derived a share in total commercial bank credit that was larger than their share in total business assets. Firms with less than $1 million of assets apiece received about 43 per cent of bank loans, although their share of business assets was about 30 per cent.[3]

The structure of the banking system, with its large number of small banks dispersed through the country, has traditionally made it easy for small and new firms to secure credit. One recent study noted that:

commercial banks are, by far, the largest single institutional suppliers of funds to small business. . . . More than any other single group in the financial community, commercial bankers have close connections with small-business men, both through their boards of directors and customers. Thus, they are familiar with the activities and problems of small businesses from daily contact.[4]

In interviews, many bankers:

pointed out that their long-view interests lay in gaining and pre-
serving the good will of small business. To some this merely represented desire for continuing good customer relations, but in many
cases it reflected a consciousness of the fact that development of
the community rested to a considerable extent on the bank's fulfilling its proper function of supplying the necessary credit to
foster economic growth. Bankers expressed a very real feeling
of obligation to accommodate credit requirements of local business, giving local concerns (the great majority of which are small)
a competitive advantage in this respect over outside firms. Banks
recognized that growth of the community, in turn, promises larger
deposits and loans. These expressions were not limited to small
country banks. Many large banks were anxious to extend branches
into suburbs and outlying areas in which deposits come largely
from small businesses and individuals. Finally, banks reiterated
the fact, borne out by statistics . . . that small business, in the
aggregate, is a big customer, and that many small businesses have
good credit ratings and are good profitable borrowers.[5]

The rapid postwar growth of motel facilities provides a
good example of bank assistance to new, small business
firms. Mortgage credit from banks has often been the chief
source of outside finance for motel construction. One survey,
based on reports from 217 banks, discovered that one-third
of them had motel loans outstanding, and that this group
had financed about 500 motels in the decade after World
War II.[6]

The great postwar development of independent super-
markets shows similar close relations to banks. One study
concluded:

As one reads through the reports on proceedings at a number of
Supermarket Institute conventions and meetings from the years
1948 to 1956 where financing was discussed, one cannot help but
be impressed by the high degree of cooperation that the pioneers
in this industry received from their banks during their development.

The comments of supermarket operators are revealing:

About a year ago, an operator told me that he had persuaded his bank to finance all his fixture requirements. I took that plan to my bank and was amazed to find them very receptive. We set up a long series of notes over a period of years, at a very reasonable rate. . . . (1952)

Working with the bank has been fine. I can go to the bank and do almost anything I want within reason, and have done that in the past. My business has been built from borrowed bank money and I have paid back every bit of it. (1956)

As small operators, we have to get close enough to our local bankers so they will lend us a certain amount of money on our reputation. . . . You can build up your credit to where your banker will lend you more money than you are really justified in getting. (1953) [7]

For a great many business borrowers, bank credit is a resource to meet substantial short-run variations in inventories or accounts receivable which arise chiefly from seasonal factors. The apparel industry, for instance, is heavily seasonal; it contains a large number of small firms each of which may specialize in a limited range of items—swim suits, heavy coats, summer sportswear, etc.

Of course, the economy as a whole goes through a substantial seasonal upsurge as the Christmas season approaches, and bank credit figures prominently in business preparations—first by manufacturers and subsequently by retailers (and finally by consumers, one might add). Bank credit as a whole expands substantially each December, a movement facilitated by Federal Reserve measures to enlarge bank lending power temporarily at that time.

Bank credit is also commonly used to finance current production expenses which may affect individual firms in an irregular or "bunched" manner, whether seasonal or not. Construction operations commonly rely on bank loans to meet current payroll and materials costs; the loans are paid off when the finished structure is sold or used as collateral for a mortgage loan (which may also come from a bank, of course).

In one outstanding case, a bank's financing of construction ended up creating major competition for itself. Phoenix, Arizona, builder David Murdock developed his business with loans from the Valley National Bank; he ultimately ended up founding the Guaranty Bank in 1959. As *Time* described it:

After a World War II stint in the Air Force, [Murdock] drifted into Phoenix with a young wife, a trailer, and a $12,000 stake he had earned running a short-order restaurant in Detroit.

Plunging into partnership with a small-time Phoenix housing contractor, Murdock quickly lost most of his savings when his partner skipped town. Though he knew nothing about either building or real estate, Murdock was determined to pay off the money the partnership had borrowed at Arizona's Valley National Bank, finished the houses by working on them himself. So impressed was Valley National that it backed him on more houses, and in 1952 helped him move into commercial building. Two years later, at 31, he was worth a million. . . .

Murdock likes to become his own tenant. The Guaranty Bank was born when Murdock idly remarked at a cocktail party: "I wish I had a bank in my building." Huddling over a punch bowl, his companions leaped at the idea, joined Murdock in pledging $960,000 toward the founding of the bank. . . .[8]

In the postwar years, commercial banks have also provided a substantial amount of funds for fixed-capital expenditures through the use of term loans. These may run from one to ten years and are usually amortized by instalments. Term loans have accounted for about one-third of member-bank loans to business in the postwar years. Term loans tend to be fairly large and go heavily into industries which make extensive use of fixed capital—metals, petroleum, coal, chemicals, rubber, transportation, and public utilities. They are one of the few resources available to finance fixed-capital expenditures by small firms. Use of term loans by smaller borrowers expanded much more in the postwar period then did those to larger borrowers, and about one-third of the bank loans to small borrowers in 1957 consisted of term loans. Bank mortgage loans to business firms also supply funds for fixed-capital outlays.

American agriculture also posted an impressive record of capital formation and technological progress in the postwar years. Farm output increased more than 30 per cent from 1945 to 1960, yet the number of man-hours of farm labor required to produce it dropped from nineteen million to eleven million. This rise in productivity created downward pressure on farm prices and incomes, and the economy was not notably successful in drawing off the extra workers into industrial employment. Agriculture remained a problem sector largely because its productive performance was so good.

The other side of this, however, was the great benefit, present and potential, to the American public and the rest of the world through agricultural abundance. Americans were able to enjoy the highest standards in the world in food and fiber and to have surplus products available for foreign aid and export, yet at the same time to devote nearly 90 per cent of the labor force to non-agricultural pursuits. Despite gloomy predictions in the spirit of Parson Malthus and the "dismal science," it was apparent that farm productivity in the United States could keep step with domestic population growth and with a good bit of the "population explosion" of the rest of the world.

The revolution in farm productivity resulted from innovations in farm technology and from greatly increased use of capital. Largely through the use of $16 billion of net borrowing, farmers were able to double their use of mechanical power and machinery between 1945 and 1960, and to make use of important biological and chemical developments.

Commercial banks were the biggest single source of farm credit, supplying about one-third of farm borrowing. Farm lending remains a specialty for thousands of small banks in rural areas. Forty per cent of bank credit to farms comes from banks which are not members of the Federal Reserve System.

The number of farm borrowers is very large—indeed, they have outnumbered business borrowers. In 1956, more than two million farmers borrowed from banks, representing nearly half of the operating farmers in the country. About a million of these had borrowed for seasonal requirements related to current production—purchases of seed, fertilizer, or feeder livestock, harvesting expenses, etc. Another million borrowers drew on longer-term credit for purchases of machinery or livestock, and about 200,000 had borrowed to finance land purchases.[9]

Some banks have moved beyond a traditional role as passive lenders to exert a positive influence on farm management practices. The First National Bank of Clarksville, Tennessee, pioneered in this direction in the 1930's, under the leadership of C. W. Bailey. The bank's "Four Pillars of Income" program stressed diversification of a sort which would bring in cash income during each season of the year. As a result, the area's previous undue concentration on tobacco production was modified by enlarged production of livestock and grain.[10] The Wachovia National Bank, which operates a statewide branch system in North Carolina, has also exerted a strong influence toward improved practices by farmers and farm-related businesses.

In addition to business and agriculture, government expenditures contributed significantly to capital investment in the postwar period—particularly state and local governments. The depression and war period had caused these government units to neglect their responsibilities toward expanding the nation's supplies of schools, highways, and other vital public facilities. Beginning in 1946, however, they began to make up for lost time. Government expenditures for construction totaled $165 billion over the years

1946-1960 inclusive, with state and local governments accounting for three-fourths of the total.

To finance their capital expenditures, state and local governments increased their debts by $44 billion between 1945 and 1960, chiefly through bond issues. Commercial banks supplied $14 billion of this sum directly and an additional $4 billion through trust-fund investments, and the banks played a major role in marketing bond issues to other investors.

Many of the borrowing government units are small—school districts, counties, small cities or towns—and cannot reach a wide market for their securities. Local banks are often an important market for these issues, and also play an important role in finding other buyers for them. Long Island's Franklin National Bank confines its $80 million portfolio of municipals to Long Island issues, and the bank bids on every local securities issue, for investment or for resale.

Large city banks are usually more diversified. In 1960, Philadelphia's Central-Penn National held issues of twenty-one Pennsylvania cities, towns, counties, or other districts, but two-thirds of the dollar volume of its portfolio was out of state. Its neighbor, Girard Trust Corn Exchange, was even more diversified. Its $21 million portfolio covered forty-five jurisdictions in twenty-four different states. Its funds have helped finance schools in Cape May, New Jersey and Olyphant, Pennsylvania, water supply and conservation in Fort Wayne, Kansas City, and Los Angeles, and roads and turnpikes in Maryland, Michigan, New York, Ohio, Pennsylvania, and Washington.[11]

Just as commercial bank credit played a major role in financing productive capital formation by the nation's businesses, farms, and government units, it also provided financing for millions of families who purchased homes, automobiles, or other durable goods during the years of postwar prosperity. The trend toward increased home-mortgage and personal lending, which got under way so strongly during the depressed 1930's, was not reversed. By 1960, more than one-fifth of all bank credit was going to individual households, and such credit was more than two-thirds as large as all bank credit to business.

Consumers, like business firms, found themselves after the war with a badly depleted or deteriorated supply of such important "consumers' capital goods" as houses, autos, and appliances. During the thirties, lack of funds or uncertainty kept purchases low. During the war, supplies were short because of scarcities of men and materials. With the end of the war, both supply and demand managed to get together at a high level—with impressive results.

By 1960, the number of dwelling units had increased by twenty million over 1945, with three-fourths of the increase occurring in owner-occupied homes. Furthermore, the Census Bureau reported a steady improvement in quality and size as well.

Home building and buying were significant indicators of a fundamental tone and quality in American life in the postwar period. This was the period of the explosive growth of the suburbs. There was much evidence of a great interest and enjoyment in family life—more families decided to have three children or more, and birth rates moved up after a long decline. With higher incomes and more leisure came the desire for a place of one's own to enjoy these things—a place on the ground, with grass and trees and decent opportunities for the children to play. There can be no doubt that many Americans found a combination of freedom, independence, and security in home ownership. It is also true that widespread home ownership contributed in many ways to the "capital-intensity" of personal life, for with the house came heavy requirements for furniture and appliances, and the indispensable automobile.

Whether his house was new or old, big or small, the home buyer usually got one thing with it—a mortgage. In the 1950's, about 85 per cent of all home purchases involved credit, ordinarily mortgage loans payable in monthly instalments over a period up to twenty or thirty years. By 1960, home purchasers owed $140 billion in mortgage debt, covering about sixteen million homes.[12]

Commercial banks furnished about one-sixth of home-mortgage funds in the postwar period. By 1960, the banks' share of mortgage holdings represented loans to about three million families. Bank participation helped make the mortgage market a highly competitive one, putting credit at the disposal of the vast majority of Americans at reasonable cost. Of great importance to this objective were the government programs for mortgage guarantee and insurance, and the widespread use of the monthly-payment mortgage to protect both borrower and lender.

Although most bank mortgage loans were to individual home owners, the banks provided important financing to projects for urban renewal and reconstruction. For example, National State Bank of Newark, New Jersey, has been an aggressive leader in lending for urban renewal and other apartment construction in the Newark area. In 1960, it financed Colonnade Park Apartments, a middle-income facility designed to accommodate more than twelve hundred families and designed by the noted architect Ludwig Mies van der Rohe.

Next in magnitude to consumer investment in housing was the expansion of automobile ownership and use. At the end of World War II, after more than three years of suspended production, there were about twenty-six million cars on the road. By 1960, this had soared to sixty million, and three-fourths of American families had become car owners. About 60 per cent of auto purchases involved credit, usually in the form of instalment loans, to be paid off over a period of one to three years.[13]

To finance these and other purchases, consumer credit expanded by $50 billion between 1945 and 1960, with automobile credit constituting one-third of the rise. The com-

mercial banks were the largest single source. Directly and
indirectly, the banks furnished nearly half the consumer
credit extended. In the process, bank credit was received by
an enormous number of families. An estimate for 1956 determined that consumer instalment loans from banks were then
outstanding to more than ten million families, representing
about one-fifth of the people in the country.

Average bank borrowers had incomes slightly above the
average for instalment borrowers in general, while credit
from finance companies or from retailers was used more by
lower income groups. Still, families headed by unskilled or
service workers, farm operators, unemployed, or retired persons constituted 18 per cent of bank borrowers, and one-
fourth of the people using bank credit reported they held no
liquid assets other than currency.[14]

The differences in use of bank credit at different income
levels are in large measure a reflection of borrower choice.
Among managerial, professional, and white-collar groups,
people are more likely to have a bank account, to be familiar
with banks and their personnel, and generally to feel at ease
with bank loan officials. They also probably know that bank
loans usually cost less than credit from other sources. Lower
income persons, by contrast, are more likely drawn from
social and occupational groups who are unfamiliar with or
distrustful of banks. Many of them see no reason not to accept the opportunities offered by retailers themselves, many
of whom are willing to extend credit automatically to any
purchaser as a way of promoting sales, relying on profit
margins to cover some of the added loan risk. It takes additional effort for the borrower to obtain a separate cash
loan from a bank or finance company. However, the banks
have made a vigorous effort to broaden their range of borrowers, with some success.

Prospective borrowers may also avoid banks because they
feel a trifle guilty about borrowing. Vance Packard suggests
that:

The loan company's big advantage over the bank is its lower moral tone! The bank's big handicap is its stern image as a symbol of unemotional morality. When we go to the banker for a loan . . . we are asking this personification of virtue to take a chance on us frail humans. In contrast, when we go to the loan company for a loan, it is we who are the virtuous ones and the loan company is the villain we are temporarily forced to consort with.[15]

The great expansion of consumer debt in the postwar years caused plenty of raised eyebrows and cries of alarm. The trend conjured up visions of impecunious borrowers struggling to keep body and soul together and forced to endure the grinding exactions of heartless usurers. This vision bore little resemblance to reality.

Poverty still exists in the United States, and poor people may indeed face problems related to debt, but this is only a tiny facet of modern consumer credit. For American households, debt is overwhelmingly a middle-income phenomenon, and it is far more associated with (and a contributing factor to) increases in wealth than with impoverishment. In 1957, of families with incomes between $4,000 and $10,000, 80 per cent reported having mortgage debt, personal debt, or both. For families above $10,000 income, the proportion was 66 per cent, while for those under $2,000 income it was only 40 per cent.[16]

There was concern about the upward trend in personal bankruptcies, which numbered about 100,000 in 1960, and there were sordid tales of credit buyers victimized by a small minority of unscrupulous sellers of goods. What the critics failed to point out was that for every family pulled under by debts, there are usually two or three families whose debts have simply been written off by lenders when hard times have hit. The number of borrowers who skip or default in bad faith far exceeds the number who are innocently victimized. However, such cases constituted only a microscopic segment of the thirty-five million families having personal debt in 1960.

For many people, credit was actually aiding in the accumulation of real wealth in the form of houses or durable goods. Paradoxical as it may seem, many families use credit as a way of forcing themselves to save. Incurring debt to buy a much-desired home or automobile imposes a discipline to meet the instalment payments; there is less likelihood that the funds will be frittered away on trivialities.

It seems clear that the banks were relatively free from credit abuses. Generally, banks have a strong interest (as do other financial lenders) in protecting the borrower from going too deeply into debt, and helping him to avoid extravagance (not that this will make the banks popular!). Bank interest charges are usually the lowest available—witness the use of the phrase "low bank rates" in the advertising of credit-granting retailers.

On the whole, the financial arrangements of the postwar period worked well in aiding people to acquire houses and durable goods. Perhaps the biggest remaining challenge in financing American households lay in the area of education. To be sure, the credit system poured funds into state and local government bond issues, but higher education, much of it privately financed, offered particularly touchy problems. The rapid rise in the number of young people of college age was accompanied by a great increase in the proportion planning to attend college. Faced with severe shortages of personnel and facilities, both public and private institutions were obliged to raise their fees at an alarming rate, and the high costs of higher education caught many families ill-prepared.

Scholarship officials found themselves deluged with applications for assistance, many from families with incomes of $10,000, possibly $25,000, and even as high as $100,000. After fifteen years of relatively full employment and rising incomes, there seemed little excuse for most of these cases. Family financial statements showed clearly what had happened—an expensive home, a fancy car or two, and the bulk of current income had become obligated to meet fixed payments on the kinds of durable assets for which easy credit was available. In 1959, a Ford Foundation survey disclosed the discouraging information that only 40 per cent of parents planning to send their children to college had some savings program for that purpose, and that less than half of these programs involved current annual savings of more than $200.

Fortunately, families can also rely on credit to finance college costs, and the volume of such loans increased nearly three fold between 1957 and 1960. Many colleges have loan funds available (including federal government funds under the National Defense Education Act), and some have required that scholarship recipients take a portion of funds in loan form.

Beginning with Massachusetts in 1956, a number of state governments have set up programs to guarantee repayment on private loans to college students, and thousands of students have received bank loans under these programs. In 1958, the Indiana National Bank (Indianapolis) pioneered in setting up a program for college loans direct to the student and his family providing up to $10,000. Many other banks have followed suit. Most of the bank loan programs carry interest rates far below the average for consumer credit. In one manner or another, bank credit provided nearly half of the college-student loans by 1960.[17]

Loans are appropriate for many students. A college education enhances earning power, and may be "self-liquidating" in the same manner as a productive capital asset. The increased income provides the funds to pay off the loan with something left over. But this is not always true—especially for girls who are likely to marry rather than work, or for young people entering low-paid but vital professions such as teaching, the ministry, or government service. Ideally, increased saving by most families, plus borrowing by those for whom it is appropriate, would release scholarship funds and other financial aid for low-income applicants or those whose future occupations are not likely to yield a high money income.

By 1960, the commercial banks had about $200 billion in credit outstanding. Bank credit was going to nearly two million business firms, more than two million farmers, and more than ten million consumer households. Where did the banks obtain the funds to supply these sectors with $100 billion of additional credit between 1945 and 1960? Some came from the redemption or sale of some of the Treasury securities they had bought so heavily during World War II. One-sixth of the expansion came from growth of bank capital accounts, as the result of plowing back more than half of profits after tax. But the largest source of bank credit was the growth of deposits.

Expansion of bank credit generally took the initial form of increased checking deposits, with proceeds of loans being credited to borrowers' accounts. Such expansion is possible only if the banks have sufficient funds to meet possible increases in deposit withdrawals and to fulfill legal reserve requirements. In the postwar years, the Federal Reserve aided credit growth by reducing bank reserve requirements and by adding to bank reserves by open-market purchases of Treasury securities. The public cooperated by limiting its withdrawal of cash from the banks to a small proportion of deposit expansion.

The dollar volume of checking deposits increased by 50 per cent from 1945 to 1960. Business firms and individuals enlarged their deposit holdings to keep pace with the rising volume of receipts and payments in the economy. Business continued to hold the bulk of checking deposits—about 60 per cent—but the trend toward increased personal use continued. The proportion of families with checking accounts rose from about one-third in 1946 to 57 per cent in 1960, and banks reported forty-six million personal accounts in early 1961.[18]

A large portion of the funds created by bank lending came to rest in personal savings in the form of time and savings deposits with commercial banks. The dollar volume of time deposits grew by more than demand deposits, and the increase was much greater on a percentage basis. Such deposits have been a favorite outlet for personal saving, since they provide a maximum of safety and a high degree of convenience and familiarity. They are highly liquid—most banks will convert them into cash on demand—but still pay interest. Like demand deposits, they are covered by deposit insurance.

By 1960, the public held over $70 billion in commercial bank time and savings deposits. This represented holdings of nearly forty million accounts—substantially larger than the number held with any other type of thrift institution.

In their role as trust institutions, commercial banks also played an important part in the accumulation and management of savings. One of the most important and dramatic financial developments of the postwar period was the spread of private pension programs for employees. Coverage increased from about six million workers in 1945 to more than twenty million in 1960.

Some private pension plans are managed by insurance companies on principles similar to those used in annuities, but the majority of workers—some sixteen million in 1960—are covered by non-insured plans. These are set up as trust funds into which the contributions are paid; reserves are invested in earning assets, and benefits paid out as they fall due.

Commercial banks manage, as trustees, about three-fourths of the volume of non-insured funds. By 1960, non-insured pension funds held about $26 billion of assets, mostly stocks and bonds. They have became a major force in the postwar financial markets. From 1946 through 1960, they absorbed more than $20 billion of savings, and their securities purchases amounted to more than one-fourth of securities issues during this period.

In addition to their new responsibilities toward pension funds, the banks maintained their more traditional role as managers of personal trust funds. By 1960, these accounted for nearly $60 billion of assets. Corporate stocks constituted two-thirds of trust-fund assets, and their holdings exceeded stock holdings by all other types of financial institutions combined.

In sum, the period 1946-1960 found commercial banks playing the role of the largest and most diversified type of financial institution in a high-productivity, high-consumption economy. Bank credit provided a substantial portion of the credit used to purchase productive capital goods for business, useful durable assets for government units, homes and durable consumer goods for individual households. Bank loans furnished one-fourth or more of external finance by business firms, farms, and state and local governments, and the proportion rises to more than one-third if bank-administered pension and trust-fund investments are included. Bank credit provided nearly one-half of consumer credit and about one-sixth of home-mortgage funds. While continuing to perform their traditional role as suppliers of short-term credit for business and agriculture, commercial banks enlarged the scope of their personal lending and also participated increasingly in financing fixed-capital outlays by business through term loans.

Bank deposits continued to provide an important outlet for personal saving where safety and liquidity were to be stressed. Pension and trust funds grew to major proportions by meeting somewhat different savings objectives. Nearly three-fourths of American families held funds in one or more of these bank-related forms.

Bank deposits also provided most of the spending money in the economy. Consequently, the operations of the banking system were continually in the spotlight as they affected the flow of expenditures and economic activity. Inflation, unemployment, economic growth, and monetary policy received a great deal of attention in the postwar years, as the next chapter will indicate.

CHAPTER

11

MONETARY POLICY
AND CONTROVERSY
SINCE WORLD WAR II

Aᴄᴛᴇʀ 1945, the money supply of the United States, already swollen to record proportions by war finance, continued to grow, but at a rate more in harmony with the transaction needs of a growing economy. The quantity of money rose from about $100 billion in 1945 to about $140 billion in 1960. The commercial banks continued to play the leading institutional role as managers of the nation's money. Checking deposits accounted for almost all of the increase in money occurring in the fifteen postwar years, bringing their share in the money supply to 80 per cent by 1960, and the volume of check payments rose from $1.2 trillion to $3.9 trillion in the same period.

The aspect of money which attracted the greatest concern was its relation to the business cycle—to fluctuations in expenditures, output, and employment. By 1945, the American people had endured fifteen years of disequilibrium. In the 1930's, expenditures were inadequate to provide full employment. Then came World War II, which eliminated unemployment but swung the economy too far in the direction of inflation. Yet widespread fear persisted that the end of the war would plunge the economy once again into stagnation and unemployment. This fear led Congress to adopt an extremely generous program of benefits for discharged servicemen, and in the Employment Act of 1946, the government's resources were pledged to promote "maximum employment, production, and purchasing power."

The financial reforms of the 1930's had greatly reduced the vulnerability of the economy to deflationary shock. The stock market was quiescent and the banks were highly liquid and enjoyed increasing confidence from depositors, partly because of the extent of deposit insurance. Bank failures were virtually nonexistent. However, the economy had witnessed very little experience with *flexible* monetary policy under the reorganized Federal Reserve System. The Reserve banks had functioned chiefly as money factories to assist Treasury finance by supporting prices of government securities, and they continued to perform this function after the war.

The fears of a postwar depression proved misplaced. When federal spending dropped sharply, the slack was taken up by private expenditures, the biggest increases going for business capital goods, houses, and consumer durables. Expenditures for current output moved upward from $214 billion in 1945 to $260 billion in 1948. While much of the increase was financed out of liquid-asset accumulations and out of rising incomes, credit expansion also played an important role. Private debt in the economy rose from $140 billion to $200 billion. A large part of the new loan funds came from reduction in the national debt, by means of which large sums of Treasury deposits were transferred to private depositors.

The expenditure upsurge enabled the economy to absorb returning servicemen without difficulty, and aided the nation's business firms to switch from war to peace production. But this was achieved at the cost of continued rapid inflation. In 1946, most wartime controls were removed, and the excess of demand over supply drove prices up, until in 1948 they were 30 per cent above 1945 levels (and nearly 80 per cent above 1940). Many observers felt that this was excessive. The rise in total expenditures need not have been so large in order to give the desired results in output and employment. Had total spending been less exuberant, prices could have better been held in check.

In particular, criticism fell on the Federal Reserve for not making a more vigorous anti-inflationary stand. During the postwar boom, the Federal Reserve continued its policy of supporting prices of Treasury securities, thus keeping interest rates down. The Treasury was no longer a heavy current borrower, but the existing national debt included an immense volume of short-term securities which had to be continually refunded into new issues as they fell due. Should security prices be allowed to fall, the Treasury would be obliged to pay higher interest on its refunding issues, and its total interest costs would rise rapidly. In addition, Federal Reserve officials feared disorderly price fluctuations in the market for government bonds if price supports were removed—fluctuations which might adversely affect individuals and financial institutions holding securities. And there were some officials in the government who desired easy credit to stimulate high levels of investment and who feared that credit tightening would choke off the boom and bring on the much-feared depression.

Actually, the bond-support responsibility did not require the Federal Reserve banks to make large net purchases of securities. But a more vigorous counter-inflation program would have required that they sell securities on balance, to absorb bank reserves and slow down the expansion of private loans.

Federal Reserve officials were not happy with their position. They tried to persuade the Treasury to offer higher interest rates on new security issues, and short-term rates were increased somewhat. Reserve officials also tried to restrain credit by keeping high requirements for member-bank reserves and stock-market credit, but these were no substitute for a vigorous open-market policy.

The immediate postwar inflationary surge came to a halt at the end of 1948, but when war broke out in Korea in the summer of 1950, the economy sustained a new burst of inflation. Consumers, fearful of a repetition of wartime shortages and price increases, responded by a wave of scare buying. Business firms rushed to enlarge their inventories before prices should rise. The surge of spending reduced unemployment, and production rose by 10 per cent from mid-1950 to mid-1951. But prices moved up at about the same rate, as sellers encountered rising costs or merely took advantage of the panic atmosphere.

The government's own expenditures rose only gradually, and did not set off much further inflation. Tax rates were raised, and direct controls of prices were imposed again. Further rises in total expenditures were pretty well matched by higher production, and prices rose only slightly after the middle of 1951.

The spending spree of 1950-1951 was financed to a substantial degree on credit. To expand loans, the banks sold government securities, many of which had to be absorbed by the Federal Reserve banks to prevent their prices from falling. In consequence, the Federal Reserve System was creating extra bank reserves to fuel the flames, instead of being able to dampen down the expansion by selling securities. Federal Reserve officials tried to compensate with other policy instruments—they raised reserve requirements and stock-market margin requirements, and when authorized by Congress, imposed direct controls over down payments and maturities for consumer credit and certain real-estate loans. But these actions were not adequate.

Disgusted with the results, Reserve officials forced a showdown with the Treasury, and in March 1951, the two agencies reached a momentous "accord." The Treasury agreed to stop trying to maintain artificially low interest rates on new bond issues. The Federal Reserve renounced any commitment to support security prices at any given level, although it promised to help prevent "disorderly conditions" from developing in the bond market—that is, wild speculative movements of bond prices.

The Federal Reserve gained an important confirmation of its freedom of maneuver in the elections of 1952. General Eisenhower had vigorously condemned the inflation of the previous decade and had promised more vigorous use of monetary policy to prevent further price increases.

Inflation was not a problem when the new administration took office, however; instead, cuts in defense expenditures started the economy into a mild recession, which was held in check by tax reduction. Monetary policy moved in the right direction: Reserve requirements were cut, consumer and housing credit controls were abandoned. The Federal Reserve banks purchased securities and lowered discount rates. Thus virtually every available technique was utilized. The economy soon righted itself in 1954, and a new wave of prosperity, less tainted by defense exigencies, was under way.

During these years of the early 1950's, the Federal Reserve leadership attempted carefully to take stock of its responsibilities and techniques. In 1952, William McChesney Martin, chairman of the Board of Governors, set forth his view of the principal goal the system should pursue: "to minimize economic fluctuations caused by irregularities in the flow of credit and money, foster more stable values, and thus make possible the smooth functioning of monetary machinery so necessary to promote growth of the country and to improve standards of living." [1] By 1955, ten years after V-J day, the evidence was clear that the nation's monetary and credit system would no longer serve as a major source of disturbance to the economy. There were no unwholesome speculative run-ups of commodity or stock prices, no waves of panic in securities markets or banks. During the mild recessions, there was none of the perverse behavior of earlier times, when worried depositors lined up to draw their funds out of shaky banks, which in turn were obliged to press their harassed debtors for payment. Large-scale bank suspensions and failures were a thing of the past.

This achievement—a monumental one, from the perspective of the previous century and a half—reflected in part the superior quantitative controls of the Federal Reserve System, in part the existence of deposit insurance, the high liquidity of the banking system arising from holdings of Treasury securities, and the improved controls of bank assets and entry into banking maintained by regulatory authorities.

But from this level of achievement, a still more ambitious role was being staked out for the banking and monetary system—to act as the lever by means of which the government might regulate and stabilize the flow of total expenditures in the economy. In this role, monetary policy would not rest content to prevent the banks and money supply from acting as a source of disturbance, but would attempt to use money and credit to counteract disturbances arising anywhere else in the flow of expenditures. Federal Reserve officials had caught a vision of this role in the 1920's, but when the crisis came the system had failed even to achieve the more limited goal of neutralizing the disturbance-creating potential of the banks. Now the experiment was to get a full scale trial.

On numerous occasions, Federal Reserve officials described their role as "leaning against the wind"—that is, providing some resistance to strong movements in total expenditure, whether they were heading up or down. But this role raised some difficult questions. How hard should monetary policy lean? Should vigorous credit restraint be applied during economic upswings before the economy might reach relatively full employment?

Particularly ticklish was the problem posed if the economy were afflicted simultaneously with substantial unemployment and rising prices—how can one be sure which way the wind is blowing? By 1961, Chairman Martin had confronted this problem repeatedly, and wryly remarked, "the problem, it now appears . . . is to lean against crosswinds, and lean against them simultaneously." [2]

In earlier years there was a widespread conviction that control of total expenditure would provide satisfactory solutions for major problems. If there were substantial unemployment, it would indicate that total expenditures were inadequate. Expansion of the money supply and easing of credit would be appropriate. Such actions would not have inflationary consequences on the price level, it was felt, so long as business firms could easily expand production by taking back unemployed workers. If the price level did rise appreciably at any time, it would be a safe sign that total expenditures were too large. Credit could be appropriately tightened and the money supply held in check to keep the flow of expenditures equal to the flow of production at existing prices.

This attitude toward expenditures, unemployment, and prices was a reasonable one, and it was well supported by the experience of the 1930's and 1940's. Unfortunately, the experiences of 1955-1960 ended the hope that things could be managed so simply.

After the 1951 accord, the top leadership of the Federal Reserve System also went to work to streamline and organize the techniques available for influencing the flow of expenditures. The accord freed open-market policy for whatever operations seemed economically appropriate. And open-market policy is the most flexible and potent of Reserve instruments. By purchasing securities, the Reserve banks can feed additional reserves into the commercial banks in the desired amounts at the appropriate times. Reductions in Reserve bank securities holdings can produce desired restraints.

Termination of Federal Reserve "price-support" operations through the accord also reduced the ease with which commercial banks could obtain added reserves by selling securities. Consequently, after 1951, the member banks became increasingly willing to borrow directly from the Federal Reserve to meet temporary exigencies in reserves. This revived demand for loans gave increased importance to the Federal Reserve discount rate as an instrument of flexible policy. During periods when credit restraint was desired, Reserve banks raised the interest rate charged on loans to member banks. Easing of credit brought lowering of the discount rate.

Able to control the amount of bank reserves through these revived techniques, the monetary authorities moved away from the high reserve requirements which had been maintained during the 1940's. Reductions were made during the business recessions of 1954 and 1958; and in 1960, member banks were given authority to count as legal reserves their holdings of cash in vault. These actions brought reserve requirements to their lowest effective level in twenty years, and placed member banks on a more equitable basis relative to non-member banks.

With the restoration of their traditional policy instruments, the Federal Reserve authorities withdrew gracefully from the exercise of direct control over the terms of consumer and housing credit. The authorities preferred to direct their attention to the aggregate supply of money and credit, allowing free market forces to allocate the supply among various claimants.

On the whole, the "new look" in Federal Reserve policy was a streamlined one, which concentrated attention on a limited range of both objectives and techniques, in order to do a better job within the limited range. The emphasis on economic stabilization as goal and open-market policy as technique represented a wise choice. However, the conditions which developed in the economy from 1955 on posed extremely difficult problems for monetary policy, and exposed it to strong criticism from many quarters.

The year 1955 witnessed a vigorous recovery from recession. Much of the force came from record levels of auto sales, stimulated by aggressive selling techniques which included substantial "easing" of credit terms by reducing down payments and extending maturities. One result was an increase of $5 billion in consumer instalment debt during the year—a rise of 15 per cent. More serious, the auto industry had clearly oversold its market. Auto sales dropped off in the years following, and that industry was faced with declining employment and difficult adjustments.

A second difficulty appeared in 1956 when the price level began to move upward at a rate of about 3 per cent a year. This occurred when the level of unemployment was still fairly substantial and most industries were not pressing the limits of their productive capacity. The Federal Reserve responded by restricting credit. Market interest rates moved steadily upward to levels which had not been experienced since the 1920's.

While total expenditures in the economy rose in 1956 and 1957, production did not keep pace, and unemployment, which averaged 4.4 per cent of the labor force in 1955, did not fall appreciably below this level.

To be sure, the economy did experience a vigorous boom in business capital investment in 1956 and 1957, adding valuable productive capacity, much of it of a highly efficient quality. However, this achievement was marred by substantial (demand-induced) price increases in machinery, and the increase in capacity made it increasingly urgent that demand and output generally keep pace.

Instead, the boom petered out in 1957 and the economy

entered another mild recession—which brought another disturbing trend. Prices kept right on rising, even while total expenditures were declining and unemployment was rising to more than 7 per cent in early 1958. Between the summer of 1957 and spring of 1958, while output was falling, consumer prices increased nearly 3 per cent. By mid-1958 they were more than 8 per cent higher than in 1955.

How can you lean against the wind if you do not know which way it is blowing? That was the predicament of the Federal Reserve authorities in late 1957. With prices rising, they chose to maintain a vigorously restrictive policy. Discount rates went higher and more securities were sold. Interest rates therefore trended steadily upward even though the economy was receding. At the end of 1957, the symptoms of recession were clearcut enough to bring a reversal of policy, and credit eased rapidly.

The economic downswing was fortunately brief and total expenditure soon turned upward. Increased government spending furnished one support, and easier credit helped raise housing expenditures. Higher government transfer payments to consumers helped total consumption expenditures to keep rising throughout the recession, thus providing a major sustaining force and preventing business expectations from becoming very pessimistic.

The upswing proved brief and not very satisfactory, however. The major steel strike which began in the summer of 1959 helped bring it to a halt. A brief upsurge followed in early 1960, only to give way to a renewed downswing which lasted through the remainder of that year.

This rather spotty behavior was accompanied by further increases in prices, though at a very slow pace. From 1958 through 1960, the rise totaled about 3 per cent, but at the same time the level of unemployment was generally high. From an average of 6.8 per cent in 1958, it fell only to about 5.5 per cent in 1959, and rose again above 6 per cent for most of 1960.

By this time, a new complication had developed, this one in the international sphere. Beginning in 1958, gold began to flow out of the country in substantial amounts. Both the explanations and implications were complex. The United States had been paying more to foreigners than it was receiving in payments from them throughout most of the fifties. The excess of outpayments (referred to in the trade as a "deficit in the balance of international payments") resulted mainly because large outlays for foreign investment and foreign aid were not fully offset by the consistent surplus of United States export sales over import purchases. During most of the 1950's, this international deficit did not lead to a gold outflow; instead, foreign countries added to their holdings of American assets—deposits in American banks, United States Treasury securities. In the late fifties, a number of factors changed the situation. The countries of Western Europe removed many of their foreign-exchange controls, thus making their currencies more freely convertible into one another for international purposes. These countries desired to build up their gold holdings as reserves for settling international imbalances which might arise. Further, interest rates in Europe were generally much higher than in the United States, and after the relaxation of currency controls, investors found it more convenient and less risky than before to keep funds invested in European assets, rather than American. And once the gold flow began, it gave rise to speculative sales of dollars based on fears that the dollar would be devalued.

The gold outflow posed no immediate threat, for United States gold holdings were still nearly half those of the entire free world, and some redistribution was probably healthy and desirable, but if the flow were to continue indefinitely, the United States would face the unpleasant choice of permitting the international value of the dollar to decline or of imposing direct controls on foreign-exchange transactions. Either of these would entail a radical shift in policy. After

World War II, the United States played a leading role in bringing the major countries of the free world nearer to a system of relatively unrestricted international trade, based on stable exchange rates and on currencies readily exchangeable for one another. By 1960, this policy had borne abundant fruit. By encouraging international specialization and exchange, it contributed greatly to efficient and expanded production in Western Europe and in Japan. Maintenance of an adequate gold supply in the United States appeared to be a necessary foundation for continuing this country's constructive influence on the character of world trade and finance—an influence rendered the more important for its relation to military and diplomatic objectives.

The loss of gold posed very specific problems for monetary policy during the recession periods of 1958 and 1960. Easing of credit was clearly called for to support the domestic economy, but this meant lower interest rates, which encouraged the outflow of loan funds. And indeed, the major outflows of gold tended to concentrate in periods when United States interest rates were low for counter-recession purposes.

Thus the years 1956-1960 were not as successful as economists might have hoped. Prices increased too much, unemployment was too high, and in addition the country obviously suffered from disguised unemployment in agriculture. The growth of the economy was disappointing; real output per capita rose only about 3 per cent from 1955 through 1960. The possible criteria for monetary policy were in conflict—should it try to minimize gold outflow, reduce unemployment, or prevent price increases?

Yet these were not bad times. More people had jobs than ever before—non-agricultural employment reached sixty million by the end of 1960—and most of them were earning high incomes indeed. Average factory wages were running around $2.25 an hour in 1960, implying a weekly paycheck of about $90 for those fortunate enough to work a full week.

Many of the unemployed were sustained by compensation benefits. If prices were rising most people were not adversely affected. For one thing, the quality and variety of products were also improving. Quite possibly this was sufficient to match price rises of 1 or 2 per cent per year and leave most people no worse off. For another thing, most wages and salaries had become more flexible upward—perhaps too much so. The long-suffering college professors and government employees were more likely to find that their money incomes would advance at least as fast as the cost of living, and generally faster. For retired people, Social Security benefits were revised upward periodically, and more and more employees were being covered by pension plans which invested funds in stocks rather than fixed-value assets, so that retirement benefits stood a better chance of keeping pace with living costs.

Yet, the economy's performance was marred by the injustices arising from the job problem. The employee on the job in the steel, auto, or coal industry earned an impressively high wage, but such well-paying jobs were increasingly hard to come by. Young people just entering the labor force, people trying to leave farming, Negroes, and displaced older workers all found the going rough. At the same time, the economy was plagued with shortages of certain vital services—schools, urban transportation, medical care, and recreational facilities.

Many explanations were forthcoming to account for the sluggish performance of the economy. Some critics felt the trouble arose from the upward pressure of wage costs on prices, resulting from labor union activity. In some industries, such as autos and steel, the wage-cost-push undoubtedly caused employers to curtail job opportunities by substituting capital goods for labor, and higher product prices probably sacrificed some sales volume, particularly in export markets.

However, wage-cost-push was only one aspect of a bigger

problem—in many sectors of the economy, market forces were not successfully equating supply and demand. Artificially high wage rates caused the demand for labor to fall below the supply, while artificially high prices in farm products caused supply to exceed demand. There was not a deficiency of total spending in the economy as a whole, but the pattern of demand did not match up well with the existing distribution of labor and productive capacity. The demand for durable goods—business capital, housing, and automobiles—weakened in the late 1950's as a proportion of total demand. The great postwar capital buildup was pretty well completed. Instead, consumers and business firms displayed increased demands for specialized services such as medical care, education and research.

As a result, the economy was afflicted with "structural disequilibrium," in the fancy phrase employed by the chairman of the Federal Reserve Board. Labor and other productive resources were not moving very successfully from areas of excess capacity to the areas of excess demand. Unemployed steel workers or underemployed farm laborers were of little use in meeting the needs for more teachers and more doctors. Inadequate mobility of labor, both occupationally and geographically, was part of the problem, and this immobility was related in part to inadequate educational facilities.

To see the problem as one of structural disequilibrium is to see it as a problem in the detailed adjustment of demand and supply in individual markets, rather than a problem in the flow of aggregate demand. Nevertheless, there remained a widely-held conviction that the economy's performance could be improved by massive increases in the flow of total expenditures. We might call this the "Farragut" or "damn-the-torpedoes-full-speed-ahead" school, which included Harvard's Alvin Hansen, former presidential adviser Leon Keyserling, and many leaders of organized labor. In this view, higher total spending, achieved by means of easier credit, tax reductions, and higher government expenditures, would lead business firms to increase production and hire more workers. With demand pressing on capacity, producers would also add to their capital equipment, thus spurring a more rapid rate of economic growth. Leaders of this school considered it unlikely that prices would rise very much, or believed the potential harm to be inconsequential.

The Farragut school was probably correct in its conviction that higher total spending would have raised production and employment in 1958-1960. Higher spending would have raised the demand for cars and houses and put excess productive capacity to use in producing them. But the low-pressure conditions of 1958-1960 had some advantages, too. Business firms were forced to be more competitive in price and quality—certainly auto buyers were getting a lot more for their money in 1961 then they had gotten in 1957. Slack demand held in check the excessive rate of increase in wage rates, and brought home to many people the urgency of productivity gains to support wage increases. A forced-draft increase in total spending would probably have aggravated the excess demand for the already-scarce services of education and medical care. Prices and costs would have risen more than they did, with adverse effects on the country's import-export position.

The theory of structural disequilibrium suggested that the problems were partly on the supply side. It gave more emphasis to such possible remedies as improved facilities for general education and vocational training, or financial support and information for moving workers to other areas. Even so, accepting the fact of structural disequilibrium did not rule out the possibility that some of the problems might be better solved if total demand were higher.

The problems of inflation, unemployment, economic growth, and monetary policy provided much grist for the political mill in 1956-1960. The Democrats, who were the "outs" in 1956 and 1960, concentrated much fire on monetary policy. In 1956, their platform attacked the "hard-money policy" as "the first time-bomb of the Republican crusade against full prosperity for all." Monetary policy in the next four years was hardly designed to please them, for the money supply had increased barely 1 per cent per year, and interest rates on long-term Treasury bonds moved up from about 3 per cent to 4 per cent.

In their 1960 platform, the Democratic Party argued that if elected, "The new Democratic Administration will confidently proceed to unshackle American enterprise and to free American labor, industrial leadership, and capital, to create an abundance that will outstrip any other system. . . . The recent slow pace of American growth is due not to the failure of our free economy but to the failure of our national leadership. We Democrats believe that our economy can and must grow at an average rate of 5 per cent annually, almost twice as fast as our average annual rate since 1953.

"As the first step in speeding economic growth," the platform continued, "a Democratic President will put an end to the present high-interest, tight-money policy."

The Republican platform also accepted the principle that "We must quicken the pace of our economic growth." But the document added, "We reject the concept of artificial growth forced by massive new federal spending and loose money policies," and stressed the importance of "maintenance of a stable dollar as an indispensable means to progress."

During the 1960 campaign, the presidential candidates referred repeatedly to monetary policy. Despite some differences in emphasis, however, their positions were not widely dissimilar. In particular, Senator Kennedy adopted a much more moderate tone in reference to monetary policy than that of his party's platform. Both he and Mr. Nixon agreed on the necessity for budgetary and monetary policies to promote economic stability, reduce unemployment, and promote economic growth.

By the time of Mr. Kennedy's election and inauguration, monetary policy had become even less controversial. Federal Reserve authorities had eased credit to deal with recession conditions in the economy. As economic conditions improved in the spring of 1961, the new administration was not obliged to treat economic policies as urgent. Harmonious relations were generally maintained with the Federal Reserve, but no one could be sure what would happen to this harmony when a new boom might bring higher interest rates and tighter credit.

Outside the political arena, the problems of economic conditions generally and monetary policy in particular were also undergoing extensive scrutiny. Economists and public figures were trying to find out more about the possible means of achieving full employment and higher rates of economic growth without inflation. In 1959-1960 the Joint Economic Committee of Congress sponsored a massive inquiry into "Employment, Growth, and Price Levels" which produced more than three thousand pages of learned testimony and monographs. It proved conclusively that the problems were complex and controversial. There were wide differences of opinion among the contributors, and the Committee itself produced a final report in which the majority and minority were in sharp disagreement along party lines. In 1961, the privately sponsored Commission on Money and Credit produced its own report, which was followed by the vast array of staff research reports on which it was based. The Commission members (chiefly representatives of business and labor) managed to agree, but at a level which produced little new theoretical insight or imaginative policy recommendations.

From all the evidence and conclusions of these studies, some essential features could be distilled. First, there was fairly impressive general agreement on the importance of economic stability and growth, on the undesirability of unemployment and price inflation. But where these objectives might be in conflict—where more growth might be achieved at the risk of more inflation, or where price stabilization appeared likely to raise unemployment—agreement was lacking. At a more subtle level, there was a wide gap between those who confidently believed the federal government was capable of maximizing the economic welfare of everyone in the nation, and those who more cautiously limited the role of government to one of protecting the economy against the serious evils of mass unemployment or rapid price inflation.

At the technical level, there was general agreement on the over-riding importance of total expenditures for current production. There would be no danger of mass unemployment or serious inflation so long as wide fluctuations in expenditures could be avoided. Furthermore, there was little doubt of the power of the federal government to prevent serious instability in total expenditures. During boom periods, for instance, tighter credit and higher tax revenues (even at constant tax rates) would help prevent excess demand and serious price inflation. During recessions, easier credit and reduced tax revenues would help cushion the decline, and government transfer payments (such as unemployment compensation) would help to sustain consumer spending. Should disequilibrium prove stubborn, deliberate changes in tax rates or expenditure programs could be made. Tax cuts would be appropriate for recession periods, in order to feed spending power into the private economy; tax increases would be suitable for booms, to siphon off spending power when it threatened to outrun productive capacity. The record of the 1950's indicated that, in the absence of external shocks like the Korean War, economic policy could keep total expenditures from making excessively sharp movements up or down.

By 1960, however, the economy faced the problems of structural imbalance in the mechanism for allocating resources into particular employments and industries. And these problems did not lend themselves to easy solutions through manipulation of total expenditures. Acting on the assumption that wherever there is a problem, there must be a solution, some economists urged the government to grapple more directly with the supply problems. Special programs were initiated for depressed economic areas, and measures were set in motion to subsidize retraining and mobility of individual workers, but no dramatic improvements seemed likely.

Granting that the government can and should maintain some control over the flow of total spending in the economy, what techniques should it use? Three choices commonly present themselves, and preference among them may properly rest on considerations both of effectiveness and manageability. The most effective choice probably is fiscal policy—variation in the government's own receipts and expenditures. Fiscal policy is directly a part of the flow of total expenditures and produces major influences on private incomes and private expenditures as well. Experience of the 1940's and 1950's repeatedly demonstrated that substantial changes in tax or expenditures policies could move the economy up or down. To some degree, fiscal policy adapts automatically to stabilize fluctuations. Tax revenues rise in booms and fall off in slumps; transfer payments tend to rise in recessions and fall when prosperity returns. Beyond this, however, the main limit on fiscal policy is its management. Taxation and expenditure policies of the government involve a multiplicity of goals, not merely economic stabilization. Fiscal policy-making must pass through the heart of the political process, since it generally involves legislation. Substantial delays in making policy changes may make these changes effective at the wrong times. Spending increases enacted under the spur of recession may come to fruition just as subsequent boom conditions threaten to become excessive.

By contrast, monetary policy is highly manageable. The policy-making process is carried on outside the heart of the political arena, and monetary policy can be directed toward the primary objective of economic stabilization without being burdened with many competing objectives. However, Federal Reserve actions may be less potent than fiscal policy.

In periods of economic downswing, Federal Reserve banks can supply the commercial banks with excess reserves, but this does not assure that bank loans to prospective spenders will increase. If commercial banks have a pessimistic outlook on business conditions, they might merely accumulate excess reserves. Nowadays they are more likely to buy government securities in the open market. This would still tend to create demand deposits, but not deposits likely to be spent for current production. The money supply would rise, but its velocity would fall.

In boom periods, on the other hand, Federal Reserve actions can reduce banks' reserves, but the banks might still increase loans by selling government securities in the open market. By selling securities at low prices and high yields, the banks might attract idle cash away from investors and put these funds into active circulation through loans. In this manner, the velocity of money would increase.

Thus monetary policies do not have the same sharp and clearcut influence on total spending as do fiscal measures; still, monetary measures are far from impotent. They have had a substantial effect on some types of expenditure, such as residential construction. And considering the difficulties of fiscal policy-making, monetary measures are often the best measures practically available to deal with the early stages of economic fluctuations.

Policy instruments of a different type have sometimes been regarded as appropriate means of influencing total spending. These include direct manipulations of particular price or wage levels, as in farm price supports or minimum wage laws. Such measures are generally ineffective in changing total expenditure, however, and are likely to worsen supply-demand imbalances in particular markets. Higher minimum wages, if they affect very many workers, raise business costs and encourage substitution of capital goods for labor. Thus, they are likely to reduce output and employment in the affected industries. Even if they do not, product prices are likely to rise, or business profits be reduced. In either case, any increase in the flow of income to wage earners is offset by reduction of income elsewhere in the economy.

It is worth noting that if the government fails adequately to deal with fluctuations through its monetary and fiscal measures, pressures will increase for it to take interventionist measures of this latter sort.

Monetary and fiscal measures emerge, then, as complementary. Fiscal policy is strong, but major changes are hard to manage. Automatic variations in tax revenues and transfer expenditures serve as important first-line stabilizers requiring no deliberate action. Monetary policy is of uncertain strength, but it is highly flexible and not plagued with too many conflicting objectives. It thus can be used also as a first-line stabilizer. If serious disequilibrium occurs, these first-line defenses will be inadequate, and deliberate changes of tax rates or expenditures become appropriate. If the disequilibrium is serious (as it was in 1933), there is little danger that policies will be "out of phase" with the business cycle, but it is important that major fiscal changes be limited to cases of substantial disequilibrium—else they run the risk, through poor timing, of aggravating instability rather than reducing it.

What about growth? How are total expenditures, and the means of controlling expenditures, related to economic growth? Certainly there is some connection. If total expenditures are inadequate for high levels of production and employment, growth will be impeded. Business firms will have no incentive to add to their productive capacity, if they already have more than they need. The stagnation of the 1930's demonstrates this most clearly.

Some observers have gone further to argue that growth is

best promoted by a "high-pressure" economy, in which total demand is high enough to keep production at capacity levels and minimize unemployment—even if this does produce inflation. Historical evidence indicates, however, that industrial nations have maintained impressive growth rates at times when high-pressure conditions did not exist in the flow of total expenditure. Growth depends in part on effective competition among business firms and on maintenance of efficiency in production, and these conditions are too often lacking in a chronically high-pressure economy.

In a free-market economy, growth is heavily dependent on the existence of adequate business profits. Current profits provide funds for capital investment, and the prospect of future profits is essential as an incentive for such investment. Profits are effected by the flow of total spending through the economy, but they also depend on a vast variety of other factors, including government policies toward labor unions, wage rates, and taxation. Probably the government would do better to encourage a "high-profit" rather than a "high-pressure" economy as a means of promoting growth without inflation, without international disequilibrium, without a softening of competition and efficiency.

The roots of economic growth go deeper than matters of credit, expenditures, and profits. Vitally important is the rate of innovation, which may depend in turn on the educational standards and the research expenditures of business, government, or nonprofit institutions. Growth depends on the entire pattern of incentives and public attitudes toward work, family responsibility, present *vs.* future, consumption *vs.* saving, etc. There are many things that governments can do to promote beneficial economic growth—improving the educational system, promoting research, reducing tax burdens on saving, investment, and risk-taking, preventing abuse of monopoly power by business or labor groups. If conditions in these areas are favorable, monetary policy and the flow of total expenditure can best promote growth by promoting stability. So long as business firms need not fear a big drop in total spending, nor a rapid rise of prices and costs, a favorable environment for growth will exist.

It is probably a mistake for monetary policy to be based primarily on such variables as prices, unemployment, or the country's international position. The simplest basis for monetary policy is to focus on the flow of total expenditures in the economy, particularly the relation of spending to existing productive capacity. The ideal monetary policy would produce a flow of spending just sufficient to purchase at existing prices the output the economy is capable of producing at relatively full employment.

Such a policy would not avoid some price increases nor prevent unemployment, if these ills arise from structural imbalance. But monetary policy cannot cure such ills; their solution lies in measures to improve the adjustment of supply to demand in individual markets. If such measures are beyond the competence of the government (as they probably are), then the maladjustments may simply have to be left to work themselves out as best they can. No serious harm will attend such a fatalistic solution, provided aggregate demand is not deficient and there are unemployment benefits, relief payments, and opportunities for education and training which insure that no one will suffer undue hardship nor be deprived of the opportunity to improve his own condition.

Over the long run, however, it probably is desirable to have the quantity of money increase at about the same rate as the level of production and productive capacity in the economy. This should facilitate the needed increases in total expenditure without requiring increases in interest rates or in monetary velocity.

Monetary policy has demonstrated great progress since the dark days of the 1930's. Money and the banking system no longer serve as independent sources of economic disturbance nor as amplifiers of disturbance originating elsewhere. Since 1951, monetary policy has aspired to a more positive role as a force to counteract disturbances in the flow of expenditures, whatever their origin. Although managed by the Federal Reserve authorities, this policy depends for its operation on the actions of the commercial banks, who have thus become participants in the government's vital task of economic stabilization. However, the limitations of such a policy have been clearly shown. Although valuable for protecting the economy against violent changes in total expenditures, it cannot prevent price increases or unemployment which arise from the malfunctioning of individual markets. Perhaps nothing can.

The problems confronting the 1960's were partly results of progress. Consumers and business firms had achieved the abundance of durable assets they so vigorously pursued during the postwar years. Consumers began increasingly to seek higher standards of education, health, and recreation—commodities not so effectively mass-produced by an industrial system. In business, a technological revolution rapidly altered the pattern of demand for different types of labor. Both at home and abroad, the 1960's promised to be a period of increased competition, in which enterprise, efficiency, and imagination would be rewarded, but in which many competitors would fall behind. It was a healthy challenge.

CHAPTER

12

COMMERCIAL BANKING AND THE
NATION'S ECONOMIC DEVELOPMENT

THE STORY OF AMERICAN BANKING has been meshed, from start to finish, with the story of American economic development as a whole. Quantitatively, this development has carried the nation from a thinly populated strip of the Atlantic coast, containing four million people whose main pursuit was subsistence farming, to a mighty continental power of 180 million people, participating in an intricately diversified high-consumption industrial economy.

Qualitatively, American development has brought to the average person the opportunity to live without deprivation of physical needs for food, clothing, and shelter, and to achieve a comfortable livelihood without back-breaking physical effort. Economic development has enabled Americans to assure their children adequate food and medical care and excellent educational opportunities. The American economy of the 1960's offers the average man unprecedented opportunities for self-development in work and leisure. All these achievements are nonetheless impressive for the fact that no one feels we should rest content with existing conditions.

The underlying source of our country's economic growth and progress has been enterprise. The willingness, even eagerness, to take a chance, to experiment, to innovate in hopes of finding a better life and a better way of doing things has been characteristic of American society since colonial times. It required enterprise and courage for people to immigrate to this country, to endure the hardships of travel and the uncertainties of the new life. It took enterprise to leave the settled parts of the country and to dare the risks and opportunities of the frontier. And of course, it has taken enterprise to risk one's capital in productive enterprise instead of working for someone else, and to experiment with new methods and new products rather than follow the customary pattern of production.

To harness enterprise to the benefit of society has required a variety of favorable circumstances. One was a system of money and prices to serve as a guide to specialization and exchange. Since the early years of the nineteenth century, the commercial banks have furnished the largest portion of the country's money supply, at first chiefly bank notes, and later, deposits.

The effective use of enterprise also required a supply of capital. Sometimes the man of enterprise could supply it himself, but often he was not a man of wealth. For the economy to take advantage of the initiative and talent arising in all strata of society, sources of outside funds were necessary. The commercial banks served as the chief institutional source of such funds during the years of America's industrialization. Although no accurate generalizations are possible, it seems safe to conjecture that commercial bank credit provided funds for at least 10 per cent of the country's productive capital formation over the century ending in 1930, and that this contribution ranked next in importance to reinvested business income and the personal savings of wealthy individuals.

The American banking system was itself a striking symbol of the spirit of enterprise which was so marked during the nineteenth century. The system embodied the principle that substantial additions could be made to *capital* through the extension of *credit* based on the creation of *money*. Bray Hammond's comments, although directed primarily at the 1830's, are applicable to most of our banking history:

Banks in general were under stronger pressures to lend on easy terms than to meet their obligations. . . . They were run for borrowers who were tortured with a thirst for credit; and the credit was sought not for the facilities of trade but for the exploitation of capital resources. At the same time they were relied on to furnish the circulating media. There were certain persons who felt strongly that the banks should be confined to the monetary function, but their efforts in the main were unconstructive. They ignored the fundamental legitimacy of the demand for long term credit, and seemed to think that it could be deflected from the banks without being given direction elsewhere. This failure to provide adequate functional specialization in the field of credit put a great undifferentiated burden upon the banks, and their survival in consequence was always dependent upon their ability to be both fish and fowl at the same time.[1]

The alliance between credit and money was always an uneasy one. Efforts to improve banking performance in one sphere have frequently prejudiced the other. Much of American financial history appears as a series of alternating efforts to stress abundant credit, on the one hand, or a money supply of high quality and relatively stable quantity, on the other.

Banking history has always stressed the monetary debasements arising from the demand for credit. It has not given much attention to the other side of the story. Frequently the measures that were imposed to improve the monetary performance of the banks interfered with the extension of credit of the kinds that the economy most needed. To insist that entry into banking be limited to men of proven character and competence, that new banks open only with an abundant cash capital, that loans be made only on low-risk opportunities, and that the total quantity of credit be held firmly under control—each of these seems eminently reasonable. Certainly a banking system operated on this basis would present little danger to monetary stability. Yet such an "aristocratic" banking system would have been less favorable to enterprise than the unsafe and unsound tactics which frequently prevailed.

Contrasting American banking patterns with those prevailing elsewhere, economist Kenneth Boulding concluded that "the United States has had in the past a worse record of bank failures, but on the other hand, the local banks have been more active in promoting and encouraging local enterprise, and it may well be that the greater dynamism of the American economy may be in part a result of the high degree of local autonomy in the banking system." [2]

Subject to varying degrees of restraint, the characteristic pattern of American banking for approximately a century was free banking. (By free banking we mean the relatively automatic granting of banking charters when certain technical requirements are met, and also the freedom to engage in private banking without incorporation.) This ended with the depression and financial revolution of the 1930's.

It is no accident that the century of free banking coincides with the most rapid and revolutionary period of the nation's economic development. Economic historians now date the "take-off" into industrialization as coming during the fifteen years preceding the Civil War. At the other end, the 1930's brought economic growth to a temporary halt. Free banking was symptomatic of the spirit of enterprise which provided the driving force for economic growth and change, and it contributed directly to that force.

We have observed that the establishment of the national

banking system extended free banking as a national policy but subject to rather stringent restraints in the form of minimum capital requirements and lending limitations. The total banking reforms of 1863-1865, including the bank-note tax, were consequently a restraining, rather than an expansionary force. The next expansion came through the enormous growth of state-chartered and private banks, particularly after 1880. The spirit of free banking is evident in the liberal opportunities available to private banks and to trust companies. Non-national institutions flourished by meeting the various needs which national banks were prevented from fulfilling—needs for small-scale country banking, for mortgage loans, for trust services.

The monetary instability displayed by the banking system at the turn of the century brought about the creation of the Federal Reserve System in 1913. Unlike the banking measures of the 1860's, this was not fundamentally a restrictive measure. Instead, it embodied a new approach, through which the liquidity of the banks could be protected directly. It took a long time for the Federal Reserve to master this technique; in the meantime, the economy suffered the drastic inflation of 1914-1921, the painful deflation of 1921-1922, the runaway bull market in stocks, and worst of all, the financial and economic collapse of 1929-1933. But with new powers and with new attitudes engendered by these experiences, the basic approach to banking stability embodied in the Federal Reserve System has proved effective.

The financial changes arising out of the depression of the 1930's display two other noteworthy features. Through the deposit-insurance program, the government extended to deposits the sort of protection it had conferred on bank notes in 1863. And the program, though voluntary, achieved virtually unanimous membership among the banks—a goal sought in the 1860's but never achieved. The incentive to have insurance protection is great for existing banks, and establishment of new non-insured banks is difficult. (Many state banking authorities will not grant charters to new banks unless they become insured.)

The depression of the 1930's also provided the stimulus for ending the long-standing policy of free banking. Federal and state banking authorities, impressed by the need for fewer and more secure banks, became much less liberal in granting new charters and greatly reduced the opportunities to engage in private banking.

Free banking had its faults and its virtues. The opportunity to start a new bank with relatively little capital and to make loans by creating money did much to make American banking borrower-oriented. Many banks originated with a group of business men in a given locality or trade who found existing credit opportunities unsatisfactory. Easy entry made commercial banking highly competitive. It contributed to the ease with which men of enterprise could gain the capital needed to put their ideas and talents to the test of performance.

Sometimes the banks were relatively passive aids for the driving performances of men like Carnegie, Eads, Vanderbilt, and Rockefeller. At times, a banking position served as the point of departure for entrepreneurs such as Erastus Corning and William C. Ralston. A bank might become a sort of rallying point for a group of "capitalists-at-large," through which they sought out new and promising fields of enterprise, new men, and ideas to back. The National City Bank of New York filled this role in the heyday of James Stillman and the "Standard Oil crowd"; so did the various elements of J. P. Morgan's financial realm. In Pittsburgh, the Mellon bank played a vital role in a remarkable variety of important industrial ventures. In short, free banking created a banking system that was willing to take a chance.

One can only look with wonder and amazement at the variety of banking institutions that American enterprise created at one stage or another. These ranged from the staid commercial enterprises of the cities to the furtive wallpaper factories of the frontier; they included canal and banking companies, railroad and banking companies, insurance and banking companies. There have been national banks and state banks, Granger banks and labor banks, industrial banks and immigrant banks, Hibernian, Germanian, and Scandinavian banks, and a wide variety of styles of private banks. When a group of bank customers felt themselves inadequately served, the way was usually open to start a new bank. In the process, the banking system as a whole was made more receptive to innovation. Note particularly the dynamic role of newly-formed trust companies around the turn of the century, and the influence of the Morris Plan and labor banks in enlarging consumer lending facilities.

Consequently, the century of free banking witnessed a gradual but far-reaching expansion in the scale and variety of commercial banking services. Before the Civil War, most banks concentrated on business lending through bank-note issues. From the 1850's, there developed a great increase in the use of checking deposits by business, a trend which entailed day-to-day continuing service by banks. By the turn of the century, banks were increasingly cultivating trust services to corporations and individuals. The first quarter of the twentieth century witnessed a great expansion in personal savings deposit business by the banks. And since 1925, the banks have extended their personal lending services until at present they embrace millions of families. By these developments, the number and proportion of people served by banks have grown greatly, and the banks themselves have become the source of general financial service on a continuing basis.

Free banking had its disadvantages. A banking system which was itself easy to enter was necessarily vulnerable to abuse by cheats or incompetents. Bank lending policies based on a willingness to take a chance were sometimes a vehicle for unwholesome speculation and farfetched promotions, to the detriment of bank solvency. The periods when bank credit was permitted to expand rapidly were often periods when serious distortions were introduced into the economy, through price inflation or through capital accumulations running too far ahead of prospective demand and production.

In any event, the era of free banking has passed. Shall we lament its passing? Probably not. The more rigorous controls of entry and of bank lending have in the past thirty years reduced the incidence of bank failure almost to zero. Credit needs which were once met by free banking are now served in other ways. Competition within banking has become more intense, rather than less, during the past thirty years, as improvements in transportation and communications have reduced the scope for local banking monopoly.

In recent years, the rapid expansion of branch banking has helped to extend the geographic scope of bank services and to add to the vigor of competition—two important functions formerly performed by free banking. While the number of banks in the country has remained static or declined slightly, the number of banking offices has risen steadily through the establishment of branches. In 1920 commercial banks had 1,000 branches. By 1946 the total exceeded 4,000, and by 1960 it had risen to 10,000. We have already noted the importance of branch banking as a vehicle for such pathbreaking bankers as Giannini, Roth, and Bimson.

Even granting these facts, we must still be on guard against the danger that government measures to curb entry into banking and to moderate the intensity of competition may be carried too far.

Aside from the spread of branch operations, the structure of the banking system has not changed much since the 1930's. In 1960, there were about 13,000 banks operating a total of about 23,000 offices. Of these, 11,000 were unit banks, operating in one facility. Even branch systems are, with few exceptions, confined within state boundaries.

About one-third of American banks operate under national

charters, while the remainder (save for a few private banks) are state-chartered. The terms of national charters are generally somewhat more onerous in such matters as minimum capital requirements and lending restrictions, but many bankers feel that national status carries the sort of prestige which may help attract deposits. One banker remarked, "If I were starting a bank, the best name I could pick for it would be the First National Bank."

State-chartered banks tend to be the smaller banks in smaller communities. There are state banks in Happy (Texas), What Cheer (Iowa), Pleasureville (Kentucky), and Paradise (Pennsylvania), but Mount Joy (Pennsylvania) has a national bank. There is a state bank in Arp (Texas), but national banks in Opp (Alabama), Gap (Pennsylvania), and Hop Bottom (Pennsylvania).

Slightly under half of the banks are members of the Federal Reserve System. Members include all national banks, plus such qualified state banks as choose to join. This membership may confer prestige on a commercial bank and provides it with access to short-term loans and other Federal Reserve services. It also carries responsibilities; member banks must abide by Federal Reserve regulations prescribing minimum cash reserves and other phases of bank operations. Though more than half of the nation's banks do not belong to the Federal Reserve system, non-members account for only one-sixth of total bank assets. The banks of Evening Shade (Arkansas), Summer Shade (Kentucky), and Travelers Rest (South Carolina) are not members, but both banks of Sleepy Eye (Minnesota) are members, though one is national and one state.

National or state, member or non-member, commercial banks are eligible to come under the insurance protection of the Federal Deposit Insurance Corporation. This government agency insures deposits up to $10,000 for each depositor. Insured banks must pay a premium and must agree to submit to examination by the insurance authorities. Only a handful of banks remain outside the insurance program. Insurance covers the banks of Protection (Kansas), Plain Dealing (Louisiana), and Honor (Michigan), but not the banks of Fairplay (Colorado), or Braggadocio (Missouri).

The number of communities with bank offices is roughly equal to the number of banks—about 13,000. There are, appropriately, banks in Enterprise (Alabama), Industry (Illinois), Commerce (Georgia), and Prosperity (South Carolina). Banks operate head offices in Deposit (New York), Wampum (Pennsylvania), Greenback (Tennessee), Windfall (Indiana), and Dime Box (Texas), but Coin (Iowa) rates only a branch.

Banking offices serve more than 5,000 communities with less than 1,000 persons each—towns as small as St. Elizabeth, Missouri (population 57). There are banks in such small towns as Calico Rock (Arkansas), Ball Ground (Georgia), Gravel Switch (Kentucky), and Marrowbone (Kentucky). Many of the banks are small, too. A thousand of them have less than one million of total assets each—banks such as the Bank of Speed (Missouri), the Embarrass State Bank (Wisconsin), and the Winona State Bank (Texas) which musters about $80,000 of assets.

Most of the banks range between one and fifteen million dollars in total assets—more than 10,000 of them fall between these limits. At the top level, about 500 banks have more than $50 million in assets, and about 25 have assets exceeding one *billion* dollars each.

The ten largest banks account for about one-fifth of the nation's banking resources. Although each bank's offices are limited to one state, these are "national"—even international —banks in a functional sense. They provide credit and deposit facilities for the largest non-financial firms whose operations cover the entire nation. Six of the "big ten" are Wall Street banks, reflecting the concentration of finance and company headquarters in New York.

By contrast to the financial giants, the great majority of

American banks are "main-street" banks of modest size. Their clientele is more local or regional in character, and in the past they have seldom felt direct competition with the banking giants of the big cities. In recent years, however, as commercial banking has increasingly cultivated consumer and mortgage loans and personal deposit business, the big banks have been eager to operate branches close to the consuming public, especially in fast-growing suburban areas. Moves to open branches or to buy out existing local unit banks have produced much friction, and the resulting controversy over branches and mergers is currently one of the more hotly debated issues in banking circles.

A lot of banking is carried on by the big banks. About two-thirds of all bank assets are held by the (roughly) five hundred banks with more than $50 million assets apiece. However, the smaller banks furnish an impressive proportion of the *number* of loans and are particularly important in meeting credit needs of large numbers of small business and farm borrowers. Control of banking is much less concentrated than in most manufacturing industries, where a single firm may control 25 to 50 per cent of industry facilities. On the whole, commercial banks face intense competition from each other and from other financial institutions.

Cooperation among banks through correspondent relationships improves their ability to cope with an integrated national economy. Banks in smaller communities maintain deposit accounts with banks in larger cities, and city banks keep accounts in other cities. The small-town banks receive many services from their city correspondents—loans, investment advice, participation in making large customer loans, collections, foreign-exchange services. The city banks benefit by having the use of deposited funds. Cooperation among correspondents helps to direct loan funds where they are needed, and enables small banks to obtain benefits from the specialization and expertise which the large banks have achieved.

In many of their operations, commercial banks face competition from other types of financial institutions. In competition for savings, interest-bearing deposits with commercial banks are pitted against deposits with mutual savings banks and savings shares in savings and loan associations and credit unions. The market for home-mortgage loans involves not only the commercial banks and the mutual thrift institutions named previously, but also life insurance companies on a considerable scale. In personal loans, banks must share the market with sales-finance and consumer-loan companies. In farm lending, the principal competition comes from the great variety of credit agencies sponsored by the federal government.

However, commercial banks are still the principal source of short- and medium-term loans to business, although life insurance companies, sales-finance companies, and specialized firms such as factors participate to some degree.

In a broader sense, bank credit services to business are not matched by other financial institutions. Although individual loans may come and go, the relationship of bank to borrower is likely to be a continuing one, and at best entails much more than impersonal extension of funds. Good banks recognize the potential benefits they can receive from association with an up-and-coming business firm. Such an association can produce a flow of income from repeated loan business and from trust and other services to the firm and its members. And as the firm expands, it is likely to bring steadily increasing deposits to its bank connections.

The bank is often in a position to provide helpful advice and counsel to its customers. In one recent survey, more than four-fifths of the business men participating rated advice as one of the important functions of banks. One commented, "Advice and money are the two commodities banks have to sell. We don't need their money, but we do need, and do get, excellent advisory service from them." [3] And of course banks perform important functions in obtaining credit information on firms elsewhere in the country and in helping to collect accounts due.

The unique character of bank loans to business, and of the attendant services, is particularly important in view of the predominant place of bank credit in supplying funds for small business borrowers. Also, though commercial banks face institutional competition in many credit markets, they are unique in their diversity of credit services. Savings and loan associations and mutual savings banks concentrate on home-mortgage lending; credit unions and consumer-loan companies deal almost entirely in personal loans. Life insurance companies invest in long-term bonds and mortgages, and investment trusts specialize in stock ownership. By their diversity, the commercial banks can influence the flow of loan funds into the areas of greatest current demand. Without some such diverse institution, the availability of funds in particular credit markets might rise and fall arbitrarily, in response to such unrelated factors as the choice by savers whether to hold savings and loan shares or buy more life insurance.

Finally, commercial banks are unique in furnishing demand deposit services. Handling checks represents the chief work of the employees of commercial banks. Here are involved all the bookkeeping and paper work entailed by accepting deposits, collecting checks, and transferring funds from demand to time deposits and back again. In these activities, the banks are truly the operating managers of the money supply. And they manage not only their own demand deposits, but do much of the work involved in putting currency in or out of circulation. By means of the transfer and record-keeping activities of the banks, the nation's system of money and payments is able to do the job of financing the complex pattern of output, employment, and financial adjustments required to support a productive industrial economy based on specialization and exchange.

It is also in connection with management of checking deposits that the bulk of bank expenses are incurred. Available accounting data suggest that managing demand deposits cost the commercial banks from $1.4 billion to $1.6 billion in 1954.[4] This represented about 40 per cent of their total costs.

To be sure, most banks levied service charges on holders of checking deposits, but these charges yielded only $300 million in 1954—one-fifth of deposit management costs. The remainder of deposit costs were financed out of the income from loans and securities. In effect, the willingness of the public to hold bank deposits enabled the banks to make loans and buy securities by creating such deposits. The earning assets thus acquired provided the funds to pay lending costs themselves, pay interest and management costs of time deposits, and to cover most of the expenses of managing demand deposits and the money supply.

Fortunately for the banks, recent technological advances have shown great promise for cutting costs of deposit management. Electronic data-processing equipment can be used to carry out most of the formerly tedious and time-consuming bookkeeping operations entailed in check handling. Increasing numbers of banks are making provisions for the special types of imprinted figures and ink required to put checks through electronic processing.

Judged by the returns paid to bank employees and stockholders, the banks have provided their services to the public at low cost. Wages and salaries paid by banks have been relatively modest. So have bank profits. Over the years 1946-1960, commercial banks averaged 8.4 per cent profit on their capital accounts, after taxes. By comparison, American manufacturing corporations over the same period recorded after-tax profits of 11.7 per cent of capital—more than one-third higher.

The generally low level of bank profits made it difficult for them to attract new capital by stock issues. Despite the heroic reinvestment of earnings, bank capital accounts remained low in relation to total assets, a situation not conducive to willingness to undertake risky loans. Access to added capital limits the ability of the banks to meet the rising demands for loans as the economy expands.

One banker has taken his colleagues severely to task for their performance, arguing that on balance they have served the public *too* well, with inadequate attention to their own profits. He urges them to try to raise their earnings, so that they can pay their employees more adequately and yield dividends which will attract more capital to meet future needs for credit expansion. In particular, he is critical of the low level of service charges on demand deposits and suggests that service charges should cover full costs of deposit management. We need not evaluate his detailed suggestions, but his criticism certainly attests to the fact that the banks have functioned mainly for the benefit of the general public rather than that of their own employees or stockholders.[5]

Thus, it can be argued that a public interest inheres in commercial banks because of their unique diversity of credit and savings functions, because of the unique quality and importance of their business loans and related services, and because of the public-service character of their management of the nation's money. In addition, they bear a unique responsibility insofar as they are the means through which Federal Reserve monetary policies affect the economy.

This is not to argue that the banks should be the recipients of special favors or subsidies. In particular, individual banks should stand or fall on their own merits, subject to the judgments of a competitive market. But questions concerning the competitive status and profitability of banks should be dealt with analytically, and banks should not be unduly discriminated against on the basis of misinformation or ideology.

A question deserving particular emphasis is whether the present network of regulations designed to preserve bank solvency has not been carried too far. The following are some of the detailed inquiries which need consideration:

1. Do reserve requirements for commercial bank time deposits serve any useful purpose? Several impartial studies have recently answered this in the negative. Present regulations hamper the ability of the banks to compete with thrift institutions not subject to such requirements.

2. Are the present restrictions on entry into the banking business too stringent in this age of deposit insurance, of insured and guaranteed mortgages, and of government policy pledged to economic stability?

3. Is there any real justification for a legal ceiling on interest rates that commercial banks are allowed to pay on time deposits?

4. Should mutual thrift institutions be virtually exempt from federal taxation of business income, while commercial banks are heavily taxed?

5. Do present restrictions on the amount of mortgage loans a bank can hold serve any useful purpose?

Many of these questions raise complicated issues, and there is not general agreement among bankers or financial scholars about particular proposals. But a good case could be made for giving freedom and competition the benefit of the doubt and putting the burden of proof on the proponents of restriction and control.

The prospects presented by the 1960's confront the American economy with serious challenges. As always, further growth of output and productivity is urgently needed to increase the economic welfare of the consuming public and to provide adequate employment opportunities. Furthermore, the economy must find some way to meet the growing demand for such bottleneck services as medical care and education. The educational problem is particularly critical because of its relation to the needs of the economy for highly trained and skilled personnel.

These needs for economic growth and adaptation have been powerfully supplemented by the exigencies of the international situation. The indefinite continuation of the Cold War gives rise to the immediate burdens of national defense and foreign aid. It also requires that the performance of the American economy provide a continuing demonstration of the productive vigor and moral integrity that are possible in a free society.

Our country's international economic position has been greatly altered as a result of the economic recovery and rapid growth of the countries of Western Europe. This trend, which resulted in part from assistance by the United States, added greatly to the strength of the free world. However, it also contributed to the international payments problems of the United States. As the decade of the 1960's opened, a rapid movement toward economic integration was under way in Western Europe, and it was apparent that the United States would have to find some sound basis for continued economic relations with the emerging entity.

The United States will probably become increasingly an "open economy," with international transactions becoming more important for many producers. On the one hand, this prospect implies the possibility of vastly enlarged markets for American farm and industrial products; on the other, it foreshadows increased competition from foreign suppliers.

Ultimately, the kind of performance needed to meet the new challenge of the world economy is what has always been required for growth and progress within the domestic economy. As much as ever, we need enterprise and initiative in the business world, combined with financial institutions which will supply capital where it is most needed to give scope and effectiveness to these qualities. The commercial banking system has a distinguished record of performance in meeting the financial needs of enterprise and growth. Its continued success is a matter of vital concern to all.

APPENDIX I

Founding Date	Original Title	Present Title	Location
1781	Bank of North America	First Pennsylvania Banking and Trust Co.	Philadelphia, Pa.
1784	Bank of New York	Bank of New York	New York, N. Y.
1784	Massachusetts Bank	First National Bank of Boston	Boston, Mass.
1791	Providence Bank	Industrial National Bank of Providence	Providence, R. I.
1792	Hartford Bank	Hartford National Bank and Trust Co.	Hartford, Conn.
1792	New Haven Bank	First New Haven National Bank	New Haven, Conn.
1792	Union Bank	Union Bank and Trust Co.	New London, Conn.
1795	Bank of Baltimore	Union Trust Company	Baltimore, Md.
1795	Merrimac Bank	Merchants National Bank	Newburyport, Mass.
1796	Gloucester Bank	Gloucester National Bank	Gloucester, Mass.
1799	Manhattan Company	Chase Manhattan Bank	New York, N. Y.
1800	Washington Bank	Washington Trust Company	Westerly, R. I.
1802	Beverly Bank	Beverly National Bank	Beverly, Mass.
1803	Plymouth Bank	Plymouth National Bank	Plymouth, Mass.
1803	Strafford Bank	Strafford National Bank	Dover, N. H.
1803	New York State Bank	State Bank of Albany	Albany, N. Y.
1803	Philadelphia Bank	Philadelphia National Bank	Philadelphia, Pa.
1803	Newport Bank	Newport National Bank	Newport, R. I.
1804	Worcester Bank	Worcester County National Bank	Worcester, Mass.
1804	Cheshire Bank	Cheshire National Bank	Keene, N. H.
1804	Newark Banking and Insurance Co.	National Newark and Essex Banking Co.	Newark, N. J.
1804	Trenton Banking Co.	First Trenton National Bank	Trenton, N. J.

APPENDIX II

Banks Surviving out of the First Fifty National Charters Issued in 1863

Original Charter Number	Present name of bank	Location
1	First Pennsylvania Bank and Trust	Philadelphia, Pa.
2	First New Haven National Bank	New Haven, Conn.
4	State National Bank of Connecticut	Stamford, Conn.
8	First National Bank of Chicago	Chicago, Ill.
10	Third National Bank and Trust Co.	Dayton, Ohio
12	First National Bank of Erie	Erie, Pa.
17	First National Bank of Richmond	Richmond, Ind.
19	First National Bank of Portsmouth	Portsmouth, N. H.
20	Fifth Third Union Trust Co.	Cincinnati, Ohio
23	Purdue National Bank	Lafayette, Ind.
24	First National Bank of Cincinnati	Cincinnati, Ohio
25	First National Bank of Marietta	Marietta, Pa.
28	National City Bank	Evansville, Ind.
29	First National City Bank of New York	New York, N. Y.
30	First National Bank of Wilkes-Barre	Wilkes-Barre, Pa.
31	First Grange National Bank of Huntingdon	Huntingdon, Pa.
35	Fishkill National Bank	Beacon, N. Y.
36	First National Bank of Findlay	Findlay, Ohio
39	First National Bank of Towanda	Towanda, Pa.
42	First National Bank of Strasburg	Strasburg, Pa.
43	First National Bank of Salem	Salem, Ohio
45	First National Bank and Trust Co.	Ellenville, N. Y.
46	First National Bank of McConnelsville	McConnelsville, Ohio
47	Terre Haute First National Bank	Terre Haute, Ind.

APPENDIX III

The Centennial Commission for the Observance of the 100th Anniversary of the National Currency Act and the Dual Banking System

CHAIRMAN
BEN H. WOOTEN, Chairman of the
Board
First National Bank in Dallas
Dallas, Texas

VICE CHAIRMEN

GIBBS LYONS
Chairman of the Board
State National Bank of Connect-
icut
Stamford, Connecticut

LOUIS E. HURLEY, President
The Exchange Bank and Trust
Company
El Dorado, Arkansas

TREASURER

EVERETT D. REESE
Chairman of the Board
City National Bank and Trust
Company
Columbus, Ohio

EXECUTIVE SECRETARY
RAYMOND M. CHESELDINE, JR.
Secretary, Public Relations Com-
mittee
The American Bankers Association
New York, New York

Members

Carl F. Bahmeier, Jr.
Executive Manager
California Bankers Association
San Francisco, California

Frank L. King
Chairman of the Board
United California Bank
Los Angeles, California

[281]

NOTES

NOTES · CHAPTER 2

1. Amasa Walker, *The Nature and Uses of Money and Mixed Currency* (1857), p. 53 quoted by George R. Taylor, *The Transportation Revolution* (New York: Rinehart & Company, Inc., 1951), p. 311.
2. Whitney's loan from the New Haven Bank is described by Jeanette Mirsky and Allan Nevins in *The World of Eli Whitney* (New York: The Macmillan Co., 1952), pp. 310–311; Allan Nevins, *Abram S. Hewitt, with Some Account of Peter Cooper* (New York: Harper & Brothers, 1935), pp. 92, 141, 171–174.
3. Quoted by H. E. Miller, *Banking Theories in the United States before 1860* (Cambridge: Harvard University Press, 1927), p. 194.
4. Andrew M. Davis, *The Origin of the National Banking System* (Washington: Government Printing Office, 1910), p. 14, quoting *Hunt's Merchants' Magazine* for January 1863.
5. Quoted by H. E. Miller, *op. cit.*, p. 8.
6. Bray Hammond, *Banks and Politics in America from the Revolution to the Civil War* (Princeton: Princeton University Press, 1957), p. 608; H. E. Miller, *op. cit.*, p. 20.
7. Hammond, *op. cit.*, p. 180.
8. Bessie Pierce, *History of Chicago* (New York: Alfred A. Knopf, Inc., 1937), II, p. 124.
9. A relatively complete list of private banks operating in 1863, with their average deposits, appears in *Report from the Commissioner of Internal Revenue, Accompanied by an Abstract of the Banks, Associations, Corporations, and Individuals Doing a Banking Business*, 38th Congress, 1st Session, Senate Executive Document 50, 1864.
10. Lance E. Davis, "The New England Textile Mills and the Capital Markets: A Study of Industrial Borrowing 1840–60," *Journal of Economic History*, March 1960. The conclusions cited in the text

were derived from materials kindly supplied by Professor Davis to the author.

11. Davis R. Dewey, *State Banking before the Civil War* (Washington: Government Printing Office, 1910), p. 156.

NOTES · CHAPTER 3

1. *Congressional Globe*, 1862, p. 455.
2. "City of Frederick, Maryland," Hearings before Subcommittee No. 2 of the Committee on the Judiciary, House of Representatives, 1961.
3. *Congressional Globe*, 1864–1865, p. 1139; February 1865.
4. *Annual Report of the Comptroller of the Currency*, 1866, p. 71.
5. *Annual Report of the Comptroller of the Currency*, 1876, p. CXLIV.
6. Address to ABA, quoted in Marquis James and Bessie R. James, *Biography of a Bank: The Story of Bank of America* (New York: Harper & Brothers, 1954), pp. 41–42.
7. See David M. Cole, *The Development of Banking in the District of Columbia* (New York: The William-Frederick Press, 1959), pp. 303–308, 340–347.
8. *Annual Report of the Comptroller of the Currency*, 1864, p. 49.

NOTES · CHAPTER 4

1. Allan Nevins, *John D. Rockefeller* (New York: Charles Scribner's Sons, 1941), I, pp. 194, 248–249.

    The banker was undoubtedly Dan Eells, president of the Commercial National Bank, and later founder and president of the (now) Bucyrus-Erie Co., manufacturers of construction equipment.

2. Florence Dorsey, *Road to the Sea* (New York: Rinehart and Company, Inc., 1947), pp. 216–217.

    Much of this account of Eads's adventures is derived from this source. See also John Ray Cable, *The Bank of the State of Missouri* (New York: Columbia University Press, 1923); and T. P. Kane, *The Romance and Tragedy of Banking* (New York: The Banker's Publishing Co., 1922).

3. Julian Dana, *The Man Who Built San Francisco* (New York: The Macmillan Co., 1936), p. 243.
4. *Ibid.*, p. 230.
5. Ethel Manter, *Rocket of the Comstock* (Caldwell, Idaho: Caxton Printers, 1950), p. 216.

6. Leonard J. Arrington, "Banking Enterprises in Utah, 1847–1880," *Business History Review,* December 1955, p. 326.

7. See Marriner S. Eccles, *Beckoning Frontiers* (New York: Alfred A. Knopf, Inc., 1951).

8. On the copper kings, see Stewart Holbrook, *The Age of the Moguls* (Garden City, New York: Doubleday and Company, Inc., 1953), pp. 156–180; Ira B. Joralemon, *Romantic Copper, Its Lure and Lore* (New York: Appleton-Century-Crofts, 1934); *Notes on Your Banks . . . Historical Sketches of Montana Banks and Bankers,* Helena Branch, Federal Reserve Bank of Minneapolis, 1946.

9. Quoted (without identification) by Henry Oliver Evans, *Iron Pioneer: Henry W. Oliver (1840–1904)* (New York: E. P. Dutton & Co., Inc., 1942), p. 121. Mellon enterprises are described by Harvey O'Conner, *Mellon's Millions* (New York: The John Day Company, Inc., 1933).

NOTES · CHAPTER 5

1. Lewis Atherton, *Main Street on the Middle Border* (Bloomington, Ind.: Indiana University Press, 1954), pp. 23–28.

2. *Historical and Biographical Annals of Columbia and Montour Counties, Pennsylvania* (Chicago: J. A. Beers and Co., 1915), p. 338.

3. Wayne D. Angell, "A Century of Commercial Banking in Kansas," unpublished Ph.D. thesis, University of Kansas, 1957, p. 235.

4. Walter Whitmore Chadbourne, *A History of Banking in Maine, 1799–1930* (Orono, Maine: Maine University Press, 1936), p. 157.

5. William Allen White, *Autobiography* (New York: The Macmillan Co., 1946), p. 317.

6. Atherton, *op. cit.,* p. 150.

7. Allan G. Bogue, *Money at Interest: The Farm Mortgage on the Middle Border* (Ithaca, N.Y.: Cornell University Press, 1955), pp. 7–75.

8. *Ibid.,* pp. 77–204.

9. Earl Sylvester Sparks, *History and Theory of Agricultural Credit* (New York: Thomas Y. Crowell Company, 1932), p. 374.

10. White, *op. cit.,* p. 127.

11. A. R. Reynolds, "Sources of Credit for a Frontier Lumber Company: The Daniel Shaw Lumber Company as a Type Study," *Bulletin of the Business Historical Society,* December 1950, pp. 189–190.

12. L. H. Langston, *Practical Bank Operation* (New York: National City Bank, 1921), I, p. 313.

13. *Credit Service,* (Philadelphia: First National Bank of Philadelphia, 1913).

14. L. F. Swift, *The Yankee of the Yards* (New York: A. W. Shaw and Co., 1927), pp. 43–44.

15. Bessie Pierce, *History of Chicago,* III, pp. 113–114.

16. Norman Gras, *The Massachusetts First National Bank of Boston, 1784–1934* (Cambridge: Harvard University Press, 1937), p. 151.

17. Quoted by John D. Hicks, *The Populist Revolt* (Minneapolis: University of Minnesota Press, 1931), p. 83.

18. Stewart Holbrook, *The Age of the Moguls,* pp. 114–115.

19. Hicks, *op. cit.,* p. 23.

20. *Ibid.,* p. 82.

21. Data from the United States Department of Agriculture, Releases 1047 and 1048 (1921, 1922); Raymond W. Goldsmith, *A Study of Saving in the United States* (Princeton: Princeton University Press, 1955–1956); and *Historical Statistics of the United States, Colonial Times to 1957* (Washington: Government Printing Office, 1960).

22. On the early years of the bank, see Alvin Tostlebe, *The Bank of North Dakota* (New York: Columbia University Press, 1924).

 At the end of 1960, the bank held assets of $120 million. Its deposits are almost entirely those of the state and local governments, while its assets consist chiefly of government securities plus some government-guaranteed mortgages. It accepts private deposits, but does not make ordinary commercial loans. The bank has extended loans to local governments to help them prepare facilities to attract industry. It also administers the state's program of low-cost loans to college students.

23. Case studies from Federal Reserve Board, Committee on Branch, Group, and Chain Banking, *Materials Prepared for the Information of the Federal Reserve Board* (Washington, 1933), VI, pp. 53, 55, 65, 82, 100.

24. James and James, *Biography of a Bank,* p. 81.

25. *Ibid.,* p. 113.

NOTES · CHAPTER 6

1. W. G. Rule, *"the means of wealth, peace, and happiness": The Story of the Oldest Bank West of the Mississippi* (St. Louis: The Boatmen's National Bank of St. Louis, 1947), pp. 58–59.

2. Ellis P. Oberholtzer, *Jay Cooke, Financier of the Civil War* (Philadelphia: George W. Jacobs and Co., 1907), II, 85–95.

3. Louis F. Cahn, "Sesqui-Centennial, The Farmers National Bank of Annapolis," (Annapolis, Md.: The Farmers National Bank, 1955), p. 23.

4. Julius Grodinsky, *Jay Gould, His Business Career, 1867–1892* (Philadelphia: University of Pennsylvania Press, 1957), p. 346.

5. Frederick Lewis Allen, *The Great Pierpont Morgan* (New York: Harper & Brothers, 1949), p. 265.

6. Irene D. Neu, *Erastus Corning, Merchant and Financier, 1794–1872* (Ithaca: Cornell University Press, 1960).

7. Nicholas B. Wainwright, *History of the Philadelphia National Bank* (Philadelphia: The Philadelphia National Bank, 1953), pp. 116, 144, 193; "This Is Our Story," (Philadelphia: Central-Penn National Bank, 1954), pp. 21–24.

8. Edward C. Kirkland, *Men, Cities and Transportation* (Cambridge: Harvard University Press, 1948), I, 369–378; II, pp. 464–465.

9. *Report of Senate Committee on Failed National Banks*, 52nd Congress, 2nd Session, Senate Report No. 1286 (1893), pp. 6, 81–82. The failure of the bank was not directly related to these loans and securities holdings.

10. A list of active participants in marketing industrial securities included Guaranty, Farmers, Franklin Trust Co. of Brooklyn, and Boston's Old Colony Trust, as well as the First National Banks of Chicago and St. Louis. Thomas R. Navin and Marian V. Sears, "The Rise of a Market for Industrial Securities, 1887–1902," *Business History Review*, June 1955, pp. 122–123.

11. House Committee on Banking and Currency, *Money Trust Investigation*, U.S. Congress (1913), pp. 2049 ff.

12. F. Cyril James, *The Growth of Chicago Banks* (New York: Harper & Brothers, 1938), II, p. 1116.

13. Professor Ulmer's estimates suggest that railroad capital expenditures in 1865–1900 totaled between $5 and $6 billion, and that the total book value of railroad assets in 1900 was $10 or $11 billion. Banks held $500 million of rail bonds in 1900. Bank loans on securities collateral totaled $800 million, of which probably three-fourths was on rail securities. Thus the share of bank credit in rail capital might have been as high as one-fourth, or as low as 10 per cent. A good guess would probably put the estimate between 15 and 20 per cent. Melville J. Ulmer, *Capital in Transportation, Communications, and Public Utilities: Its Formation and Financ-*

ing (Princeton: Princeton University Press for the National Bureau of Economic Research, 1960), pp. 256–259, 502; Raymond Goldsmith, *Financial Intermediaries in the American Economy since 1900* (Princeton: Princeton University Press for the National Bureau of Economic Research, 1958), pp. 338 ff.

In the years 1901–1902, inclusive, railroads raised about $5 billion by securities sales—a total which accounted for one-third of all corporate securities issued for cash in this period. In the same period, the banks added $400 million to their holdings of rail bonds and expended their loans on collateral of rail securities by about the same amount. This suggests that bank credit provided as much as 15 per cent of rail finance in 1901–1912. In addition, bank-administered trust funds appear to have bought about 10 per cent of the rail bonds issued in 1901–1912. See Goldsmith, *A Study of Saving in the United States,* I, pp. 489–496; *Financial Intermediaries,* pp. 227, 338 ff., 227. The proportion of security loans on rail collateral is simply my guess.

14. Andrew Carnegie, *Autobiography* (Boston: Houghton Mifflin Company, 1920), pp. 87–88.

15. On Tredegar, see Allan Nevins, *History of the Bank of New York and Trust Company, 1784 to 1934* (New York: The Bank of New York, 1934), p. 82; and E. Merlin Coulter, *The South During Reconstruction* (Baton Rouge: Louisiana State University Press, 1947), p. 255. Harold F. Williamson and Kenneth H. Myers, *Designed for Digging; The First 75 Years of Bucyrus-Erie Company* (Evanston, Ill.: Northwestern University Press, 1955); Henry Oliver Evans, *Iron Pioneer,* pp. 193, 225–226.

16. Goldsmith, *Financial Intermediaries,* pp. 231, 339.

17. *Money Trust Investigation,* pp. 2049 ff.

18. Goldsmith, *Financial Intermediaries,* pp. 231, 339.

19. Ralph M. Hower, *History of Macy's of New York, 1858–1919* (Cambridge: Harvard University Press, 1943), pp. 323–326.

20. House Committee on Banking and Currency, *National Banks,* Report No. 2342, 52nd Congress, 2nd Session, (1893), pp. 254–266.

21. *Money Trust Investigation,* op. cit., pp. 2049 ff.

22. Estimates of business capital are summarized in *Historical Statistics of the United States, Colonial Times to 1957,* p. 151. Business indebtedness is shown in Goldsmith, *A Study of Saving in the United States,* III, pp. 42–43. Estimates of credit from banks and other sources are from Goldsmith, *Financial Intermediaries,* esp. pp. 339 ff.

NOTES • CHAPTER 7

1. David Kinley, *The Use of Credit Instruments in Payments in the United States* (Washington: Government Printing Office, 1910), p. 57; *Special Report from Banks of the United States* (Washington: Government Printing Office, 1910), p. 56.
2. W. G. Rule, *"the means of wealth, peace, and happiness,"* p. 68.
3. Secretary of the Treasury, *Annual Report on the State of the Finances,* 1866, p. 16.
4. Hugh McCulloch, *Men and Measures of Half a Century* (New York: Charles Scribner's Sons, 1888), p. 201.
5. *Annual Report of the Comptroller of the Currency,* 1868, p. xiii.
6. *Congressional Globe,* 39:1, p. 1452, March 1866.
7. Richard Bernhart, *Economics* (Boston: D. C. Heath and Company, 1954), pp. 319–320.
8. Bray Hammond, *Banks and Politics in America,* p. 34.
9. Raymond Goldsmith, *A Study of Saving in the United States,* I, pp. 382, 385; *Financial Intermediaries in the American Economy since 1900,* p. 349.
10. Estimate obtained by applying to all banks the expansion ratio for national banks as obtained from *Special Report from Banks of the United States,* p. 114. Since the share of national banks in total deposits declined, it is not likely that this procedure overstates the increase in number of accounts.
11. Russell A. Stevenson (ed.), *A Type Study of American Banking: Non-Metropolitan Banks in Minnesota* (St. Paul: University of Minnesota Press, 1934), pp. 21–23.

NOTES • CHAPTER 8

1. Donald A. Moore, "The Automobile Industry," in Walter Adams (ed.), *The Structure of American Industry* (2nd ed.: New York: Macmillan Co., 1954), pp. 279–280.
2. Allan Nevins and Frank E. Hill, *Ford, The Times, The Man, The Company* (New York: Charles Scribner's Sons, 1954), p. 229.
3. Quoted in Lawrence Seltzer, *Financial History of The Automobile Industry,* (Boston: Houghton Mifflin Co., 1928), pp. 29–30.
4. Nevins and Hill, *op. cit.,* pp. 233–239.
5. Arthur Pound, *The Turning Wheel* (Garden City, N.Y.: Doubleday, Doran and Co., 1934.), pp. 125–130.
6. John B. Rae, *American Automobile Manufacturers, The First Forty Years* (Philadelphia: Chilton Company, 1959), p. 88.

7. Alfred Lief, *The Firestone Story* (New York, Whittlesey House, 1951), pp. 17, 32; Harvey S. Firestone, *Men and Rubber* (Garden City, N.Y.: Doubleday, Page, & Co., 1926), pp. 40–44.

8. Warren Scoville, *Revolution in Glass-Making* (Cambridge: Harvard University Press, 1948).

9. See the report of the Immigration Commission in 61st Congress, 3rd Session, Senate Document 753.

10. Bascom N. Timmons, *Jesse H. Jones, The Man and the Statesman* (New York: Henry Holt & Co., Inc., 1956).

11. Arthur J. Morris in *Personal Finance Law Quarterly Report*, quoted by Hillel Black, *Buy Now, Pay Later* (New York: William Morrow & Co., Inc., 1961), p. 165.

12. Thomas C. Boushall, "Banking for Main Street, U.S.A.," (Richmond: The Bank of Virginia, 1959).

13. *The Labor Banking Movement in the United States* (Princeton: Industrial Relations Section, Princeton University, 1929), p. 201.

14. "Labor Banking; It Still Survives," *Business Week*, November 17, 1956, pp. 108–113. The United Mine Workers Union owns a controlling interest in the National Bank of Washington as an investment.

15. Roger W. Riis, "Here's A Banker with Imagination," *Reader's Digest*, February 1945.

16. Data in foregoing paragraphs are drawn from various sources in Goldsmith, *A Study of Saving in the United States* and *Financial Intermediaries*.

17. *Annual Report of the Comptroller of the Currency*, 1920, p. 32.

18. James and James, *Biography of a Bank*, pp. 245–247, 429–430.

19. *Special Report from the Banks of the United States*, p. 38; *Annual Report of the Comptroller of the Currency*, 1929, p. 114.

NOTES · CHAPTER 9

1. Robert A. Gordon, "Population Growth, Housing, and the Capital Coefficient," *American Economic Review*, June 1956.

2. Bernhard Ostrolenk and Adrian M. Massie, *How Banks Buy Bonds* (New York: Harper & Brothers, 1932), pp. xii, 3.

3. C. O. Hardy and Jacob Viner, *Report on the Availability of Bank Credit in the Seventh Federal Reserve District* (1935), p. vi.

4. Quoted in Ernest J. Hopkins, *Financing the Frontier* (Phoenix: 1950), pp. 217–218. The following material is derived from this source.

5. Hopkins, *op. cit.*, pp. 246–247.

6. Information on these developments is found in the following unpublished theses prepared for the Stonier Graduate School of Banking at Rutgers: Andrew T. Maloney, "Bank Financing of the Quick-Frozen Foods Industry," 1947; Highland C. Moore, "Financing Aviation Equipment," 1942; John Ware, Jr., "The Supermarket, Its Growth and Financing," 1958.

NOTES · CHAPTER 10

1. Statistical data computed from *Flow of Funds/Saving Accounts, 1946–1960*, Board of Governors, Federal Reserve System (Washington: Government Printing Office, 1961).
2. George Katona, *Business Looks at Banks* (Ann Arbor: University of Michigan Press, 1957), p. 93. This survey covered firms with assets of more than $1 million each.
3. Author's estimates of assets of non-financial firms by size of assets were derived from *Statistics of Income, 1955*, and "What is Small Business," by Eleanor J. Stockwell, in *Financing Small Business*, Report to the Committee on Banking and Currency and the Select Committee on Small Business, U. S. Congress, by the Federal Reserve System, p. 167. Bank loans by size of borrower were estimated from processed data on member-bank loans supplied by Federal Reserve.
4. David Eastburn and John J. Balles, "Commercial Banks," *Financing Small Business*, p. 396.
5. *Ibid.*, p. 401. A survey among small and medium-sized firms in 1955 revealed that bank loans constituted 79 per cent of the number of all loans received. In 1957, Federal Reserve member banks reported they had 107,000 loans outstanding to firms newly established within the past two years. *Survey of Current Business*, October 1955; *Federal Reserve Bulletin*, April 1958, p. 408.
6. Rine G. Winey, "A Study of Motel Financing," unpublished thesis, Stonier Graduate School of Banking, 1956.
7. Quoted in John Ware, Jr., "The Supermarket, Its Growth and Financing," unpublished thesis, Stonier Graduate School of Banking, 1958, pp. 63–64.
8. *Time* Magazine, June 9, 1961, pp. 85–86.
9. Raymond Goldsmith, *Financial Intermediaries in the American Economy since 1900*, p. 339; *Federal Reserve Bulletins*, November 1956, pp. 1163 ff.; August 1960, pp. 855, 934–944; *Flow of Funds/Saving Accounts, 1946–1960*.
10. *Burroughs Clearing House*, February 1943, pp. 13 ff.

11. Annual reports for 1960 of Franklin and Girard; Central-Penn port-folio courtesy of the bank.

12. *Flow of Funds/Saving Accounts, 1946–1960; 1960 Survey of Consumer Finances,* Survey Research Center, University of Michigan, 1961, pp. 49–71.

13. *Historical Statistics of the United States, Colonial Times to 1957,* p. 462; *1960 Survey of Consumer Finances.*

14. *Federal Reserve Bulletin,* July 1956; John J. Croteau, "Sources of Consumer Credit: Instalment Debt Among Institutional Creditors," *Journal of Finance,* December 1960, pp. 531–545.

15. Vance Packard, *The Hidden Persuaders* (New York: David McKay Co., Inc., 1957), pp. 66–67.

16. *Federal Reserve Bulletin,* June 1957, p. 644. Personal debt is defined in this survey to exclude charge accounts and service credit. It thus consists mainly of instalment debt.

17. *The New York Times,* June 18, 1961.

18. *Federal Reserve Bulletin,* April 1961, pp. 405–407; *1960 Survey of Consumer Finances,* p. 78.

NOTES • CHAPTER 11

1. *Monetary Policy and the Management of the Public Debt: Replies to Questions,* Joint Economic Committee, United States Congress, 1952, part 1, p. 212.

2. *January 1961 Economic Report of the President and the Economic Situation and Outlook,* Hearings before the Joint Economic Committee, United States Congress, 1961, p. 464.

NOTES • CHAPTER 12

1. Bray Hammond, "Long and Short Term Credit in Early American Banking," *Quarterly Journal of Economics* (1935), pp. 102–103.

2. Kenneth Boulding, *Principles of Economic Policy* (New York: Prentice-Hall, Inc., 1958), pp. 229–230.

3. George Katona, *Business Looks at Banks* (Ann Arbor: University of Michigan Press, 1957), pp. 51–65, quotation at p. 53.

4. Costs of deposit management were estimated from data in "Trends in Bank Costs," (New York: American Bankers Association, 1956); and "A Complete Service Charge Program For Smaller Banks," (New York: American Bankers Association, 1955).

5. Clifford Hufsmith, *Profitable Banking* (Boston: Bankers Publishing Company, 1959).

INDEX

INDEX OF BANKS AND BANKERS

[300]